S0-AHR-648

DISCARD

When the Earth Roars

ASIA/PACIFIC/PERSPECTIVES
Series Editor: Mark Selden

Crime, Punishment, and Policing in China edited by Børge Bakken

Woman, Man, Bangkok: Love, Sex, and Popular Culture in Thailand by Scot Barmé

Making the Foreign Serve China: Managing Foreigners in the People's Republic by Anne-Marie Brady

Marketing Dictatorship: Propaganda and Thought Work in China by Anne-Marie Brady

Collaborative Nationalism: The Politics of Friendship on China's Mongolian Frontier by Uradyn E. Bulag

The Mongols at China's Edge: History and the Politics of National Unity by Uradyn E. Bulag

Transforming Asian Socialism: China and Vietnam Compared edited by Anita Chan, Benedict J. Tria Kerkvliet, and Jonathan Unger

Bound to Emancipate: Working Women and Urban Citizenship in Early Twentieth-Century China by Angelina Chin

The Search for the Beautiful Woman: A Cultural History of Japanese and Chinese Beauty by Cho Kyo, translated by Kyoko Iriye Selden

China's Great Proletarian Cultural Revolution: Master Narratives and Post-Mao Counternarratives edited by Woei Lien Chong

North China at War: The Social Ecology of Revolution, 1937–1945 edited by Feng Chongyi and David S. G. Goodman

Little Friends: Children's Film and Media Culture in China by Stephanie Hemelryk Donald

Beachheads: War, Peace, and Tourism in Postwar Okinawa by Gerald Figal

Gender in Motion: Divisions of Labor and Cultural Change in Late Imperial and Modern China edited by Bryna Goodman and Wendy Larson

Social and Political Change in Revolutionary China: The Taihang Base Area in the War of Resistance to Japan, 1937–1945 by David S. G. Goodman

Rice Wars in Colonial Vietnam: The Great Famine and the Viet Minh Road to Power by Geoffrey C. Gunn

Islands of Discontent: Okinawan Responses to Japanese and American Power edited by Laura Hein and Mark Selden

Masculinities in Chinese History by Bret Hinsch

Women in Early Imperial China, Second Edition by Bret Hinsch

Chinese Civil Justice, Past and Present by Philip C. C. Huang

Local Democracy and Development: The Kerala People's Campaign for Decentralized Planning by T. M. Thomas Isaac with Richard W. Franke

Hidden Treasures: Lives of First-Generation Korean Women in Japan by Jackie J. Kim with Sonia Ryang

North Korea: Beyond Charismatic Politics by Heonik Kwon and Byung-Ho Chung

Prosperity's Predicament: Identity, Reform, and Resistance in Rural Wartime China by Isabel Brown Crook and Christina Kelley Gilmartin with Yu Xiji, edited by Gail Hershatter and Emily Honig

Postwar Vietnam: Dynamics of a Transforming Society edited by Hy V. Luong

From Silicon Valley to Shenzhen: Global Production and Work in the IT Industry by Boy Lüthje, Stefanie Hürtgen, Peter Pawlicki, and Martina Sproll

Resistant Islands: Okinawa Confronts Japan and the United States by Gavan McCormack and Satoko Oka Norimatsu

The Indonesian Presidency: The Shift from Personal towards Constitutional Rule by Angus McIntyre

Nationalisms of Japan: Managing and Mystifying Identity by Brian J. McVeigh

To the Diamond Mountains: A Hundred-Year Journey through China and Korea by Tessa Morris-Suzuki

From Underground to Independent: Alternative Film Culture in Contemporary China edited by Paul G. Pickowicz and Yingjin Zhang

Wife or Worker? Asian Women and Migration edited by Nicola Piper and Mina Roces

Social Movements in India: Poverty, Power, and Politics edited by Raka Ray and Mary Fainsod Katzenstein

Pan Asianism: A Documentary History, Volume 1, 1850–1920 edited by Sven Saaler and Christopher W. A. Szpilman

Pan Asianism: A Documentary History, Volume 2, 1920–Present edited by Sven Saaler and Christopher W. A. Szpilman

Biology and Revolution in Twentieth-Century China by Laurence Schneider

Contentious Kwangju: The May 18th Uprising in Korea's Past and Present edited by Gi-Wook Shin and Kyong Moon Hwang

Thought Reform and China's Dangerous Classes: Reeducation, Resistance, and the People by Aminda M. Smith

Japan's New Middle Class, Third Edition by Ezra F. Vogel with a chapter by Suzanne Hall Vogel, foreword by William W. Kelly

The Japanese Family in Transition: From the Professional Housewife Ideal to the Dilemmas of Choice by Suzanne Hall Vogel with Steven Vogel

The United States and China: A History from the Eighteenth Century to the Present by Dong Wang

The Inside Story of China's High-Tech Industry: Making Silicon Valley in Beijing by Yu Zhou

When the Earth Roars

Lessons from the History of Earthquakes in Japan

Gregory Smits

ROWMAN & LITTLEFIELD
Lanham • Boulder • New York • Toronto • Plymouth, UK

Published by Rowman & Littlefield
4501 Forbes Boulevard, Suite 200, Lanham, Maryland 20706
www.rowman.com

10 Thornbury Road, Plymouth PL6 7PP, United Kingdom

British Library Cataloguing in Publication Information Available

Library of Congress Cataloging-in-Publication Data Available
ISBN 978-1-4422-2009-6 (cloth : alk. paper)
ISBN 978-1-4422-2010-2 (electronic)

Contents

Acknowledgments

It is a pleasure to acknowledge the support and assistance of friends and colleagues. This book is part of a line of research that began in 2004. At that time, my main research focus was the Ryukyu Kingdom, but thanks to a collaboration on an article with Ruth Ludwin, I discovered the fascinating world of earthquake history.

Mark Selden has long been a supporter of my work, both on Ryukyu and on earthquakes. The initial plans for this book were the result of discussions with Mark, and he has provided me with a variety of useful leads and advice. I thank Susan McEachern at Rowman & Littlefield for her editorial guidance and patience and for always answering my questions quickly. An anonymous outside reader provided extensive and helpful comments on an earlier draft. Robert Geller provided invaluable advice about key scientific journal articles. My work on earthquakes has also benefited from the support of Brian Atwater, Steve Phipps, Frank Chance, Philip Brown, Garrit Schenk, and others. My brother, Jeffrey Smits, of Cherokee Drafting Specialists, produced two maps for this book. Michele Tomiak has improved this manuscript with her fine copyediting. Any shortcomings that remain are, needless to say, entirely my own responsibility.

I thank my colleagues and the administration at Penn State for creating an environment conducive to academic pursuits. I especially thank my wife, Akiko, for her good cheer and enthusiasm. Finally, I would like to express my appreciation for my network of music friends, especially the good folks who gather at Paul's cabin in Hampshire County. You folks help keep me sane, happy, and productive.

Introduction

For millennia, Japan has suffered the effects of earthquakes, of which the March 11, 2011, earthquake was the most recent event but far from the most devastating. This book is a social and intellectual history of earthquakes in early modern and modern Japan with particular attention to Japan's unstable Sanriku coast. The northeast of Japan is known as the Tōhoku region, and the coastal area on the Pacific Ocean side is the Sanriku coast. This area is subject to megathrust earthquakes and the tsunamis these earthquakes often generate. The March 11, 2011, magnitude (M) 9 earthquake and tsunami was just the most recent example. Here, following common practice, I refer to the 2011 earthquake, tsunami, and disaster that occurred when these natural hazards intersected with human society as "3/11." This book sheds useful light on 3/11 but is not intended as a systematic analysis of that event. Instead, it contextualizes 3/11 by examining many of the major earthquakes that preceded it, beginning in 1611. There is no study in English that examines these earthquakes in an integrated manner, nor to my knowledge does any book in Japanese take the approach that I have here.

ARGUMENTS

I seek to advance arguments in three realms. The first concerns the nature of earthquakes as natural disasters. I argue that earthquakes are chaotic events. Unpredictability is the defining feature of chaotic systems: "Given an enormously complex system, it is impossible to predict how any disturbance of any size will shape the future."[1] Human societies are complex systems. No two earthquakes play out identically either as geophysical events or as social events because small variations either in the earthquake itself or in the society with which it interacts can result in vast differences in outcomes. The same applies more broadly to human history. While certain patterns of behavior recur, the way these behaviors reverberate through society and the social effects they produce are unpredictable. In this sense, history does not repeat itself.

Although I argue that each destructive earthquake is a unique social phenomenon, I do not mean to push this point so far as to deny similarities. Similarly, although the social trajectories of earthquake disasters are mostly unpredictable, it is possible and desirable to anticipate major vulnerabilities. It is in this realm, especially, that the past can be a useful guide for the future. Vulnerable behaviors, practices, and structural conditions of past disasters can manifest themselves in the future, even if not in an identical manner. Moreover, we can and should examine the data in the past record of earthquakes for patterns, recurrences, or analogues to the present and future. We will see, for example, that some seismologists warned of seismic hazards to nuclear power plants in the years and even days before 3/11. Similarly, a prescient seismologist warned of the danger of gaslights and petroleum use in Tokyo prior to the horrific seismically generated firestorms of 1923, now remembered as the Great Kantō Earthquake. Risks and vulnerabilities can be identified before disaster strikes, and a sophisticated knowledge of past disasters can provide excellent guidance in that process. Sometimes we can identify recurring patterns that provide useful insights. For example, in modern Japan, major earthquakes have often brought forth a rhetoric of renewal. This rhetoric has sought to put a hopeful spin on otherwise tragic disasters, presenting the catastrophe as an opportunity for beneficial social change. However, the experience of modern Japan suggests serious limits for natural disasters to initiate social or political change. Insofar as disasters stimulate change, it is more typically in the manner of a catalyst accelerating processes already under way.

History can provide "lessons" from the past, but rarely are these lessons obvious or easy to grasp. Early seismologists sought to discover order, regularity, and clear explanations concerning earthquakes. This endeavor was entirely reasonable and commensurate with the broader aims of science in the late nineteenth century. However, often instead of *discovering* orderliness, early seismologists, in effect, imposed it. Eventually, the earth intervened violently to expose the limits of scientific knowledge. One implicit argument here is that historians should be similarly cautious with respect to the tendency to impose order on the past. Writing a book such as this one is inevitably an act of intervention, albeit a modest one. In so doing, I strive to mediate between the chaotic condition of the world and the human tendency to reduce and simplify. One example of such reductionism is the frequent appearance in the mass media after 3/11 of cultural explanations about "the Japanese" and earthquakes. One goal of this book is to problematize culturally based explanations.

The second realm in which I advance arguments is the history of science and technology, especially the knowledge discipline of seismology and the know-how domain of antiseismic engineering. The modern science of seismology developed in parts of Europe and in Japan. Japanese seismology evolved from interactions between Anglo-European scientists, native traditions of scholarship on earthquakes, and extensive earthquake documentation. Just as every major earthquake was a unique social event, each earthquake posed a unique set of challenges to science and contributed to scientific knowledge in different ways and to different degrees. I also argue that certain ideas from Japan's early modern past continue to influence not only popular views of earthquakes but also approaches to earthquake science and resource allocation. These early modern ideas made sense in the context of their time, when the conception of earthquake mechanics was entirely different from what it is now. Particularly problematic is a continuing focus on earthquake prediction, which follows a logic that dates to the early nineteenth century. This focus potentially misleads the public about what is possible and diverts resources from more effective means of dealing with seismic hazards. I acknowledge the change after 1995 from short-term "prediction" to longer-term "forecasting," but I argue that the distinction is more semantic than substantive.

Finally, I advance general arguments about resource allocation and approaches to seismic hazards. The unique nature of specific earthquakes suggests that detailed contingency plans based on the most recent past example are unlikely to be useful, whereas the ability to mount a flexible response to seismic emergencies drawing on the historical record, especially at the local level, would be of considerable benefit. Moreover, the long and completely unsuccessful history of earthquake prediction in Japan (and elsewhere) suggests that resources invested in that realm, especially as manifest in the ever-expanding web of data collection, are unlikely to pay useful dividends in mitigating future disasters. Antiseismic engineering and other pragmatic steps to diminish damage from strong ground motion, by contrast, have a proven record of effectiveness.

It is highly unlikely that we will ever be able to say with any precision when a destructive earthquake will strike, but we do know that it will strike. If we could know the timing and locations of major earthquakes in advance, evacuation might be a viable strategy in some cases. Since we cannot, intelligent intervention to enhance human environments vis-à-vis inevitable seismic hazards makes sense. As we will see, however, such intervention can lead to overconfidence and a disregard for the potential power of natural hazards. Seawalls, for example, can reduce damage from many tsunamis. They are not completely reliable, however, and there is no substitute for coastal residents seeking high ground after the earth shakes.

SCOPE

The scope of this book is broad but not uniform. Temporally I emphasize the modern era (late nineteenth century onward), and geographically I emphasize the Sanriku coast. Moreover, I seek to complement and integrate past coverage of Japanese earthquakes, not replicate work already done. For example, because the 1923 Great Kantō Earthquake has received extensive attention in English-language scholarship, I discuss only those aspects of it relevant to the broader arguments of this study, and I analyze a representative primary source that has yet to receive sustained attention. In other words, my goal with respect to this event is to supplement the fine work of scholars such as Gennifer Weisenfeld and J. Charles Schencking. Similarly, I do not seek to write a new history of the 1891 Nōbi earthquake, which Gregory Clancey has analyzed in detail. Instead, I highlight aspects of that event especially relevant to topics in this book, such as early knowledge of the close connection between faults and earthquakes and the impact of the event on society and academic research. On the other hand, the historical literature in English on earthquakes and tsunamis along the Sanriku coast is sparse. I therefore analyze earthquakes in this region more thoroughly.

Although destructive earthquakes and tsunamis have been common along the Sanriku coast, nuclear power was not an issue prior to 3/11. Indeed, the nuclear disaster component of 3/11 seems to have brought forth a small army of atomic experts and commentators, who have produced an extensive literature. I am not one of them. My research for the past eight or so years has been earthquakes in Japan and to a lesser extent elsewhere, both in the sense of assessing the impact of earthquakes on society and from the standpoint of the history of science. The Fukushima nuclear disaster is obviously of great importance, but there is also value in a close study of the earthquakes and tsunami component of 3/11. Therefore, I have relatively little to say about the Fukushima meltdown, and insofar as I do discuss it or nuclear power plants in general, I do so in connection with relevant aspects of earthquakes and tsunamis.

Another topic that, for the most part, is beyond my expertise and thus beyond the scope of this book is commentary on contemporary Japanese politics. I am sympathetic with many of the criticisms others have leveled. For example, I second the criticism of Japanese politicians and power-plant executives who invoked the *sōteigai* (unimaginable, i.e., not something we could/should have imagined) defense for 3/11. Furthermore, I agree with the major criticisms of Japan's earthquake prediction program and the disconnect with reality inherent in the writing of earthquake prediction into legislation. Moreover, insofar as history provides insight or guidance, I make some general arguments about resource allocation and some broad statements about the ability of natural disasters to cause major social change. I am not a specialist in contemporary Japanese politics, however, and I do not offer prescriptions for systemic political or institutional change in this book.

The main organizing rubric of this book is chronology, with geography as a secondary consideration. There is considerable cross-referencing. If, for example, the discussion of an early modern earthquake leads to a point that sheds useful light on a more recent event, I discuss the connection at that point. Each chapter, therefore, includes some discussion of modern or contemporary issues and the early modern past. Most chapters address all three of the broad areas in which I advance arguments, although some emphasize one realm or another. I begin by setting the stage, examining the relevant geology of the Japanese islands and some of the major issues that have emerged in the wake of 3/11.

NOTE

1. Susan Elizabeth Hough and Roger G. Bilham, *After the Earth Quakes: Elastic Rebound in an Urban Planet* (New York: Oxford University Press, 2006), 180–81.

ONE

Setting the Stage

The March 11, 2011, megathrust earthquake off Japan's northeast coast probably released more energy than any seismic event to shake Japan in more than one thousand years. A fault (discontinuity surface) created by the convergence of two tectonic plates slipped approximately 45 meters along a 350 kilometer length. Of earthquakes striking Japan in historical times, only the Jōgan earthquake of 869 may have been on a par with the 2011 event in terms of both magnitude (M = energy released) and the reach of the tsunami waves. Recent excavations by paleoseismologists have revealed multiple layers of inundation of the Sendai Plain corresponding to tsunamis on a par with the March 11, 2011, event occurring, on average, approximately once every one thousand years during the prehistoric past.[1] We will see, however, that massive earthquake/tsunami combinations, even if not quite as large as the 2011 event, have been common in this region.

The M9.0 earthquake produced a tsunami (a train of seismic sea waves) that struck much of Japan's Pacific coast. The ground motion from the seismic land waves and the influx of ocean water from the tsunami interacted destructively with human society to create a natural disaster commonly known as "3/11." This disaster resulted in approximately twenty thousand fatalities. It was the most deadly earthquake-tsunami catastrophe since 1923, and it was almost as deadly as the tsunami that devastated precisely the same area of northeastern Japan in 1896. In addition to destruction of lives and property, 3/11 produced social, economic, and political effects that continue to play out. It remains an

1

event in progress. The most dramatic and important longer-term effect of 3/11 is the ongoing nuclear crisis. Not only did the meltdown at the Fukushima Daiichi Nuclear Power Plant wrench hundreds of thousands away from their homes, communities, and work, but it has led to serious problems and unresolved questions about energy policy.[2]

Given the subject matter of this book, it is important to clarify the basic relationship between natural hazards and natural disasters or catastrophes. Natural hazards of various types are constantly present. They produce disasters only when they intersect with human societies. The level and configuration of social vulnerability varies. Therefore, the extent and nature of a disaster and its longer-term effects depend on a complex array of social conditions. To illustrate, let us consider one rather obvious factor: typical housing construction. The domed adobe houses common in many parts of Iran are especially prone to collapse in even relatively moderate earthquakes. Since 1890, more than two hundred thousand people have died in Iran from this cause alone—roughly the

Figure 1.1. Tsunamis Have Shaped the Landscape of Coastal Japan. Kanegaike (Crab Pond) in Tosa City, Kōchi Prefecture, was created by the action of a tsunami about two thousand years ago. *Source*: Wikimedia Commons, As6022014.

total of earthquake and tsunami deaths in Japan during the same period.[3] For this and other reasons, an earthquake with the same physical parameters occurring under a major urban area in Iran is likely to be much more deadly than were it to occur the same distance beneath a comparably populated part of Japan.

The sheer quantity of energy an earthquake releases is an important variable in determining its potential hazard, but earthquakes of the same or similar magnitudes routinely produce vastly different social results. The M7.3 Kōbe earthquake took the lives of more than 6,400 people in 1995. Five years later, the M7.3 Seibu earthquake in Tottori Prefecture released approximately as much energy as did the Kōbe event but did not claim a single life.[4] Location and particular circumstances matter greatly in determining how natural disasters unfold. Moreover, broad social circumstances often determine the longer-term impacts of natural disasters and the way they are perceived in retrospect. The 1855 Ansei Edo earthquake, for example, was roughly M6.9 or M7 and killed between seven thousand and eight thousand (less than 1 percent of Edo's population). The 1703 M8.2 Genroku earthquake was of the same type as the 1923 Great Kantō Earthquake. The 1703 event killed a slightly higher percentage of the population compared with the 1855 event and was much more powerful in physical terms. The social and political impact of Ansei Edo, however, was much greater than Genroku. One reason is that in 1855, Japanese society and its system of government were under much greater stress than was the case in 1703.

The social impact of earthquakes includes such elements as prevailing scientific knowledge, popular beliefs and perceptions, technological capabilities, prevailing political issues, the nature of the political system, emergency preparedness, and a variety of random factors such as time of day. This book is a study of select interactions between seismic forces in a compressed, twisted, and fault-riddled land—the Japanese islands—and the societies that have inhabited that land.

ASSESSING RISK AND ACCEPTING LIMITATIONS

A study of past earthquakes in Japan does not reveal a singular characteristic pattern of disaster. Instead, it reveals a range of possible cause-and-effect relationships and longer-term results. It is possible, however, to identify certain problematic behaviors and ways of thinking common to many, though not all, major earthquakes. One such problem is short-sightedness in the form of a tendency to assume that the next earthquake will be like the previous one. Such assumptions are often incorrect and can lead to fatal consequences.

Although there is no characteristic pattern of earthquake disasters, the socioseismic history of Japan does reveal a recurring pattern of overconfidence and diminishing attention to recurring natural hazards such as earthquakes. A similar pattern is probably discernible in many other seismically active parts of the world. Exacerbating this tendency is the irregular occurrence of large earthquakes. Moreover, the time between such events is often greater than a human lifetime. Most geological processes, including seismicity, play out over a vastly longer period than human history and especially human attention spans. In some parts of Japan or the world, major earthquakes occur very infrequently by the standards of human time. The existence of the Rokkō-Awaji fault zone, for example, was unknown until it caused the deadly 1995 Kōbe earthquake. Subsequent research has resulted in estimated recurrence rates of 900–2,800 years for one segment of the zone and 1,800–2,500 years for a different segment.[5] The Longmenshan Fault, which caused the M8.0 Sichuan (Wenchuan) earthquake in 2008, previously ruptured between sixty-five and two hundred million years earlier.[6]

Compared with these cases, the Sanriku coast of northeastern Japan has experienced a relatively high frequency of deadly seismic events. Even there, however, short-term considerations of convenience or other hazards such as landslides and fires worked against long-term abandonment of dangerous low-lying areas as sites for communities. There was, for example, a marked increase in resettlement in hazardous areas ten years after the 1896 tsunami. While a decade is a significant part of a human lifetime, it is but the blink of an eye in geological time. Major earthquake-tsunami combinations occurred along the Sanriku coast in 2011, 1933, 1896, 1856, 1793, and 1611. Although we can use these dates to declare a tentative "average recurrence interval," such a statistic means little in reality. Notice that in some cases, the recurrence was short enough for the previous event to have remained prominent in social memory, a situation that probably saved many lives in 1933. Social and demographic change combined with a much longer time interval resulted in a fainter social memory of the 1933 event in 2011 in many (though not all) areas of the Sanriku coast. This circumstance undoubtedly added to the death toll of 3/11, although, of course, we have no way to quantify it.

In a country like Japan, located at the congested intersection of four tectonic plates pushing each other in different directions, seismicity is an ever-present natural hazard. A prerequisite for mitigating this and other hazards is a frank acknowledgment of reality. The first part of such an acknowledgment is recognizing what is possible and what is not. Risk assessment and the closely connected issue of allocation of limited resources is part of that process. Similarly, the contemporary belief that total safety vis-à-vis natural hazards is possible is both erroneous and irresponsible. Risk assessment, as detached as possible from emotional considerations or vested political and economic interests, is the route to the greatest degree of safety for the greatest number of people, even though that degree will always be less than 100 percent.

Another aspect of facing reality is accurate information about earthquakes themselves. The contemporary persistence of earthquake-related folklore in part reflects a lack of historical perspective. As we will see, lore connected with earthquake clouds, for example, or the alleged ability of animals to predict earthquakes was a product of a specific early modern understanding of earthquakes. These ideas made sense in their early modern intellectual context but make no sense outside of it. There is a romantic appeal of traditional or folk "wisdom" and the "democratization" of science. Continuing to give credence, however, to ideas that developed when earthquakes were known to be explosions caused by the buildup of yang energy within the ground is an ahistorical appeal to tradition. Such appeals may seem harmless, and indeed they often are. However, insofar as contemporary governments allocate resources based on such lore and insofar as people place confidence in it, appeals to the alleged wisdom of the past can be counterproductive. Suppose a coastal city, frustrated in the wake of 3/11 by the inability of contemporary science to predict earthquakes, allocated funds to monitor well water and animal behavior as a substitute. At least one city decided to do precisely that.[7]

My basic argument with respect to such a situation is that we must accept what is by now a well-established fact that the occurrence of earthquakes cannot be predicted or forecast in any socially useful way. Turning to folklore does not remedy this gap in our technological capabilities. A better approach is to assume that a destructive earthquake, and in coastal areas a tsunami, could strike at any time and devote local resources entirely to mitigating the destructiveness of that occurrence. This book will suggest some avenues for doing so.

NAMES

Lobbying is one reason that the official names of Japanese earthquakes can be confusing. The Japan Meteorological Agency (JMA) assigns earthquake names, but it is not immune to outside pressure. In 1983, for example, an M7.7 earthquake occurred just offshore from Akita Prefecture in the Japan Sea. Locally powerful politicians lobbied hard to keep "Akita" out of the official name of that earthquake. It ended up being designated the "Japan Sea Central Region" earthquake (Nihonkai chūbu jishin), even though the central region of the Japan Sea is not seismically active and the earthquake actually occurred at its eastern edge. The whole point of the misleading name, in other words, was to obscure the real location of the earthquake.[8]

In part because of the vagueness of some official names, many earthquakes go by more than one name in Japan. Moreover, often these earthquakes are known by yet other names outside of Japan. Sometimes scientific literature favors one name and popular literature another. The event I am calling 3/11 in this book bears the official name "Earthquake off the Pacific Coast of the Tōhoku Region" (Tōhoku-chihō Taiheiyō-oki jishin). However, almost since its occurrence, it has been known in Japan as the "Great East Japan Earthquake" (Higashi-Nihon daishinsai). In scientific papers written in English, it is often called the "2011 Tōhoku earthquake." Similarly, the January 17, 1995, earthquake that shook Kōbe and surrounding areas is officially known as the Southern Hyōgo Prefecture earthquake (Hyōgo-ken nanbu jishin), but it is more commonly known in Japan as the Hanshin-Awaji earthquake, sometimes shortened to Hanshin or Great Hanshin Earthquake. Sometimes it is also called the Rokkō-Awaji earthquake, taking its name from the fault system that caused it. However, in the English-speaking world this event is usually known as the Kōbe earthquake.

Earthquakes that took place in the distant past also sometimes possess multiple names. One potentially confusing aspect of nomenclature is the use of era names in premodern earthquakes. The 1855 Ansei Edo earthquake, for example, shook the shōgun's capital of Edo (present-day Tokyo), and until recently it was common to call this earthquake the "Ansei Earthquake." The previous year, however, the more powerful Ansei Tōkai and Ansei Nankai earthquakes and their resulting tsunami wave trains ravaged large areas of the coast of Honshū and Shikoku. In addition, there were other major earthquakes during the relatively short Ansei era (1854–1860). The use of complete and precise names for earthquakes is therefore important in cases like these to prevent confusion about different events occurring close in time during periods of particularly frequent seismic activity in the Japanese islands.

As a rule, if there is a well-established English-language name for an earthquake, I use it in preference to Japanese names. In the case of earthquakes farther in the past without English names, I use the most common Japanese name, with alternatives given parenthetically the first time the name occurs. Similarly, if a government agency has an official English name or commonly used initials, I use that name or initials, with the Japanese name given parenthetically the first time it appears. For example, I refer to the Japan Meteorological Agency as the JMA, although in Japanese it is the Kishōchō (weather bureau). Otherwise, I translate the Japanese names of agencies. I do the same for laws, book titles, and any other instances in which it is reasonable to use English terms instead of Japanese. My intention is for this book to be of use both to specialists in Japanese studies and to a broader audience, hence a bias for using English in the main text as much as possible. The notes, however, faithfully reflect Japanese-language materials, and specialists should have no difficulty looking up any cited source. In some cases, there is no obvious best choice for one name over another, and it is necessary simply to select one and use it consistently.

Another name-related issue occurs because the normal order of Japanese and East Asian personal names puts the family name first. The general practice in the humanities, which I follow, is to use East Asian order in both the main text and notes when citing works written in Japanese. In works written in English or other Western languages, or in the case of people with Japanese names based outside of Japan or East Asia, the names usually follow Western order. Because parts of this book are multidisciplinary, I should point out that there is a strong tendency in the sciences to impose Western name order on everyone, everywhere. Moreover, from correspondence with seismologists, I have learned that there are political implications to personal naming conventions in the sciences.

Therefore, I should point out explicitly that my use of native Japanese name order simply follows conventional practice in the humanities and does not imply preference or support for any political cause or orientation.

The situation with Japanese personal names becomes even more complex when dealing with times before 1868. Instead of attempting to explain some of the arcane details here, I will simply follow the usual academic conventions. Those who know them will see my logic, and other readers should be able to follow the discussion without undue difficulty because personal names are relatively few. Place names, earthquake names, and agency names may become difficult to track in some contexts, but occasional use of the maps, other figures, and the glossary should prevent confusion.

EARTHQUAKE COUNTRY

It is common for writers in Japan to claim that their country is the most seismically active in the world. There are different ways to quantify seismic activity, so it might well be possible to support this claim with creative use of statistics. However, using modern state boundaries and looking at the twenty-year period between 1980 and 2000, China experienced the greatest number of earthquakes in the world, and Japan was in fourth place, behind Indonesia and Iran. On the other hand, for this same period, Japan averaged 281.3 fatalities per year from earthquakes, whereas China averaged 92.2. Iran led the world in fatalities, averaging 2,250.3 per year for these twenty years.[9] Extending the time by ten years to include the hundreds of thousands of earthquake fatalities suffered by China during the 1970s would greatly increase the Chinese average. Claims to the title of the world's most earthquake-prone country, in other words, are difficult to quantify, and there is no universal standard for doing so. By almost any measure, Japan is among the few most seismically active countries in the world, and that point is sufficient for our purposes. Of the world's M6-class (and greater) earthquakes, 22 percent occur in or near Japan, while Japan occupies 0.6 percent of the world's surface area. In short, seismic activity is a major natural hazard in Japan.

The basic reason for this situation is that the Japanese islands lie at the intersection of four tectonic plates, two of which, the Pacific Plate and the Philippine Sea Plate, create zones of subduction by sliding underneath

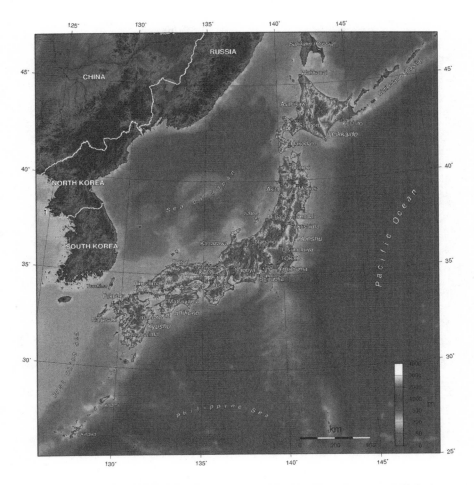

Figure 1.2. Topographic Map of Japan. Approximate tectonic plate boundaries are visible. *Source*: **Wikimedia Commons, Electionworld.**

the North American and Eurasian Plates, respectively. These zones of subduction are the sources of megathrust earthquakes that often generate trains of seismic sea waves, once inaccurately called "tidal waves" but now known around the world by their Japanese-derived name, tsunami.

In zones of subduction, two tectonic plates are moving toward each other. Oceanic plates slide under continental plates because the oceanic plates are denser. Oceanic plates travel under the continental plates offshore from the Japanese islands, but friction between the two plates temporarily locks their boundary. As strain accumulates and the boundary remains locked, the continental plate distorts, the edge bending downward. Despite our perception of rock as hard and brittle, it can and does bend. Strain accumulates behind the locked boundary as the main portions of the plates continue to move toward each other. The accumulated strain eventually becomes sufficiently powerful to overcome the friction, and the plate boundary ruptures. The oceanic plate suddenly lurches downward, the continental plate pulls free, and its edge rebounds upward. This event is a megathrust earthquake. It causes the ground over a wide area to shake owing to the release of several types of seismic waves that travel outward from the hypocenter (or focus), the area of rupture. The epicenter is the place on the surface directly above the hypocenter.

When the continental plate rebounds upward, in most cases it displaces large quantities of water. This displaced water becomes a tsunami, usually not a single wave but a series of them. 3/11 was a megathrust earthquake that occurred in an area often described as an "earthquake nest." That 3/11 occurred where it did was not surprising, but its magnitude of 9.0 exceeded most expectations. Later I will examine the question of whether an M9-class event really was or should have been "unimaginable," as many Japanese officials and scientists defensively claimed soon after the event. Of the earthquakes that shake Japan, 85 percent are ocean trench earthquakes, that is, earthquakes originating in zones of subduction. All earthquakes more powerful than M8.0 are of this type.

The geology of the Japanese islands is complex, in large part owing to the tectonic forces that have compressed, folded, twisted, and overlaid multiple layers of rock. Consider as a rough metaphor giant cosmic hands grasping Honshū and the other main islands and partially wringing them out like towels. About twenty million years ago, the northern island of Hokkaidō was actually two islands, split roughly east and west. Tectonic forces have jammed these two islands together, pressing them into a single entity whose landforms differ significantly east versus west.[10] The twisting and compression from these tectonic forces have produced more than two thousand faults, or tears in the crust, throughout the Japanese islands.

As tectonic forces continue to put pressure on the Japanese islands, these faults occasionally move suddenly, resulting in earthquakes with magnitudes as high as 8.0 but usually lower. Although these intraplate earthquakes (*chokkagata jishin*, often translated as "near-field earthquakes") typically release less energy than do those originating in sub-

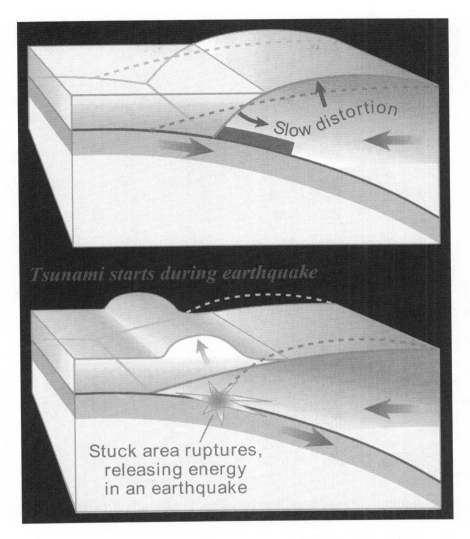

Figure 1.3. **Megathrust Earthquake and Tsunami Mechanics.** *Source*: Wikimedia Commons, Brian F. Atwater, Marco Cisternas V., Joanne Bourgeois, Walter C. Dudley, James W. Hendley II, and Peter H. Stauffer.

duction zones, the hypocenter is usually much closer to inhabited areas. Therefore, destruction from ground motion in these cases can be severe. Intraplate earthquakes generally do not produce tsunamis.

Is it reasonable to assume that any part of the Japanese islands is safe from earthquakes? The short answer is no. One reason is that despite efforts to find and map faults after 1995, many remain unknown. News-

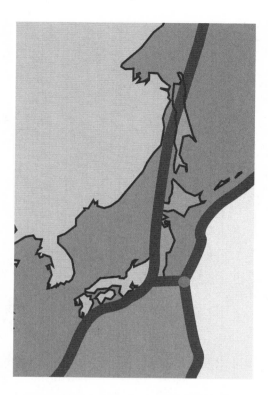

Figure 1.4. Triple Junction of Tectonic Plates. *Source*: **Wikimedia Commons, Pimvantend.**

paper articles regularly report new discoveries of faults, and many recent earthquakes have occurred where no faults were known to have existed. Examples include the Western Tottori Prefecture (2000), Niigata Chūetsu (2004), Fukui Prefecture Western Offshore (2005), Nōtō Peninsula and Niigata Chūetsu Offshore (2007), and Iwate-Miyagi (2008) earthquakes.[11] The deadly 1995 Kōbe earthquake also occurred in an area thought at the time to be free of faults. The violent shaking was the first sign of the subsequently discovered Rokkō-Awaji fault system. The likely presence of many unknown faults is one reason that destructive earthquakes may occur anywhere in the Japanese islands.

Another relevant factor is the extremely long recurrence intervals between earthquakes on many faults. We have already seen the examples of Rokkō-Awaji and Longshanmen in China. Let us consider one more. The Western Lake Biwa fault zone (Biwako seigan dansō tai) runs north-

northeast to south-southwest for about fifty-nine kilometers along the western shore of Lake Biwa. There is a danger that it will cause an M7.8 earthquake, which would release five times more energy than the Kōbe earthquake (magnitude scales logarithmically). Such an earthquake would cause severe damage to Kyoto and surrounding areas. Recent excavations of the fault indicate a recurrence interval between 1,900 and 4,500 years, and the most recent earthquake occurred 2,400–2,800 years ago.

From the standpoint of the short end of the estimated recurrence range of the Western Lake Biwa fault zone, the next big earthquake is, in a sense, "overdue." However, at the other end of the range, we still have some two thousand years to go. Calculated retrospectively using current methods, the probability for the Kōbe earthquake on the eve of its occurrence was 0.4–8 percent.[12] A very wide range in the estimated recurrence intervals of many faults is common, and it indicates that creating such estimates is far from an exact science. Given our current state of knowledge, it is prudent to assume that any part of the Japanese islands may experience a destructive earthquake at any time. Moreover, these earthquakes cannot be predicted.

PROMINENCE OF EARTHQUAKE PREDICTION IN JAPAN

A September 26, 2012, headline in a Japanese newspaper caught my attention: "4 Year Term Sought for Earthquake Prediction Failure" (*Jishin yochi shippai de yonen kyūkei*). The article was about a trial in Italy of six scientists and a government official for malfeasance in connection with the April 2009 L'Aquila earthquake in central Italy that killed 309. "Bringing a charge of criminal responsibility for failure to predict an earthquake is exceptional anywhere in the world," stated the article.[13] If indeed the article's characterization of the issue was correct, then the scientists in Italy were on trial for failing to do the impossible.

Further investigation revealed a more complex situation. The prosecution specifically rejected the notion that the scientists bore responsibility for earthquake prediction. According to reporting in the journal *Nature*, "[Prosecutor Fabio] Picuti made it clear that the scientists are not accused of failing to predict the earthquake. 'Even six-year-old kids know that earthquakes cannot be predicted,' he said."[14] In an earlier statement, Picuti reiterated that earthquake prediction was not the issue. Instead, he claimed, the scientists were negligent in performing diligent risk assessment: "Part of that risk assessment, he says, should have included the density of the urban population and the known fragility of many ancient buildings in the city centre. 'They were obligated to evaluate the degree of risk given all these factors,' he says, 'and they did not.'" [15]

This case might well be a manifestation of a modern tendency to expect more of science than it can deliver. Commentator Brendan O'Neill disagrees with the Italian action but blames the scientific community in part for it. Like the Japanese press, he also rejects the notion that the trial was not about earthquake prediction. He makes an excellent point about the mistaken modern assumption that science and the state can control nature and ensure safety:

> Fundamentally, the criminalisation of people for failing to predict an earthquake, and potentially lessen its impact, speaks to Western society's discomfort with the idea of accidents or disasters, with the idea that some things just happen and no one is responsible. Ours is an era in which we find it very hard to accept that some events have no logic behind them. And so we continually go on Medieval hunts for a malevolent force or person who might be blamed for various terrible things that occur. [16]

I second O'Neill's point and add that the notion that perfect safety is possible is itself a hindrance to genuinely effective disaster mitigation. The belief that scientists must surely be able to predict earthquakes is one specific manifestation of this modern myth of perfect safety.

It is common to claim that Japan spends more on earthquake research than on military defense. [17] Perhaps if emergency preparedness, broadly defined, is included, then the figures could be comparable, but central government funding for earthquake research is significantly less than total military spending. Nevertheless, earthquake research spending is significant, totaling approximately 35 billion yen (359,275,000 USD) in fiscal year 2012 and amounting to nearly 30 percent of total science spending. A look at the line items shows that the majority of this research budget is for monitoring and data collection. [18] The total spending figure would be larger if we included personnel salaries and certain earthquake-related construction projects. [19] As we will see in chapter 5, the spending priorities in this budget are the direct result of Japan's postwar earthquake prediction program. Japan has sunk more resources into earthquake prediction than any other country, and we will see that earthquake prediction is even written into law.

Bookstores offer a variety of volumes on earthquake prediction for general readers, most authored by university scientists, including a few seismologists. The boldest of these books actually claim that earthquake prediction is currently possible. Marine geologist Kimura Masaaki, for example, offers a four-step "Kimura method" that he says could be put to practical use right now for short-term prediction.[20] His view, however, is well outside the mainstream.

Much more common among prediction advocates is an acknowledgment that accurate short-term earthquake prediction is not currently possible. Advocates typically implore readers to keep the faith that short-term prediction will one day become a reality. Tokyo University seismologist Tsukuda Tameshige, for example, after granting that reliable seismic precursors have yet to be found, says:

> The various phenomena thought to be associated with large earthquakes occur in an apparently capricious manner. We call this "haphazard" (*detarame*). It is correct to regard earthquake precursor phenomena as "haphazard" because they do not follow a single pattern. Please, however, do not think, "This realm is nonsense." We cannot depend on any particular piece of data, but combining them all together results in useful information.[21]

This passage frankly acknowledges the chaotic nature of earthquakes, which seems at odds with the topic of Tsukuda's book: a sympathetic survey of the science of earthquake prediction. Notice that for Tsukuda, even taken together, earthquake precursors provide "information," not specific predictive capabilities. It is common in works promoting earthquake prediction for the author to imply that successful prediction may someday be possible without specifying a clear path forward to that goal. A common approach of prediction advocates is simply to list vast quantities of possible precursors and unexplained anomalies.

Similarly, prediction advocate and Osaka university physicist Motoji Ikeya specifically rejects the idea that we are currently able to predict earthquakes with precision:

> I am not arguing for earthquake prediction using the animal precursors described in *Earthquakes and Animals*, if, by prediction, we are meaning an exact forecast of time, epicenter, and magnitude of an earthquake. In that case no prediction is possible for any fracture phenomena. . . . But I

am arguing that there is a scientific basis to many of the legendary and reported precursors.[22]

Most of the rest of his book presents the case that a wide array of precursors might, taken together, indicate an increased likelihood of a near-future earthquake. In other words, even the majority of earthquake prediction advocates in Japan, when pressed, acknowledge precise prediction as a goal, not as a capability that currently exists.

Why persist in pursuing the goal of prediction after decades (or even centuries) of sustained effort have resulted in approximately zero practical capacity? In addition to legal considerations, some Japanese scientists perceive a moral imperative. "Can we give up efforts at prediction and just passively wait for a big one?" asked prediction research advocate Kyioo Mogi.[23] Although Mogi's answer was "no," those who reject the possibility of earthquake prediction tend to argue that excessive optimism in this realm and the diversion of resources accompanying it does a disservice to society.

Debates over earthquake prediction often display a linguistically slippery quality. Especially common is rhetorical movement between "prediction" in the sense of short-term, specific prediction (usually *yochi* in Japanese) with "forecasting" in the sense of longer-term probabilities (usually *yosoku* in Japanese), roughly akin to weather forecasts. Especially when pressed by skeptics, advocates of earthquake prediction often end up saying that research into earthquake prediction is a worthy endeavor because it is likely to lead to better forecasting. Many writers for a popular audience seem actively to slide back and forth between implied promises that short-term prediction could become a reality and specific claims only about long-term forecasting. Linguistic and conceptual confusion often occurs in the context of discussing past events. Many advocates of earthquake prediction, for example, tend to claim that there have been accurate predictions in the past. Not only are many of these alleged predictions poorly constrained in terms of time, location, and magnitude, but also it is common to "predict" earthquakes retrospectively, that is, after the event has occurred. In 1994, in the immediate aftermath of the Northridge, California, earthquake, "an eminent seismologist was asked if anyone had predicted the earthquake. 'Not yet,' came his deadpan reply."[24]

Views on earthquake prediction among experts constitute a spectrum. At one end is the view that earthquakes are so chaotic that research

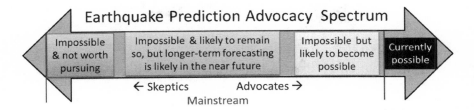

Figure 1.5. **Earthquake Prediction Advocacy Spectrum.** *Source*: Gregory Smits.

aimed at attempting to predict or forecast them is pointless and wasteful. At the other extreme are those very few people who claim precise earthquake prediction is currently possible. Closer to the mainstream would be those who acknowledge that short-term prediction is currently impossible but anticipate that with more effort it will become possible in the future. Roughly in the middle would be those who think short-term prediction is likely to remain impossible but that reasonably good longer-term forecasting is both a future possibility and a worthy goal. "It may never be that we get to the 'You're gonna have an earthquake *next Thursday*' sort of scenario," said one scientist in an interview. "But I think it's entirely possible that we'll get to a point where we can say, 'Sometime in the *next decade* we're likely to have something happen.' And I think that sort of thing is on the horizon in the not-too-distant future."[25] In the past, the actual behavior of the earth has rendered even such limited optimism problematic. On the other hand, the history of science abounds with examples of the impossible becoming possible.

SEEKING ORDER IN A CHAOTIC EARTH

Consider the following summary of 3/11 by a seismologist. It is a concise statement of the reigning idea in geology of "characteristic earthquakes" (*koyū jishin*):

> The Tōhoku Region Offshore earthquake of 2011 was a giant event of magnitude 9.0. An earthquake of this magnitude has never been recorded in Japan, nor was it conceptualized. Long-term government forecasts specified a 99% chance of an earthquake of about M7.5 occurring offshore from Miyagi prefecture within 30 years. At a minimum, [this forecast] served as a definite earthquake warning. The current earthquake greatly exceeded forecasts in terms of magnitude, but that was a result of the historical record, upon which long term forecasting

is mainly based. *Forecasting assumes that the same kinds of earthquakes will occur in the future.* The assumptions about earthquakes and tsunamis that entities like the nuclear power industry or the Central Council for Disaster Prevention adopt, and the countermeasures they implement, are based mainly on the previous largest earthquake that has occurred since the Meiji period.[26]

The Meiji period (1868–1912) or even the Tokugawa period (1603–1867) is a terribly short time geologically from which to extrapolate earthquake characteristics. Indeed, 3/11 has raised the question of whether it is even accurate to conceive of earthquakes as possessing regularly recurring characteristics.[27]

The notion that earthquakes in specific locations exhibit characteristic qualities has a long history. In most contexts, it is an assumption rather than an established fact. Earthquakes of approximately the same size, recurring at regular or semiregular intervals in approximately the same place, are characteristic earthquakes. The idea has a strong emotional appeal. Writer Jerry Thompson, for example, is typical of those who find the chaotic, random nature of earthquakes disheartening. In the context of discussing a recent theory, Thompson sums up what is surely the hope of many: "Just when chaos theory seemed to have won the day, there was a fresh reason to think that at least some seismic shocks might not be a statistical crapshoot."[28] This aversion to randomness is reminiscent of the famous assertion by Albert Einstein that "God doesn't play dice with the world."[29] In the early twentieth century, Einstein opposed the emerging theory of quantum mechanics largely because it implies that ultimate reality at the subatomic level is probabilistic in nature. At the scale of the earth, earthquakes have repeatedly confounded scientists and others seeking orderly processes.

Long-term forecasting depends on a notion of characteristic earthquakes. Using historical records when possible and literally digging out portions of faults and examining them where practical and affordable are two methods for gathering data about past earthquakes. In Japan, the Tōkai, Tōnankai, and Nankai earthquakes caused by the Philippine Sea Plate moving under the Eurasian Plate off the Pacific coast between Suruga Bay and the southwest end of the island of Shikoku are the commonly cited examples of characteristic earthquakes. Experts also regard some intraplate faults as producing characteristic earthquakes, mainly as a function of their length.[30]

Closely related to the idea of characteristic earthquakes are notions of a seismic cycle or a seismic gap. The idea of a seismic gap comes into play in the case of long faults with multiple segments. According to the seismic gap model, the segment that ruptured most recently is considered safe, and the segment that ruptured farthest in the past is thought to possess the greatest danger of rupturing in the future. Indeed, if a segment or fault remains quiet too long, there is a tendency to consider it "overdue." Many experts currently regard the segment of the Nankai Trough that borders on Suruga Bay, for example, as overdue and thus especially dangerous. This way of thinking makes intuitive sense. However, does it hold up to rigorous analysis?

Yan Y. Kagan, David D. Jackson, Seth Stein, and others have long been critics of the seismic gap theory, pointing out as early as 1991 that it has failed to predict actual earthquakes better than random chance.[31] Kagan and others have recently argued that characteristic earthquake and seismic gap models do not hold up to testing and in some iterations are too vague to test.[32] We tend to have better data, whether historical or instrumental, closer in time to the present. One statistical problem is that short sequences of events pulled from a random process can often appear quasiperiodic, especially when a broader intellectual context that assumes precisely this characteristic predisposes our thinking. Moreover, the seismic gap model has not conferred a statistically significant improvement in forecasting. Kagan and colleagues point to the uncharacteristic 2004 Sumatra earthquake and tsunami and 3/11 as "tragic failures" of characteristic earthquake models. The model also confers a false sense of relative safety because of the problematic idea that a region is immune from large shocks following a characteristic earthquake.[33]

Given that the characteristic earthquake model is both aesthetically satisfying and deeply ingrained in the way many specialists and nonspecialists think about earthquakes, it will probably remain influential despite such criticism. The main concern in this study is not earthquakes as geophysical phenomena but earthquakes interacting with society to cause natural disasters. In the subsequent chapters, I develop the argument that just as earthquakes lack characteristic qualities as geophysical phenomena, so, too, do they lack such qualities as natural disasters. We cannot predict how earthquakes will play out in society owing to a superfluity of variables. This argument is not a call for complacency or resignation but instead underlines the need for careful analysis and flexibility in disaster planning. In particular, it is essential to avoid the tendency to assume that the next earthquake disaster will resemble the previous one. It might, but we cannot know in advance.

Whether because of a flawed paradigm or for other reasons, 3/11 surprised many experts. Politicians and nuclear power officials cited the unprecedented nature of the catastrophe in defense of their haplessness in its immediate aftermath. If earthquake prediction is impossible and the basic assumptions behind long-term forecasting are quite possibly flawed, was 3/11 an unimaginable event that nobody could reasonably have anticipated?

BEYOND THE PALE?

In thinking through certain facets of 3/11, it may be helpful to divide the event into two related but different catastrophes. On the one hand, the earthquake and tsunami wreaked death and destruction all along the Sanriku coast, in some cases wiping out areas thought to have been protected by seawalls. In addition to killing some twenty thousand people, the tsunami caused massive displacement of survivors and a disruption of economic activities. On the other hand is the nuclear disaster. The 3/11 tsunami disabled Tokyo Electric Power Company (TEPCO)'s Fukushima Daiichi nuclear plant, causing meltdowns of three reactor cores.

The meltdowns did not cause any known fatalities, but they did displace hundreds of thousands from their homes and occupations. Moreover, the event prompted nationwide, even worldwide, anxieties about the possibility of nuclear contamination, a shutdown of Japan's other nuclear reactors, and a popular outcry against nuclear power. The nuclear crisis has garnered the lion's share of attention in connection with 3/11. This book deals mainly with seismic danger, but a brief examination of the intersection of seismic hazards and nuclear power will shed light on some of the themes of later chapters, especially bureaucratic inertia and resistance to change in the face of new evidence. It is this evidence that is ultimately relevant to the question of whether 3/11 should have exceeded the bounds of official imagination.

The regulatory policy for Japan's nuclear power plants dates from 1978, though it was slightly updated in 2006.[34] The regulations state that nuclear power plants must be able to withstand the equivalent of an M6.5 earthquake (now M6.7).[35] Why such a low magnitude level? The reason is that plants must be built on a foundation of bedrock and must not be located near an active fault. Faults, however, can be complex. They twist, turn, stop, and start and are difficult to detect in places. As we have seen, many recent M7-class earthquakes have occurred in areas where no faults had previously been suspected. Therefore, the standards for nuclear plants are probably set too low, and several seismologists raised this concern in published work prior to 3/11.[36]

Prior to 3/11, several prominent scientists warned specifically of seismic hazards to nuclear plants. In 2008, for example, Shimamura Hideki wrote that in the event of a major Tōkai earthquake, "the danger is not only that a nuclear plant will incur damage, but the strong likelihood that it will produce more damage."[37] Writing in 2003, Kaminuma Katsutada said, "In recent years there has been debate over the safety of active faults near nuclear power plants. . . . It is a fact that the area around nuclear power plants is subject to the occurrence of large earthquakes."[38] Only after 3/11 have messages like these received a wide hearing.

Seismic land waves from 3/11 subjected the Fukushima Daiichi Nuclear Power Plant to acceleration that exceeded its maximum design basis in an east-west direction by 20 percent. It is indeed fortunate that the plant was built on solid rock because nearby acceleration levels were nearly four times higher on sediments (unconsolidated sediments usually experience the most severe ground motion in an earthquake). Despite this high acceleration level, the plant withstood the shaking fairly well. However, it was designed to withstand a tsunami wave height of only 3.1 meters, based on the 1960 Chile tsunami. The plant was built ten meters above sea level with seawater pumps four meters above sea level. The 3/11 tsunami waves in this area reached heights of fifteen meters, overwhelming backup systems and leading to the current ongoing nuclear crisis.[39]

Could anyone in a position of responsibility for the nuclear industry have reasonably known that an M9-class earthquake, with its correspondingly high tsunami waves, was a possibility? Finance Minister Yosano Kaoru famously called 3/11 "an act of God" (*kamisama no shiwaza*), but within weeks of the earthquake, considerable evidence began to emerge suggesting human responsibility for the disaster.[40] Subsequently, we have come to learn that executives from TEPCO and other nuclear plants had received explicit warnings prior to 3/11 of the possibility of a massive earthquake and tsunami.

As early as 1990 an article on the Jōgan earthquake and tsunami of 869 appeared in *Jishin*, the journal of the Seismological Society of Japan (Nihon jishin gakkai), authored by experts at the Onagawa Nuclear Power Plant construction center. In 2009, seismologist Okamura Yukinobu asked TEPCO representatives directly about the Jōgan earthquake at a June meeting of Japan's Nuclear and Industrial Safety Agency (NISA). TEPCO representative Nishimura Isao tried to deflect the question, first implying that the Jōgan earthquake was not terribly destructive and then claiming that other, less severe earthquakes were more appropriate models. At the next month's NISA meeting, Okamura again brought up the matter, characterizing the Jōgan earthquake as a repeating event in the region and citing a seventeenth-century Chishima Trough earthquake in the Kuriles and the 2004 Sumatra earthquake as examples of what is possible. Again, TEPCO officials ignored the warning.[41] Just days before 3/11, Japan's Earthquake Research Committee was on the verge of issuing a report warning of the possibility of a massive tsunami based on its assessment of the Jōgan earthquake. We now know that officials from three power companies intervened, pleading with the committee to soften the language in its report.[42]

The broader seismic context also presented ample evidence that M9-class earthquakes and correspondingly devastating tsunamis were a possibility. The key to revealing these events was the development of moment magnitude in 1977. During the 1960s, scientists began to use seismic moment as their standard measure of earthquakes. Seismic moment takes into account the shear modus of involved rocks, the surface area of the fault rupture, and the average displacement. Seismic moment was a more precise measure than Richter magnitude, especially for large earthquakes. In the 1930s, Charles Richter and Beno Gutenberg developed a logarithmic local magnitude scale to deal with the kinds of earthquakes that strike California.[43] These earthquakes are M7 class or less and do not include megathrust earthquakes. Because the Richter scale was so common, however, Hiroo Kanamori and Thomas Hanks created a formula to convert seismic moment to the values of the Richter scale. Since the end of the 1970s, the expression "magnitude x" refers by default to moment magnitude for events above M3.5. At around 8.0, Richter magnitude and moment magnitude begin to diverge significantly.[44]

With the advent of moment magnitude, a new picture began to emerge around the Pacific region as earthquakes previously classified in the low M8 range were "upgraded" to M9 events. For example, the 1960 Chile earthquake, whose tsunami killed people in Japan, went from a Richter magnitude of 8.3 to a moment magnitude of 9.5. Stated differently, the Chile earthquake released 150 times more energy than had previously been thought (magnitude scale is logarithmic). The 1964 Alaska earthquake became an M9.2 event, and the 1952 Kamchatka earthquake became an M9.0 event.[45] In the old Richter scale, the 2004 Sumatra earthquake would have been 8.6 instead of 9.3, and the 3/11 earthquake would have been 8.2 instead of 9.0.[46]

By the 1990s, therefore, not only had an article about the Jōgan earthquake been published in a major journal, but also recent M9-class earthquakes had occurred in three places around the Pacific. Discovery of a likely M9-class earthquake in 1700 associated with the Cascadia Subduction Zone (whose tsunami struck Japan) and the 2004 Sumatra earthquake added to the evidence that M9-class earthquakes occasionally took place in or near the Pacific region.[47] Although specific earthquakes cannot be accurately forecast, long before 3/11, experts in Japan's nuclear power industry knew, or should have known, that an M9-class earthquake was possible. Indeed, industry officials actively ignored both general and specific warnings.

We should bear in mind that M8-class earthquakes and large, deadly tsunamis struck Japan's northeast coast in 1611, 1793, 1856, 1896, and 1933. Although casualty figures for the first three events are difficult to discern, the 1896 Meiji Sanriku earthquake and tsunami killed more people than the 3/11 event. Had residents of the Sanriku coast heeded warnings from 1896 and 1933 not to build in dangerous lowlands, the 3/11 death and destruction toll would have been significantly lower. Major earthquakes can strike anywhere in Japan, but large tsunamigenic earthquakes have been especially frequent along the Sanriku coast. We now turn our attention to northeastern Japan during the early modern era (the Tokugawa period, 1603–1867).

NOTES

1. Satake Kenji, "Kyodai tsunami no mekanizumu," in *Kyodai jishin, kyodai tsunami: Higashi Nihon daishinsai no kenshō*, by Hirata Naoshi, Satake Kenji, Meguro Kimirō, and Hatakemura Yōtarō (Asakura shoten, 2011), 74–82.

2. For a comprehensive guide to the damage that occurred in the 3/11 event, see Gerard K. Sutton and Joseph A. Cassalli, eds., *Catastrophe in Japan: The Earthquake and Tsunami of 2011* (New York: Nova Science, 2011).

3. Regarding adobe houses in Iran, see Susan Elizabeth Hough and Roger G. Bilham, *After the Earth Quakes: Elastic Rebound in an Urban Planet* (New York: Oxford University Press, 2006), 22.

4. Shimamura Hideki, *Nihonjin ga shiritai jishin no gimon rokujūroku: Jishin ga ōi Nihon dakara koso chishiki no sonae mo wasurezu ni* (Soft Bank Creative, 2008), 32; and Shimamura Hideki, *"Jishin yochi" wa usodarake* (Kōdansha, 2008), 138–40.

5. Jishin chōsa kenkyū suishin honbu, "Rokkō-Awajishima dansō-tai," accessed October 8, 2012, http://www.jishin.go.jp/main/yosokuchizu/katsudanso/f079_rokko_awaji.htm.

6. Shimamura, *Jishin yochi*, 164.

7. "City Looks to Base Tsunami Warnings on Animal Behavior," *Japan Times*, June 3, 2012; and "Japanese City to Watch Animal Behaviour for Disaster Signs," *Tokyo Times*, 2012.

8. For details on earthquake naming, see Shimamura, *Jishin no gimon*, 93–95.

9. Tsuji Yoshinobu, *Zukai, Naze okoru? Itsu okoru? Jishin no mekanizumu* (Nagaoka shoten, 2010), 16–17.

10. Shimamura, *Jishin no gimon*, 68. For a comprehensive survey, see Mitsuo Hashimoto, ed., *Geology of Japan* (Tokyo: Terra Scientific, 1991).

11. Shimamura, *Jishin yochi*, 164. See also see Shimamura, *Jishin no gimon*, 76.

12. Shimamura, *Jishin yochi*, 164–68.

13. "Jishin yochi shippai de 4 nen kyūkei, Itaria kensatsu, gakushara 7 nin ni iinkai no handan ga hitobito no shi ni musubitsuita," *MSN-Sankei nyūsu*, September 26, 2012.

14. Nicola Nosengo, "Prosecution Asks for Four-Year Sentence in Italian Seismology Trial," *Nature Newsblog* (blog), September 25, 2012, http://blogs.nature.com/news/2012/09/porsecution-asks-for-four-year-sentence-in-italian-seismology-trial.html.

15. Stephen S. Hall, "Scientists on Trial: At Fault?" *Nature* 477 (2011): 264–69, http://www.nature.com/news/2011/110914/full/477264a.html.

16. Brendan O'Neill, "A Disaster That Science Brought upon Itself," *Spiked*, November 6, 2012, http://www.spiked-online.com/site/printable/13016.

17. For example, see Hough and Bilham, *After the Earth Quakes*, 174.

18. For the details of spending on earthquake research for FY 2011, 2012, and 2013, see Jishin chōsa kenkyū suishin honbu, "Budget Related to Earthquake Research for FY 2012," http://www.jishin.go.jp/main/yosan-e/yosan2012b.pdf; and "Budget Request Related to Earthquake Research for FY 2013," http://www.jishin.go.jp/main/yosan-e/yosan2013a.pdf.

19. For more details on the history of Japan's earthquake research budget, see Shimamura, *Jishin yochi*, 115–17.

20. The four steps are: (1) locate the "seismic eye" of a cluster of earthquakes to determine the likely location; (2) after the seismic eye becomes manifest, the main shock will occur within thirty years, thus determining the time frame; (3) refine the time estimate with reference to volcanic activity; and (4) the size of the seismic eye determines the size of the main shock. See Kimura Masaaki, *Daijishin no zenchō o toreata! Keikai subeki chiiki wa dokoka* (Daisan bunmeisha, 2008), esp. 111–17. I should emphasize that Kimura's method has not been proved effective by rigorous testing, and I cite it here as an example of prediction theories and methods available to the public via books and mass media.

21. Tsukuda Tameshige, *Jishin yochi no saishin kagaku: Hassei no mekanizumu to yochi kenkyū no saizensen* (SoftBank Creative, 2007), 18.

22. Motoji Ikeya, *Earthquakes and Animals: From Folk Legends to Science* (River Edge, NJ: World Scientific, 2004), ix.

23. Quoted in Jerry Thompson, *Cascadia's Fault: The Coming Earthquake and Tsunami That Could Devastate North America* (Berkeley, CA: Counterpoint, 2011), 254.

24. Susan Elizabeth Hough, *Earthshaking Science: What We Know (and Don't Know) about Earthquakes* (Princeton, NJ: Princeton University Press, 2002), 123.

25. Chris Goldfinger quoted in Thompson, *Cascadia's Fault*, 264.

26. Satake, "Kyodai tsunami," 89–90. Italics added.

27. Yan Y. Kagan, David D. Jackson, and Robert J. Geller, "Characteristic Earthquake Model, 1884–2011, R.I.P.," *Seismological Research Letters* 83 (November/December 2012): 951–53.

28. Thompson, *Cascadia's Fault*, 263.

29. William Hermanns, *Einstein and the Poet: In Search of the Cosmic Man* (Wellesley, MA: Branden Books, 1983), 58.

30. For a concise summary of characteristic earthquakes, see Tsukuda, *Yochi no saishin kagaku*, 110–11.

31. Yan Y. Kagan and David D. Jackson, "Seismic Gap Hypothesis: Ten Years After," *Journal of Geophysical Research* 96, no. 13 (December 10, 1991): 21, 419–21, 431; Seth Stein, "Seismic Gaps and Grizzly Bears," *Nature* 356 (April 2, 1992): 387–88. See also Andrew Robinson, *Earthquake: Nature and Culture* (London: Reaktion, 2012), 166.

32. Kagan, Jackson, and Geller, "Characteristic Earthquake Model," 951–53.

33. Kagan, Jackson, and Geller, "Characteristic Earthquake Model."

34. It is called *Hatsudenyō genshiro shisetsu ni kansuru taishin sekkei shinsa shishin* (*Guidelines for Earthquake Resistant Design Review for Nuclear Power Plants*), often shortened to *Shishin*. A detailed analysis of these guidelines can be found at the National Diet Library, accessed October 11, 2012, http://rnavi.ndl.go.jp/research_guide/entry/theme-honbun-400230.php.

35. This magnitude corresponds to peak ground acceleration of between 450 and 600 galileos (1 Gal = 1 cm/sec^2). Peak acceleration at the Fukushima Daiichi nuclear plant was about 550 galileos. Peak acceleration at nearby areas of unconsolidated fill was about 2,000 galileos.

36. Shimamura, *Jishin yochi*, 232–39; and Shimamura, *Jishin no gimon*, 74–76. See also Robert Geller (Robaato Gera), *Nihonjin wa shiranai "jishin yochi" no shōtai* (Futabasha, 2011), 56; and World Nuclear Association, "Earthquakes and Seismic Protection for Japanese NPPs," http://www.world-nuclear.org/fukushima/earthquakes_seismic_protection_japan.html.

37. Shimamura, *Jishin yochi*, 239–43, quotation on 243.

38. Kaminuma Katsutada, "Jishin yochi to kazan funka yochi no kenkyūsha no yakuwari," in *Jishin yochi to shakai*, ed. Kaminuma Katsutada and Hirata Kōji (Kokon shoin, 2003), 15–16.

39. World Nuclear Association, "Fukushima Accident," http://www.world-nuclear.org/info/Safety-and-Security/Safety-of-Plants/Fukushima-Accident/.

40. Minoru Matsutani, "Nuclear Crisis Man-Made, Not 'an Act of God': Experts, Government, Tepco Blamed for Failure to Prepare for Tsunami," *Japan Times*, April 6, 2011.

41. David Nakamura and Chico Harlan, "Japanese Nuclear Plant's Safety Analysts Brushed Off Risk of Tsunami," *Washington Post*, March 23, 2011. For a more detailed account of this and related matters, see Geller, *Jishin yochi*, 51–66.

42. "Tsunami Alert Softened Days before 3/11," *Japan Times Online*, February 27, 2012.

43. For a thorough account of the development of Richter's local magnitude scale, see Robinson, *Earthquake*, 95–107.

44. See Geller, *Jishin yochi*, 32–35, for an account of the creation of moment magnitude. See also Robinson, *Earthquake*, 107–10.

45. Geller, *Jishin yochi*, 35–36.

46. World Nuclear Association, "Earthquakes and Seismic Protection."

47. See Brian F. Atwater et al., *The Orphan Tsunami of 1700: Japanese Clues to a Parent Earthquake in North America* (*Minashigo Genroku tsunami: Oya-jishin wa Hokubei seikaigan ni ita*) (Reston, VA: United States Geological Survey/University of Washington Press, 2005).

TWO

Early Modern Earthquakes and Their Modern Relevance

Sources as old as the fifth century occasionally mention earthquakes, but detailed documentation of earthquakes and tsunamis was not common until the late sixteenth century. In the typical periodization of Japan's past, the early modern era corresponds to the Tokugawa period, also known as the Edo period, 1603–1867. Many earthquakes occurred during these centuries, but I do not cover them comprehensively. The geographic focus in this chapter is major tsunamigenic earthquakes striking the northeast coast. I also examine other early modern earthquakes that have been especially influential in the modern era.

In the course of investigating these earthquakes, I highlight four points. First and most obvious, Japan's Sanriku coast has long been subject to tsunamigenic earthquakes. Second, in examining the reactions to these events, there was a tendency for local residents to regard the previous earthquake and tsunami as characteristic and to react (or not react) accordingly. Third, the quest for earthquake precursors that continues to this day is rooted in the experiences and intellectual atmosphere of the Tokugawa period. To illustrate this point, I consider earthquakes that were especially influential in the realm of ideas: Sanjō (1828), Kyoto (1830), Ansei Tōkai and Nankai (1854), and Ansei Edo (1855). My fourth point is that the modern tale *Rice Bale Fire* (*Inamura no hi*), based on the 1854 Tōkai and Nankai earthquakes, became emblematic of the human capability to defy and conquer natural hazards. Overconfidence in this capability had fatal consequences in 2011.

27

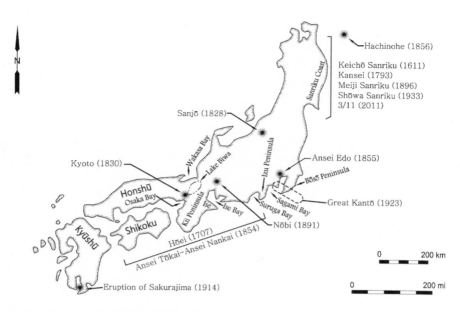

Figure 2.1. Selected Earthquakes, 1611–1933. *Source*: **Jeffrey Smits, Cherokee Drafting Specialists.**

THE KEICHŌ SANRIKU EARTHQUAKE AND TSUNAMI, 1611

Throughout the morning of December 2, 1611 (Keichō sixteen, tenth lunar month, twenty-eighth day), small earthquakes occurred along the Sanriku coast. Around 1:00 p.m., the tsunamigenic shock occurred. Some accounts of the earthquake describe it as "large" or "strong," but a close reading of available documents leaves doubt about whether and to what extent people felt the earthquake. Expert opinion varies somewhat. Usami Tatsuo, for example, describes the earthquake as "strong," with an estimated magnitude of 8.1, but also points out that no damage from ground motion has yet been discovered.[1] Indeed, the destruction described in documents from the time is the result of three large tsunami waves, not from shaking. Watanabe Hideo says that the seismic land waves produced moderate shaking in some areas and were not felt in other nearby areas along the coast. "The earthquake was extremely small, a tsunami earthquake," and Watanabe estimates a magnitude of 7–8.[2] The term "tsunami earthquake," used loosely, can simply refer to a tsunamigenic earthquake. However, it is actually a technical term for an earthquake that generates a large tsunami yet is barely felt by those in the affected area. Such earthquakes are also known as "slow earthquakes," "sliding earthquakes" (*nurunuru jishin*), and other similar names because the main reason for this phenomenon is now thought to be a slow rupture of the plate boundary. The 1611 event may have been one of these slow earthquakes, and I revisit this topic in more detail in connection with the 1896 Meiji Sanriku earthquake in chapter 4.[3]

The mild or perhaps imperceptible ground shaking would have added to the danger of the tsunami, assuming that violent shaking of coastal areas was a signal for local residents to move to higher ground. Adding up the fatalities reported in sources that provide specific numbers results in a figure of roughly seven thousand for the island of Honshū, but some sources use vague terms such as "many" or "too many to know," and this figure is probably low. All of these deaths were the result of drowning, another indication that the tsunami was much more destructive than the earthquake itself. Numerous sources list "more than 3,000" as the death toll in Nanbu and Tsugaru, domains located in present-day Aomori Prefecture. The population at the time was only 25 percent of what it is today, so that figure would be roughly comparable to twelve thousand deaths in more recent times. Extrapolating to the entire Sanriku coast, it is possible that the 1611 tsunami was more deadly on a per capita basis than either the 1896 tsunami or 3/11.[4] Pioneering seismologist Imamura Akitsune (1870–1948) estimated that the 1611 event was stronger than 1896 and on a par with the Jōgan tsunami.[5] Another point about the 1611 tsunami is that the withdrawal of the waves back out to sea appears to have been more destructive than the surge of the waves onto the shore. One tale from this event highlights this phenomenon by way of a lesson about the perils of clinging to one's possessions only to be washed out to sea with them.[6]

The Sanriku coast is full of bays and inlets. Many of them are shaped roughly like a funnel, with the wide end facing the ocean. This topography magnifies the destructive impact of tsunami waves as they rush ashore by forcing a fixed volume of water into an increasingly narrow space. Another coastal danger associated with bays and inlets is the phenomenon of people and structures sandwiched between two tsunami waves, each coming in from opposite directions. In an area along the southern coast of Miyagi Prefecture called Kuma-no-Hayashi, many local names and shop names include the elements *ori* (break, fracture) or *kawara* (roof tile). One reason is that tsunami waves came ashore directly from the ocean but also pushed into a nearby inlet, crushing buildings from both the east and west. Then, as the waters receded, roof tiles lay strewn on the ground. In other words, current local names most likely reflect the pincer movement of tsunami waves from 1611.[7] This phenomenon would have occurred up and down the coast with every large tsunami. At least one fishing village, Murohama, located at the edge of an inlet north of Sendai, has retained a living memory of this phenomenon, perhaps from as far back as the Jōgan earthquake of 869. This historical memory saved many lives in 3/11, as people fled not to the nearest high ground, which indeed became inundated by the double waves, but to an area farther away.[8]

Historical memory also manifested itself in another way. In a study of the 1611 event, Hirakawa Arata of Tōhoku University concluded that massive tsunamis have flooded the Sendai Plain every few centuries. Moreover, the rest stations along the Tokugawa-period coastal highway corresponded to areas just beyond the reach of the water from the 1611 tsunami. Hirakawa blames post-Meiji development for fostering a lack of awareness of tsunami danger in modern times.[9]

We will see, however, that historical memory and local lore are not always beneficial. There is a tendency to assume a high degree of folk wisdom in the case of earthquakes and tsunamis and a tendency to take local beliefs, especially if they are recorded in documents, at face value. I return to this issue at several points in this book. In connection with the 1611 event, for example, there was a tale from the Date household records. The basic plot is that two retainers of the lord of the Date domain had been sent to the beach to enlist fishermen to catch fish for the lord's household. However, the fishermen were uncooperative that morning, protesting, "The color of the tide is not good and the weather is bad." One retainer heeded the warning and refrained from setting out in a boat, while the other insisted on carrying out his assigned task, with tragic results.[10] This tale is an early source of the notion that abnormalities in seawater precede tsunamis, an idea that resurfaced in various forms in later centuries.

Even more common is the idea that large fish catches and other fish-related abnormalities are precursory phenomena to large tsunamigenic earthquakes. It is not certain when this idea first emerged or why, but we find it in 1611. Supposedly, catches of sardines and sweetfish (*ayu*) were high the year before the tsunami, and sardine catches were large just prior to the tsunami. In retrospect, this environmental anomaly seemed significant to many local residents as a precursor.[11] The notion of abnormally large fish catches preceding earthquakes and tsunamis, especially sardines, remained prominent in this region and reappeared in reports following the earthquakes and tsunamis of 1896 and 1933. Incidentally, the idea that catfish might be able to predict an earthquake is of much later vintage, first appearing in print in 1855.

In connection with discussing the 1611 event, Koshimura Shun'ichi makes the following claim:

> Are there really precursory phenomena before a tsunami strikes? For example, for several months preceding a tsunami sardines are numerous, strange seaweed grows luxuriantly, or large numbers of eels die. Such lore is quite difficult to believe, and because there is no scientific basis for it, we have no final word about it. However, there is a possibility that several precursory phenomena could be explained scientifically, and there are hypotheses for some of them. For example, it is not impossible scientifically to explain phenomena like abnormalities in ocean water prior to a tsunami, strong winds prior to a tsunami, and emissions of light.

He goes on to explain that water abnormalities could be the result of slippage of the sea floor, strong winds could be the result of sudden shifts in the surface of the ocean altering barometric pressure, and flashes of light could be the result of the moon reflecting off the choppy ocean surface. He concludes by stressing that these explanations are all speculative.[12]

We see in Koshimura's explanations a tendency that is common among at least some earth scientists in Japan. First, there is a belief in the existence of at least some precursory phenomena. Moreover, there is a tendency to assume that earthquake and tsunami lore from the distant past has some basis in reality. I would suggest, however, that two phenomena provide a better explanation for much of this lore. First, accidental or random occurrences that appear months or even years prior to an earthquake or tsunami are seen in retrospect as being significant because of proximity in time. Moreover, once local lore establishes a phenomenon as something that is likely to happen in connection with earthquakes or tsunamis, people experiencing subsequent events are more likely to assume that they had observed it. Moreover, early in the Tokugawa period a de facto script developed, with local variations, about what people expected to see in connection with earthquakes. Written materials tended to spread the script and focus it on certain phenomena that fit the prevailing theory of accumulated yang energy under the ground causing earthquakes. By the nineteenth century, we find a remarkable homogeneity in the retrospectively observed earthquake "precursors."

Fish stories are perhaps the most common variety of earthquake lore in Japan, and variations of them continue to the present. Soon after 3/11, for example, a newspaper article pointed out that unusually large squid catches preceded several major earthquakes between 1946 and 2011, implying a possible causal link.[13] Of course, there were also years of large fish or squid catches not followed by major seismic events. For a precursor to have any practical utility as a predictor of seismic hazards, at a minimum it must reliably precede major earthquakes close to the time of their occurrence and become manifest only prior to such events.

THE 1793 KANSEI AND 1856 HACHINOHE EARTHQUAKES

At midday, February 17, 1793 (Kansei five, first lunar month, seventh day), most of northeastern Japan began to shake. The earthquake and some of its aftershocks were felt as far away as Edo. The estimated magnitude of the main shock was 8.0–8.4, and this event was characterized by a long series of aftershocks, persisting ten months in some places. Tsunamis struck the coast in at least eight places, from Hachinohe near the top of Honshū to the Bōsō Peninsula near Edo. While the 1611 tsunami generated maximum wave heights of about twenty-one meters, in 1793 the highest waves were only four to six meters. The 1793 earthquake and tsunami affected a large area, but fatalities were few, probably between forty-four and one hundred. One factor in the low fatality rate was that the event occurred in the middle of the day. The number of houses destroyed or washed away was more than 1,730.[14]

Reports of unusually bountiful fish catches appeared in connection with the 1793 event. In addition, the 1611 disaster and the tsunami of 1793 occurred during the winter. Furthermore, an earthquake that shook the area eighteen years earlier in 1775 did not generate a tsunami. These circumstances led to the development of a local theory that a tsunami will not strike when the leaves on the trees are green. This notion was part of popular lore on August 23, 1856 (Ansei three, seventh lunar month, twenty-third day), when a strong offshore earthquake shook the Sanriku area.

Because the trees were full of green leaves, some people delayed making their way to high ground and were caught by the four tsunami waves that soon came sweeping through the coastal areas.[15] In this case, historical memory contributed to an inaccurate and potentially deadly folk theory. Fortunately, the initial wave in 1856 was modest, and most people were able to flee after its arrival.

The notion that tsunamis occur only in certain seasons was one manifestation of a more general tendency in Japan to assume links between atmospheric phenomena and earthquakes and tsunamis. Diaries describing earthquakes and aftershock series often included detailed weather reports as an integral component of the description.[16] One legacy of this way of thinking is that the national weather bureau (JMA) is the main agency charged with earthquake and volcano forecasting and warnings. Although mainstream seismology is no longer concerned with atmospheric phenomena and earthquakes, some scientists in Japan and elsewhere continue to posit the existence of "earthquake clouds" or theories about the effect of weather on earthquakes.[17]

The 1856 earthquake struck around noon, and estimates of its magnitude range from 7.5 to 8.0. Maximum wave height estimates are similar to those of the 1793 event, and fatalities were low. Shaking from this earthquake could be felt in most of the northern Tōhoku area and southern Hokkaidō. Unlike in 1793, the 1856 earthquake was not felt south of the Sanriku coast. The earthquake originated offshore from Hachinohe in Aomori Prefecture. As the four main tsunami waves washed in, residents of Ōtsuchi village fled to high ground, where the local temple and graves were located. Aftershocks continued for about three days, and four days after the main shock residents returned to their village.[18] One important characteristic of the 1856 event was that the tsunami waves arrived about an hour after the main shock and came in gradually, giving people enough time to flee. Historical memory of 1856 helped reduce the sense of urgency during the devastating tsunami forty years later. Indeed, compared with 1896, the 1856 earthquake and tsunami had precisely the opposite characteristics. In the earlier event, there was strong shaking and a relatively weak, slow train of waves. A generation later, the shaking was weak and the waves were tall, fast, and devastating.[19] Recent past earthquakes or tsunamis in an area are limited in their predictive value to suggesting possibilities. The next event is quite likely to have different characteristics from the previous one. The boilerplate warning for many modern financial investments that "past performance does not guarantee future results" applies even more in the case of major earthquakes and tsunamis.

Northeastern Japan in the early modern era was a relative backwater, consisting mainly of fishing villages. The highly destructive 1611 event occurred before a nationwide news network had developed, and the 1793 and 1856 events were not dramatic enough to warrant much attention in Japan's larger urban areas. One result is that when the 1896 tsunami struck the region, although it was part of a long line of tsunamigenic earthquakes, it was a surprise to many Japanese, including scientists. Indeed, even the 1896 event received relatively less attention than the less deadly 1891 Nōbi earthquake owing to the location of the two events. The Nōbi earthquake originated in a remote, rural area, but it shook Nagoya and surrounding areas violently and was felt in Tokyo. The extent to which earthquakes became natural disasters and the extent to which they became famous were more often a function of location and social conditions than magnitude or sheer destructiveness.

Other, smaller tsunamigenic earthquakes struck the region in 1677 and 1763, but we need not consider them here. We now turn to several other early modern earthquakes that were especially influential in their time and remain useful in the present for revealing the prevailing understanding of earthquakes during the early modern era.

THE 1828 SANJŌ EARTHQUAKE AND THE IDEA OF PRECURSORS

At about 7:00 a.m. on a market day, December 18, 1828 (Bunsei eleven, eleventh lunar month, twelfth day), the earth around Sanjō in Echigo (Niigata Prefecture) began to shake. The estimated M6.9 inland earthquake caused liquefaction, and many buildings sank about one meter into the earth. It also caused landslides and fissures in the earth from which water and sand flowed. Felt as far away as Edo, the earthquake caused roughly 1,443 people to die, 9,808 structures to collapse, and 1,204 structures to burn down. The shaking began just after many merchants in the marketplace had started their fires to prepare food, and many fled without extinguishing their fires. Soon the whole town was ablaze, and the cries of trapped victims mingled with cries of the *nenbutsu* (a short Buddhist prayer).[20] One account mentioned the anguished sounds of horses and cows amid smoke and people drowning in flooded pits that had opened in the ground.[21]

Owing to its relatively obscure location, this earthquake is not one of the more famous events of the Tokugawa period. Unlike the earthquake in Kyoto less than two years later, the Sanjō earthquake did not produce widely read works of scholarship, but it did produce moralistic literature. For example, the Zen priest and poet Ryōkan, then seventy-one years old, was walking from Wajima Village to Sanjō when the earthquake occurred. He composed two poems based on his thoughts and observations, one of which reads in part:

> Reflecting on the past forty years / The trend toward luxury in this world / Has advanced like a galloping horse. / All the more so, because for so long there has been peace and stable government / The feelings of the people have slackened / . . . / People think very highly of themselves and regard deceiving others as great talent. / Like piling up mud upon earth / There is no end to their sordid deeds.[22]

Luxurious living and stable political conditions allegedly had warped people's sense of ethics and duty. Ryōkan implies, but does not explain, a causal link between this state of moral degeneration and the earthquake.

The idea that premodern Japanese regarded earthquakes as heavenly warnings is not entirely wrong, but it is an oversimplification. This theme was muted in many earthquakes and came to the fore in a few cases. To amplify their voices, social critics typically pointed to fact of an earthquake as evidence of the correctness of their claims about degeneration. In certain circumstances, this amplification worked. The Sanjō earthquake was one example, and in its wake, blind female musicians began to sing about the earthquake in rhythmic narrative songs (*kudoki*). A major theme was that those who have grown accustomed to material prosperity in a peaceful world and who are obsessed with a desire for private gain invite earthquakes. This theme, of course, resonates with Ryōkan's poem.[23] Approximately a century later, as Tokyo and Yokohama lay in smoldering ruins, a similar discourse on morality and divine punishment arose. One reason is that the 1923 Great Kantō Earthquake struck at a point in Japan's modern history when social anxiety about urbanization and its alleged ill effects on the nation was especially high.[24]

Although the Sanjō earthquake did not produce works that became widely known and frequently cited, it did produce a masterpiece of earthquake literature, Koizumi Kimei's *Account of Chastisement and Shak-*

ing (*Chōshin hiroku*). The majority of the work is concerned with moral arguments advanced through various tales, supposedly true stories from the earthquake. What is useful for our purposes, however, is the work's detailed discussion of earthquake mechanics, especially alleged precursors. *Account of Chastisement and Shaking* begins with a summary of the earthquake. The next section is a detailed description of the geography of "our Echigo country." It was common in the early modern era for people to identify more strongly with their province than with Japan as a whole. Following the geographic details is a section titled "Earthquake Signs" ("Jishin no kizashi"). In other words, the author claims that certain observed phenomena were, in retrospect, signs of an impending earthquake. There are six main items, most connected with the weather.

First, a steamy ether (*ki*) appeared, just like a thick fog. Indeed, for a while it became impossible to see anything farther than seven or eight paces. Then, when the sky cleared, a five-colored rainbow or rainbowlike substance encircled the sun. Next, the weather turned abnormally warm, and the snow on tall mountains was no longer visible. The various trees sprouted buds (in late December), flowers bloomed, and people delighted in the springlike weather. In the evening before the day of the earthquake, clouds to the southeast took on a red color, followed by wind and rain. On the morning of the twelfth day, the sound of the wind was strong, and thick, black clouds in the southwest glowed red like the morning sun, radiating warmth. Around 8:00 a.m., a roar like thunder came from the southwest. A moment later, the earth began to shake violently.[25]

The next section describes the earthquake itself and some of its effects in considerable detail. Here I mention only a few points. When the shaking started, a great cloud of sand dust, looking like black smoke, traveled in a wavelike manner from southwest to northeast, and the ground shook. It became difficult for people to stand, and in places, sand blew out of the earth like smoke. The earthquake tore apart the earth and expelled muddy water from wells. It also disgorged fire and fiery wind from within the earth, and peasants actually were able to light lanterns with it.[26]

The inclusion in *Account of Chastisement and Shaking* of a section on earthquake signs was a relatively new development in Japanese earthquake literature. It was not radically new, because we can find earlier documents that speculate about this or that phenomenon as being connected with earthquakes. However, the formal category of "earthquake signs" made its appearance at approximately this time. Moreover, the basic idea that there are observable precursors to destructive earthquakes has remained a mainstay of earthquake literature to the present day. After every major earthquake—always *after*—scientists and others bring their reports of precursors to the media. 3/11 was no exception. "Could we have predicted the March 11 Great East Japan Earthquake was about to strike by observing natural phenomena?" begins one newspaper article.[27]

In the geology blog *Highly Allochthonous*, Chris Rowan wrote on May 21, 2011:

> There is currently no reliable way to predict exactly when a big earthquake will occur. Nonetheless, whenever a large earthquake does wreak havoc on some unfortunate corner of the globe, there is an almost one hundred percent certainty that at some point over the following couple of months, someone will publish some research which will indicate that there was some physically measurable precursor signal detected in the days before the earthquake. The Tohoku earthquake is no exception, and this time the "precursor" of choice is an ionospheric temperature anomaly that a study just uploaded to the arXiv (and therefore yet to be peer reviewed) claims to have detected above the epicentre of March's magnitude 9 earthquake off the coast of eastern Honshu, in the three or four days just before the rupture.

Rowan goes on to make a key point that often gets lost amid the post-earthquake clamor to proclaim this or that item as a precursor:

> This study perfectly illustrates one of the major issues that plagues every study of possible earthquake precursors that I've ever seen. Whatever the proposed signal is—be it radon gas, low frequency radio waves, ocean temperature, or even animal behavior—it usually proves to not be *uniquely* associated with earthquakes. In other words, although you may sometimes see the "precursor" prior to some sort of seismic activity, there are also many occasions where you see the signal and nothing of any significance happens.[28]

It is beneficial to take a closer look at the specific items that Koizumi Kimei put forth as precursors in 1828. The first is ether (*ki*). In modern Japanese, the term "*ki*" has a wide range of meanings, including feelings or sensations, attention, disposition, will, psychological or physical makeup, and, by extension, weather (*tenki*, the *ki* of the heavens). In premodern usage, it often referred to a nebulous raw energy, roughly like concepts of ether, which often manifested itself as mist or steam. It was a common term in academic and scientific discourse until approximately the 1870s. That warm *ki* would arise from the earth prior to an earthquake is precisely what any educated person in Japan in 1828 would have expected. By that time, there was a strong consensus about the basic mechanical cause of earthquakes. Simply stated, it was that yang energy (often called "yang *ki*") accumulates within the earth, which is normally the realm of yin. Clay soils trap this energy, which naturally seeks to expand upward. Just before an earthquake, some of this hot yang energy seeps to the surface and warms the air. The majority of it bursts forth explosively, causing the earth to shake, collapsing mountains, tearing the earth, and so forth.[29]

With this theory in mind, therefore, one would expect that just before an earthquake, the weather would become unusually warm because the earth itself functioned as a giant heat source, radiating warm yang energy upward. Steamy emissions would be common, and this warm energy would accumulate as clouds or among the clouds, transforming their appearance. Thus was born "earthquake clouds," a mainstay precursor of earthquake advocates to this day.[30] In a book on the latest science of earthquake prediction, Tsukuda Tameshige takes earthquake clouds (*jishin kumo*) seriously, describing them as caused by emissions of steam from fissures in underlying rock.[31] Although the modern version is grounded in notions of water seeping into cracks in rocks formed by their expansion, the basic explanation of earthquake clouds today would have made perfect sense to educated people in 1828.

The altered coloration of the sun and sky and the appearance of rainbows or rainbowlike phenomena were also the result of emissions of hot ether from the earth. Ikeya Motoji is a contemporary scientist who takes such lore seriously at face value. He begins a discussion of it by citing a Mother Goose rhyme: "Red sky at night, shepherd's delight / Red sky in the morning, shepherd's warning." Ikeya then explains:

> A red sky in the evening indicates fine weather, but a red sky in the morning suggests rain. There is a scientific explanation. In Japan, the weather changes from west to east because of the region's prevailing mid-altitude westerlies. High cloud is usually associated with rain fronts. A red sky in the morning means the light of the rising sun is reflecting off the frontal cloud approaching from the west and there will be rain. . . . Red sky in the evening means that the setting sun is

reflecting off the frontal cloud that has just passed and there will probably be a period of calm weather before the next front approaches.

Not only the clouds, but the sky itself is said to look different from normal before earthquakes, particularly the reds and yellows of morning and evening skies.[32]

This passage closely reflects parts of the 1828 account of earthquake signs, but Ikeya is not making specific reference to this work. The idea of changes in cloud and sky color prior to earthquakes recurred so often in earthquake accounts that it had become common sense by the end of the Tokugawa period. Notice also a sleight of hand, common in works of this sort. Ikeya proposes an explanation of why certain cloud formations are "warnings," but of rainstorms, not earthquakes. He then jumps to the topic of earthquakes (note the vague "is said to") in the next paragraph, but without any indication of whether or how rainstorms are in fact connected with earthquakes.

Recall that a connection between storms, especially thunderstorms, and earthquakes was a common assumption in the Tokugawa period. It was common in earthquake accounts to posit either actual thunder or "a sound like thunder" just before the earth began to shake. Therefore, another common assumption was that the weather must have been at least somewhat conducive to the production of thunder in the hours prior to the earthquake. Tokugawa Japanese regarded the explosive accumulation of yang energy within the earth as the same phenomenon as thunder in the atmosphere. Because so many old texts assumed links between atmospheric phenomena and geological phenomena, modern and contemporary advocates of earthquake lore often assume (or rely on readers' assumptions) that such links reflect some kind of folk wisdom. What they reflect, however, is a model of earthquake causality that made sense in the early nineteenth century but is meaningless today.

Account of Chastisement and Shaking is a window into the prevailing patterns of thought in its day. There is no evidence that the text was widely read or otherwise influential. To locate an influential text that other writers frequently cited, we need to examine an earthquake that struck the imperial capital of Kyoto (Edo was the capital of the military government) less than two years later.

THE 1830 KYOTO EARTHQUAKE

At roughly 4:00 p.m. on August 19, 1830 (Bunsei thirteen/Tenpō one, seventh lunar month, second day), an earthquake of approximately M6.5 shook Kyoto. The epicenter was slightly to the northwest of the city. Damage to earthen storehouses was extensive, but damage to houses did not even reach one in one thousand. Larger structures such as temples and shrines also fared well. The death toll from this event was around three hundred. Heavy shaking was limited to the city itself, although some outlying areas experienced minor damage and the earthquake was felt in nearby cities such as Osaka. Nijō castle suffered serious damage, and liquefaction was widespread throughout the city.[33] As was usual by this time, there were reports of light flashes in the sky and bursts of light issuing forth from the earth.[34] The idea that light flashes just as the earth shakes was the result of regarding earthquakes as essentially underground thunder and lightning.

Clearly, the earthquake was a major event, but compared with other large earthquakes in the Tokugawa period, including earthquakes in or near Kyoto, the death toll and property destruction were modest. The event, however, dragged on for months owing to a long train of aftershocks. This situation kept Kyoto's residents on edge and created an ideal atmosphere for the spread of rumors. Diaries, letters, and other accounts of the days following the main shock frequently mention aftershocks. One chronicle records one or more aftershocks almost every day for three months after the main shock.[35] "The shaking did not stop for consecutive days," according to another typical report.[36] A letter from two days after the main shock mentions rumors about a second earthquake and about massive fires. It then explains, "Such rumors, spread amidst the aftershocks, increase people's unease all the more."[37]

Another factor relevant to perceptions of the earthquake was that by 1830, the popular press had become a major presence in urban Japan. News networks connected all the major cities, and publications competed for readers. One strategy was to offer potential print buyers increasingly lurid accounts of death and destruction. For example, "At four in the afternoon [the day after the main shock] another great earthquake occurred, and Kyoto is turned upside down. Even if the (second) earthquake had not occurred, the whole city would have burned down from the fires that were raging."[38] There were even reports of landslides and devastation in places far from the city that could not have experienced significant shaking. Indeed, in Wakasa, on the Japan Sea coast, some eighteen villages were rumored to have sunk into a sea of mud caused by a (nonexistent) tsunami. In his detailed study of the Kyoto earthquake, seismologist Miki Haruo speculates that the rumors of sinking villages came directly out of literature published 130–170 years earlier about severe floods and other disasters in that area, including the Kanbun earthquake of 1662. Miki's conclusion is that the mass media were responsible for rumormongering by exaggerating the destruction in 1830.[39] In short, the relatively modest 1830 earthquake became a media circus.

That Kyoto was the imperial capital was one reason for the oversized psychological impact of this earthquake. Another was that 1830 was a year of special religious significance (an *okage* year), featuring popular religious pilgrimages with millenarian overtones. Even people far from Kyoto regarded the earthquake with unease. Matsuzaki Kōdō, for example, was a Confucian scholar living near Edo. He took anxious notice of both the earthquake in Kyoto and the unseasonable blooming of cherry trees. Writing in his diary a day after the Tempō era started, he said, "Our ruler is virtuous, and our habits upright . . . so there should be no reason for any disasters. . . . All we can do is pray for the Heavenly Protection of yesterday's new era name."[40] Indeed, the Kyoto earthquake is one of several seismic events that prompted a change in era names, in this case from Bunsei to Tenpō.

This atmosphere helped produce what was likely the most important early modern book on earthquakes in Japan, Kojima Tōzan's *Thoughts on Earthquakes* (*Jishinkō*). He wrote it with the explicit purpose of calming fears of a breakdown in social order by explaining earthquakes in a rational manner. Although "Tōzan sensei" appears prominently on the cover as the author, the book came out after his death. Tōzan indeed wrote the first half, but an anonymous student wrote the more interesting second half.[41] "People are shocked and terrified," Tōzan wrote, and "for the purpose of calming people," he pointed out that "since antiquity, historical records in Japan have recorded the occurrence of earthquakes." His first example is from 887, and the context of subsequent examples indicates that they are earthquakes that shook Kyoto. In this way, he tried to normalize the 1830 earthquake by putting it into the context of a long line of seismic events shaking the capital. Another calming function of these examples was to point out that aftershocks are a normal part of earthquakes. At the end of the section, Tōzan explains that in each series of shaking, the first shock was always the most severe and the intensity of subsequent shocks decreased afterward.[42]

The next section is a basic explanation of earthquakes, and it contains little that was new at the time. It is instructive for our purposes, however, because it provides a useful summary of prevailing ideas. The first point is that earthquakes occur when yang energy within the earth seeks to rise but is trapped by the force of yin, the normal characteristic of the earth. Citing an influential Chinese text, it explains that there are holes in the earth like a bees' nest or the cap of a mushroom and that the contact of fire and water creates a force that seeks to rise and causes the earth to shake when blocked. Geography matters. Cold northern regions and hot equatorial areas, as well as areas of sandy or muddy soil, experience few earthquakes. By contrast, warm areas with rocky soil suffer the highest frequency of earthquakes.[43]

Although it relied on the conventional understanding of the basic mechanics of earthquakes, *Thoughts on Earthquakes* contains innovative ideas about ground motion and the center and periphery of earthquakes. It explains the circumference of the earth and that the distance from the center of the earth to its surface is approximately 2,500 Japanese *ri*. In this physical context, the current earthquake shook only a small area of the surface, and areas of shaking in any earthquake are actually quite small in relative terms. Next, earthquakes have a center, where the shaking is most severe. The shaking propagates outward from the center in all directions, attenuating as a function of distance.[44] Subsequent earthquake literature, especially in connection with several large earthquakes between 1848 and 1855, frequently drew on *Thoughts on Earthquakes*, with or without attribution.

Thoughts on Earthquakes contains two extended discussions of precursors. Its overall argument is that earthquakes are predictable because certain signs precede them. In the absence of such signs, people need not worry that a main shock will strike. Notice in the context of social unease caused by the earthquake that a claim of predictability serves as a rhetorical device to calm anxieties. In other words, the author was, in effect, saying, "See, no precursors are evident now, so the main shock is in the past." The section "Indications of Earthquakes" ("Jishin no shirushi") explains the details. First, soon before the shaking starts, numerous holes appear in the earth at night. Dirt issues from these holes, resembling the activity of rats or moles. In addition, when farmers plow fields, smoke will arise from the furrows, a further indication that shaking is imminent. Well water will become turbid and agitated. Clouds appearing closer than normal are one sign of an earthquake. The text explains, "These are not really clouds, but upwellings of ether that resemble clouds or smoke."[45] Notice that these precursors are all consistent with the prevailing theory of earthquake mechanics. The holes and rising of smoke indicate that considerable upward strain has developed from the accumulated yang energy in the earth.

In the second half of the book, we are told that people reported seeing smoke rise from the center of the city just as the earthquake began. The discussion then returns to earthquake signs. For example, the setting sun might shine an abnormally bloodred color in the morning and evening. Next are tales from 1803 (Kyōwa 3) (but the correct date is 1802) on Sado Island, of a boat captain and someone named Hiroshima observing strange atmospheric phenomena. Based on lore passed on from his father, Hiroshima realized that what they were observing was not clouds but upwellings of "earth ether" and that an earthquake would soon occur. They rushed back to their lodge at the inlet of Oki and sounded the warning. Lodgers secured their possessions and moved to a safe location. The earth then shook and undulated like a wave. In another case, a mineshaft conducted large quantities of "earth ether" upward, appearing like steam or smoke. The ether obstructed everyone's view from the waist up. Knowing it was a sign of an earthquake, nobody went into the shaft, and all escaped unscathed. Just before the shaking started, several thousand herons took flight at once because birds in the sky can also detect upwellings of earthly ether. Another warning sign would be the appearance of a rainbow in places or circumstances where it would not usually be seen.[46]

Once again, we see that earthquake clouds, strange weather, and the behavior of birds made sense as precursors only because of the understanding that accumulations of upward moving yang energy or ether within the earth caused earthquakes. It is common for contemporary earthquake prediction advocates to claim that old texts often mentioned such phenomena and therefore to imply that there must be some basis to observations made convincing by virtue of their age and frequent mention. Ikeya, for example, surely referring to *Thoughts on Earthquakes*, says:

> Another old book published in 1830 tells the story of the Sado Earthquake (M6.6) in 1802 (Musha, 1957). Sado Island in the Japan Sea was

once famous for its gold mines, and the miners used to leave the mine whenever fogs appeared, interpreting them as pre-earthquake phenomenon. The fogs were thought to have been formed by the emanation of "earth air" (gas). [An inserted diagram of six types of earthquake clouds breaks up the text.] A boatman noticed strange weather and clouds he had never seen before, close to the ground. There was no wind, and it did not rain. Soon after there was an earthquake.[47]

One point that is clear in reading *Thoughts on Earthquakes* is that these tales of precursors are all hearsay. In some cases, there is a name attached to the tale, such as "Mr. Hiroshima" regarding the strange clouds at the lodge, or simply "somebody" (*aru hito*) in the case of the rainbow. None of these tales are verifiable, but their inclusion in *Thoughts on Earthquakes* helped condition what others expected to see in connection with earthquakes. Clouds, fog, and smoke would have been common sights in the nineteenth-century countryside, and they would have been visible before any earthquake—as well as when no earthquakes took place.

Because *Thoughts on Earthquakes* became so widely read, the text encouraged the notion that earthquakes could be predicted by careful attention to their precursory signs. It also specified what those signs should be. Notice that except for the flock of herons (hardly a reliable precursor, since herons take flight when no earthquake is imminent), there is no mention of animals or animal behavior as earthquake precursors. The text discusses fish, but not as earthquake precursors.

Today, the claim that a variety of animals can predict earthquakes is perhaps the most common assertion of earthquake prediction advocates writing for a popular audience. In the wake of 3/11, the mass media duly conveyed the inevitable reports of strange animal behavior, claimed in retrospect as precursors. A July 2011 newspaper article began, "Just before the recorded magnitude 9.0 Great East Japan Earthquake, multiple eyewitnesses report having seen strange behavior in wild animals." These beasts allegedly demonstrated uncanny "wisdom" not understood by science. A flock of crows, for example, took flight and emitted screeching sounds of a kind never heard before, and a pod of whales were cast up on the beach near Kashima (Bōsō Peninsula, northeast of Tokyo) a week before the earthquake.[48] In a manifestation of 3/11 rekindling fears of a Tōkai earthquake, the city of Susaki in Kōchi Prefecture investigated ways to use animal behavior and well-water levels as a basis for issuing evacuation recommendations.[49]

We have seen some evidence of local lore in northeastern Japan such that large fish catches preceded tsunamigenic earthquakes as precursors. If *Thoughts on Earthquakes* makes no mention of the predictive powers of fish, when did the idea enter popular consciousness? It was literature from the 1855 Ansei Edo earthquake that suggested catfish have the ability to predict earthquakes. Moreover, the creation of hundreds of varieties of catfish-themed broadside prints from that earthquake later helped popularize a different but related notion that early modern Japanese believed catfish caused earthquakes. Because this notion is still common, we turn to it now.

CATFISH?

Over the course of the Tokugawa period, catfish, especially giant, whale-like imaginary catfish, gradually became symbols of earthquakes. By the early eighteenth century, academic books began noting this curious item of folklore and proposing possible explanations for the symbolism. The most common explanation was that fish flop around and that they are yang creatures living in a yin environment. Therefore, they nicely symbolize the causal mechanism of earthquakes. While it is true that people sometimes take metaphors literally, I have seen no evidence that such confusion was widespread in Tokugawa Japan. In other words, I have seen no evidence of widespread early modern belief that catfish cause earthquakes.

Despite the lack of evidence that anyone regarded catfish as the cause of earthquakes, modern and contemporary writers frequently claim otherwise. For example:

> Until the Emperor Meiji dragged Japan into the modern age in the late nineteenth century, most Japanese believed that their archipelago rested on the back of a temperamental creature whose tantrums resulted in convulsions of the earth. Some said that it was a whale; others believed that it was a dragon, a snake, or a spider. The most commonly accepted version of the myth held that Japan perched on a giant catfish.[50]

This claim appears in a journalistic account of the Great Kantō Earthquake and is a recycling of the same notion from an earlier, albeit slightly better informed, journalistic account:

In the old days—unlike the Indians who thought earthquakes were caused by an underground cow, or the Chinese, who credited a subterranean turtle—the Japanese believed that quakes were caused by an enormous catfish, lying curled up under the sea, upon whose back all four of the islands rather precariously reposed. When the catfish wiggled, the earth shook. Some etymologists, upon rather sketchy grounds, have argued that the archaic Japanese word for earthquake, which is *nai*, had some common root with the word for catfish.[51]

The claim that premodern Japanese thought a giant catfish caused earthquakes is not limited to English-language literature. Since the Meiji period, many Japanese have also taken the popular prints featuring catfish produced in 1855 at literal face value. In other words, they overlook the metaphoric nature of these prints. Musha Kinkichi, for example, wrote in the 1950s, "Today nobody believes the absurd notion that a catfish causes earthquakes," after explaining at some length that premodern Japanese did indeed believe such a thing.[52]

This misconception about catfish is not simply an amusing case of modern beliefs about the alleged foolishness of our ancestors. The problem is that focusing on the nonexistent "catfish theory" of earthquakes, which supposedly held sway in the early modern era, obscures the dominant theory of earthquakes that did prevail at that time. Moreover, the claim that Japanese in past eras believed that catfish cause earthquakes implies the existence of some kind of folk wisdom. For example, Musha follows up the sentence quoted above with, "However, it is not necessarily the case that there is no connection at all between catfish and earthquakes," to segue into an idea that he vigorously supports: catfish (and other fish) can predict earthquakes.[53]

I discuss Musha and other modern fish advocates in later sections and chapters. As for Japan's earthquake catfish, its origins are complex, and I have examined them in detail elsewhere.[54] Very briefly, the ultimate ancestor was a Chinese mythical creature that resembled a cross between a giant fish, a turtle, and a snake or dragon. Transplanted to Japan, this creature transformed into the earthquake catfish during the late sixteenth century in the region around Lake Biwa. Variations of the metaphor of the earthquake catfish did not become widely known, however, until approximately the late eighteenth century.

In the wake of the 1855 Ansei Edo earthquake, publishers produced hundreds of varieties of "catfish prints" (*namazue*), in which catfish in various guises symbolized aspects of the earthquake or other recent earthquakes. The catfish was a convenient symbol, sufficiently flexible to enable printmakers to comment on the state of society under the guise of reporting on the earthquake. Commentary about contemporary affairs was technically illegal at that time and therefore required some degree of encoding. Apparently, the production of these prints is the basis for the modern misconception that Tokugawa Japanese thought that their country rested atop a giant catfish. By this same logic, the appearance of images of Santa Claus, reindeer flying through the sky pulling a sleigh, and so forth each year as the winter solstice approaches would indicate that modern denizens of the United States believe that deer can fly. Obviously, manifestations of fantastic mythology in human societies do not necessarily mean that adults hold a literal belief in these entities.

With the symbol of a giant catfish so well established by the nineteenth century and given the vast outpouring of catfish prints in 1855, it is hardly surprising that the idea emerged at this time that actual catfish could predict earthquakes. Before examining this matter more closely, we need to move back approximately one year in time, when the entire Nankai Trough ruptured over the course of two days.

THE ANSEI TŌKAI EARTHQUAKE OF 1854

At 9:00 a.m. on December 23, 1854 (Kaei seven/Ansei one, eleventh lunar month, fourth day), an M8.4 megathrust earthquake occurred along the subducting edge of the Philippine Sea Plate offshore between the Izu Peninsula (Shizuoka Prefecture) and the Kii Peninsula (Wakayama Prefecture). Shaking could be felt as far south as northern Kyūshū and as far north as the Tōhoku region. Tsunamis struck areas between the Bōsō Peninsula east of Edo (Chiba Prefecture) and the Pacific side of the island of Shikoku (Kōchi Prefecture), with wave heights ranging from four to twenty-one meters. The most severe shaking occurred along the coast between Numazu and Ise Bay. In some places, damage to structures approached 100 percent. The estimated death toll from the Ansei Tōkai earthquake was 2,500–3,000, and the shaking, fires, and sea waves destroyed more than sixty thousand structures.[55]

Of the many events connected with this earthquake, perhaps the most famous is the tale of the Russian vice admiral Euphimy Putiatin. Nearly every Japanese book dealing with historical earthquakes discusses the tale in considerable detail, perhaps in part because there is a rich array of eyewitness accounts and in part because of the dramatic and exotic nature of the situation. Putiatin was in the midst of treaty negotiations with shogunal officials in Shimoda when the shaking started. The chaplain of the Russian vessel *Diana* interpreted the event by claiming, "God has visited upon us, and especially upon the Japanese, divine punishment."[56] Conversely, some local residents blamed the earthquake on cosmic revulsion at the presence of the Russian vessel.[57] A series of seismic sea waves arrived shortly thereafter, the second of which was approximately 6.4 meters high. The waves swirled the *Diana* around forty-two times in the space of thirty minutes, causing great damage that eventually caused the ship to sink. With the assistance from the recovered cargo of a magazine containing ship diagrams, local shipwrights working in the nearby village of Heda built what most historians regard as Japan's first Western-style ship. Named *Heda*, the vessel returned the Russian crew safely, and Putiatin arrived in Moscow on November 10, 1855, with a treaty in hand.[58]

OVERCONFIDENCE AND THE ANSEI NANKAI EARTHQUAKE

The day after the Ansei Tōkai earthquake, at approximately 4:00 p.m., an adjacent segment of the subducting edge of the Philippine Sea Plate ruptured off the eastern coast of the island of Shikoku. This M8.4 Ansei Nankai earthquake was essentially a continuation of the previous day's seismic event. Some areas, such as the southern tip of the Kii Peninsula, were shaken by both earthquakes. In the village of Koza, for example, residents spent the night after the Tōkai earthquake in the hills. They came back to what was left of their houses the next day and were shaken by the Nankai earthquake that afternoon. Seeing the sea recede, they escaped a second tsunami just in time. The Ansei Nankai earthquake shook a wide area, and ground motion was especially severe in Shikoku and adjacent coastal areas of Honshū. The death toll from the shaking and seismic sea waves amounted to several thousand. Subduction-zone earthquakes often cause uplifting and subsidence, and this one was no exception. Major earthquakes during the Hōei, Ansei, and Shōwa eras raised the port of Murozu 1.4, 1.2, and 1.1 meters, respectively. Other areas of Shikoku sank. The Tōkai earthquake caused uplift along the coast of present-day Shizuoka Prefecture, permitting construction of the Satta Pass to reconnect the Tōkaidō highway, which the earthquake had blocked.[59] Today, the Tōmei Expressway and Tōkaidō honsen train line both pass through this uplifted area.[60]

The most famous tale from the Ansei Nankai earthquake came from the village of Hiro in the Kii Peninsula (Wakayama-ken, Arita-gun, Hiro). A tsunami washed away four hundred of one thousand houses in the village and killed three hundred following the 1707 Hōei earthquake. Thereafter, the village residents fled to higher ground whenever the ground shook.[61] Owing to this precautionary custom, the tsunami following the Ansei Nankai earthquake killed only 36 out of a population of nearly 1,400.[62] Another reason for the low casualty count was the leadership of Hamaguchi Goryō, a young man from a prominent merchant family that brewed Yamasa soy sauce and operated coastal ships. Goryō had returned to his boyhood village of Hiro to open a school.

Owing to the Tōkai earthquake, the villagers had already fled to high ground around the Hachiman shrine the previous day. When the Nankai earthquake struck, there was a general tendency for people to return to higher ground, but the much stronger shaking had caused disorientation and obstructions. It was winter, and the days were short. The sun was setting behind the mountains, so darkness in the lower areas of the village compounded the difficulties. Leading a group of ten young men, Goryō used bales of rice stacked up by the side of fields (*inamura*, hulled rice prior to being processed) as fuel to light bonfires to illuminate the escape route. He also provided food for the 1,400 evacuees and later sought a tax reduction for the village. Moreover, Goryō put those idled by the disaster to work constructing a double seawall, which later proved effective against tsunami waves caused by the 1946 Shōwa Nankai earthquake.[63]

In a tale entitled "Rice Bale Fire" ("Inamura no hi," first published in 1932), Goryō's deeds edified fifth-graders throughout Japan between 1937 and 1946 as part of the official reading curriculum. "Rice Bale Fire" has a peculiar pedigree. It was based on Lafcadio Hearn's "A Living God," a chapter in his larger work *Gleanings in Buddha-Fields: Studies of Hand and Soul in the Far East* (1897). Hamaguchi Goryō served as the basic model for the protagonist Gohei in "A Living God." Nakai Jōzō translated and reworked Hearn's tale to create "Rice Bale Fire." Japanese writers have pointed out that in creating Gohei, Hearn changed some details about the real Hamaguchi Goryō, perhaps to appeal to his presumed readership. For example, the thirty-five-year-old Goryō, as Gohei, became an old man in Hearn's account, and Hearn shrank Goryō's 1,322-person village to a quaint 400. In Hearn's account, Gohei was the only villager wise and experienced enough to suspect that a tsunami was on the way, and he lit the fire as a ruse to cause the unsuspecting villagers to rush toward it. In reality, most villagers knew to flee, but darkness and debris impeded their progress. [64]

Hamaguchi Goryō's heroic deeds are important for our purposes in two respects. First, let us consider the account of the earthquake Goryō himself reported in his memoir. In the afternoon, just before the Nankai earthquake, two villagers reported "abnormalities" in well water, which made Goryō think that some "abnormality in the earth" would soon occur. The moment the ground started shaking, "suspicious clouds" of a black and white color could be seen in the southwestern sky, and they emitted a golden light. "It was as if something abnormal was flying upward." [65] Notice the close resemblance to the accounts of precursors we have seen in the 1828 *Account of Shaking and Chastisement* and the 1830 *Thoughts on Earthquakes*.

Goryō wrote his memoir during the Meiji period, and his retrospective account of conditions just before and at the moment of the earthquake is so similar to other late Tokugawa period accounts that it almost seems scripted. Modern earthquakes have never been so cooperative as to present the same set of precursors repeatedly. Depictions of earthquakes in the Tokugawa period, by contrast, typically follow the script of hot yang energy rising into the sky from the earth. Strange clouds in the southwest, strange colors in the sky, and well-water abnormalities appear whenever there is an earthquake, at least in retrospective accounts. Clearly, people of the time knew what they expected to see prior to and at the moment the earth shook, and that is what they usually said they saw.

Amid the strong atmosphere of patriotism that prevailed in the 1930s, Hamaguchi Gohei (as his name remained in "Rice Bale Fire") exemplified virtues such as wisdom, bravery, and generosity. Because he did battle with nature, not with opposing armies, he retained his heroic status in the postwar years. Today there is a website devoted to "Rice Bale Fire," and the tale is available in multiple languages in both adult and children's versions. [66] It is problematic.

Insofar as "Rice Bale Fire" helps promote the message to seek high ground after an earthquake, it serves a useful purpose. In the context of Japan, however, the dominant theme in the portrayal of Hamaguchi

Goryō is that he was a man who heroically defied or did battle with the destructive forces of nature. The title of a recent biography, for example, is *Tsunami to tatakatta hito: Hamaguchi Goryō den*, literally, "*The Person Who Battled a Tsunami: The Biography of Hamaguchi Goryō*." Sangawa Akira takes a similar approach in a recent book, titling the section on "Rice Bale Fire" as "Tsunami no tachimukatta otoko," that is, "The Man Who Stood Up to a Tsunami." [67] In other words, in Japan, at least, Hamaguchi Goryō is portrayed less as a man with enough sense to flee to high ground and more as someone who led his village in a tactical retreat and then stood up to nature's fury by constructing a giant seawall. That the seawall proved effective in 1946 added to this legacy of defiance.

Assuming people will dwell in low-lying coastal areas, there are two basic approaches to tsunami protection. One is to facilitate evacuation to safe areas, possibly by constructing escape routes or places to gather on high ground. The other is to construct barriers. In the face of moderate tsunamis, barriers can be effective, but they can also lead to overconfidence. The 1960 Chile tsunami sparked a rush of seawall projects in northeastern Japan, all of which failed dramatically in the 3/11 event because the waves overtopped and often destroyed the barriers. The most famous example of bold defiance vis-à-vis tsunami hazards was the town of Tarō on the Sanriku coast. As a fishing village, the tsunamis of 1611, 1896, and 1933 washed it away, killing most of its residents. After a tsunami swept away 500 of 599 houses in 1933, the village decided not to relocate but to borrow money to begin constructing a seawall. Tarō exemplified the defiant interpretation of "Rice Bale Fire."

Impressed by the village's resolve, the prefectural and national governments soon picked up the tab for construction. By the end of 1940, 960 meters of the wall had been built. In 1952, the wall performed well in the face of a modest tsunami. The second phase of construction, finished in 1958, brought the wall to 1,350 meters in length, and it rose 10 meters above sea level (the wall itself was 7.7 meters high). It saved the town from the 1960 Chile tsunami, and people from all over the world came to see and learn from the wall. A third and final phase was completed in 1966, bringing the total length to 243 meters and enclosing the town in what people referred to as the Great Wall [of China]. [68]

Reflecting the spirit of defiance modern writers have attributed to Hamaguchi Goryō, on March 3, 2003, to commemorate the seventieth anniversary of the 1933 tsunami, the town of Tarō publically declared itself a "tsunami defense town." The official declaration (Tsunami bōsai no machi sengen) was as follows:

> Large tsunamis such as the ones in 1896 and 1933 have wreaked devastation on Tarō Town, causing a loss of precious life and property. However, the indomitable spirit of our ancestors who resided here and a great love of home place permitted us to transcend [this tragic past] and achieve a revival that is nearly miraculous and serves as the foundation of the present.
>
> In 1944, the reborn Tarō, to commemorate tsunami recovery, changed from a village to a town. To this day, we continue to train in tsunami evacuation and have constructed a tsunami defense wall unlike anything in the world. Moreover, we have installed the newest disaster information facilities.
>
> We constantly bear in our minds the many lessons of tsunami disasters and never forget our history of tsunami destruction. We do not luxuriate in modern conveniences, but along with civilization, we endeavor to deal with dynamic disasters, to enhance the ability of the region to withstand disasters, and to pass on our accumulated wisdom to the next generation.
>
> Praying for the repose of the spirits of the deceased and vowing that there will be no repeat of past disasters, to encourage all the people of the town courageously to face the inevitable battle with tsunamis, on this seventieth anniversary of the great Shōwa Sanriku Tsunami, we hereby declare [Tarō to be the] "Tsunami Defense Town."[69]

The 3/11 tsunami wiped out Tarō once more, reducing much of the town to debris. The tsunami even tore apart the wall in several places. In retrospect, the declaration seems a tragic case of overconfidence. There have been many others.

Returning to 1854, as in the case of Hiro Village, there is abundant evidence that in many rural coastal areas, residents sought high ground after the Tōkai and Nankai earthquakes, saving many lives when the tsunami waves arrived. One reason is that knowledge of the Hōei earthquake 147 years earlier had been passed down through the generations. For example, a letter describing the Nankai earthquake and aftermath mentioned, "There are prior examples of tsunamis in this place. They are found in the tales the elderly tell and in written records." Another writer, living in the Kii Peninsula explained, "Fearing a tsunami, people set up lean-to shelters in the mountains," and letters, diary entries, and other documents dealing with rural areas regularly describe lowland villages in terms such as "Owing to tsunamis, everyone had set up huts in the mountains, and not a single person was dwelling there." In the village of Wagū on an outcropping of the Kii Peninsula near Ise, most residents fled for the hills, but some returned to retrieve "gold, silver, clothing, et cetera" and drowned in the tsunami. Letters and diaries routinely report villagers heading for high ground and remaining there after the earth shook.[70] Houses and other structures suffered damage and destruction, but knowledge of the relationship between earthquakes and tsunamis mitigated the human tragedy in rural areas of the coast such as the Kii Peninsula and Shikoku. Indeed, the total number of deaths from both earthquakes of five thousand to seven thousand was remarkably low, considering the power of the seismic upheavals.

By contrast, in Osaka, where many residents had the option of fleeing to boats to wait out aftershocks and possible fires, much of the population seemed oblivious to the link between earthquakes and tsunamis. An order by the Osaka city magistrate's office prohibiting onboard drinking parties clearly indicates that the city authorities regarded fleeing to boats as a viable option, provided the refugees remain sober. Responding to an

Figure 2.2. Ansei Nankai Tsunami Monument at Nakahama, Shimizu City, Kōchi Prefecture. *Source*: **Wikimedia Commons, As6022014.**

earthquake in Osaka by fleeing to boats in the rivers began with the 1662 Kanbun earthquake, which did not generate a tsunami. The experience six months before Ansei Nankai of the nontsunamigenic Iga-Ueno earthquake reinforced this course of action. The Ansei Tōkai earthquake produced some shaking in Osaka but no tsunami. Therefore, recent experience in the city supported the idea that vessels in the river were a good place to flee during and immediately after an earthquake, especially considering the likelihood of aftershocks.

There is no evidence from Osaka in 1854 of widespread knowledge of the Hōei earthquake, even though it caused heavy tsunami damage there. One likely reason is demographic. In Osaka between 1707 and 1854, there had been a substantial changeover in townspeople households. In rural areas, village households tended to remain stable over the generations and were thus better able to pass down earthquake-related knowledge. One effect of this incomplete collective memory of past earthquakes in Osaka was to magnify the tsunami death toll in 1854.[71] Some reports from the time give figures as high as eight thousand crushed boats and seven thousand deaths, but those figures are certainly too high.[72] It is instructive to compare Osaka with the nearby port city of Sakai. In 1707, its residents also fled to boats and were killed in large numbers by the tsunami. Thereafter, they erected a large stone monument warning against such action in the future. In 1854, the townspeople fled to a temple on high ground and suffered no fatalities.[73]

Some documents describing the carnage of crushed boats and drowned victims in Osaka characterized the situation as "unprecedented" (zendai mimon),[74] but residents of rural areas along the coast were well aware of relevant precedents. Indeed, one writer began a short essay with, "There is a saying that complacency is the greatest enemy," and went on to criticize people of the present for ignoring the lessons of the Hōei earthquake "as if it were an ancient tale" and not currently relevant knowledge.[75] The tsunamigenic Ansei Tōkai and Nankai earthquakes produced a range of responses, some highly beneficial and others tragically mistaken. Tsunamigenic earthquakes in the modern era, including 3/11, also led to a range of responses. Although we find no characteristic response to earthquake and tsunami disasters, some form of complacency has usually played a role in the tragic outcomes. I return to that point in later chapters.

CATFISH, MAGNETISM, AND DOUBTS: 1855

The Ansei Edo earthquake struck at approximately 10:00 p.m. on November 11, 1855. Estimates of magnitude vary slightly, but 6.9–7.0 is typical. Deaths for civilian and military personnel combined were in the range of eight thousand to ten thousand. The Ansei Edo earthquake was an inland earthquake that caused choppy coastal waters but did not generate a tsunami. Estimates of the epicenter consistently place it between the northern part of Tokyo Bay and Etō-ku, at approximately the mouth of the Arakawa River as it empties into Tokyo Bay.[76] This earthquake is arguably the most influential in Japanese history, and I have written a book-length study of it.[77] In this section, I briefly examine two new alleged precursors that originated in 1855. I also survey the reason that the very occurrence of the Ansei Edo earthquake cast doubt on the prevailing theory of trapped yang energy within the earth seeking to expand upward as the proximate cause of earthquakes.

One tale that circulated right after the earthquake was that a giant magnetic stone located in a spectacle shop called Nanigashi lost its magnetic properties roughly two hours before the main shock. The tale appeared in a work of popular journalism, *Ansei Chronicle* (*Ansei kenmonshi*) and in *Fujiokaya Diary* (*Fujiokaya nikki*), a blog-like work about contemporary events written by a well-connected owner of a used bookstore. It is important to note at the outset that this story of the stone was part of a vast outpouring of fantastic tales from the earthquake, and no reliable source verifies it. Moreover, ideas about magnetism and electricity were becoming very popular at this time in Japan, as they were in Europe, and there was a general fascination with magnets and electrical gadgets in Japan's urban areas.

Modern authors sometimes cite this 1855 "fact" of the magnetic stone losing its properties as evidence supporting the hypothesis that electromagnetic anomalies often precede earthquakes.[78] In 1855 or 1856, the tale resulted in the design of several warning devices. Most famous is a sketch of an earthquake alarm clock (*jishinkei*) that theoretically might provide brief advance warning. Its basic mechanism was a magnet releasing a metal ringer.[79] There is no evidence that the device advanced beyond the drawing stage, despite claims by some modern writers that it existed.[80] A sketch of a different device appears in Murayama Masataka's 1856 *Thoughts on Earthquakes and Electricity* (*Shinden kōsetsu*). Masataka's explanation reads, "In our country, from ancient times to the Ansei era, there have been instances in which earthquakes were connected with electricity [or thunder and lightning]. The diagram here describes an earthquake warning device based on a magnetic stone."[81]

Recall that thunder and peculiar light flashes had long been part of the standard repertoire of earthquake precursors. What seems to have started in the 1850s was a tendency to think of these phenomena in terms of electricity, not the similar but vaguer notion of yang energy. Scientists such as Masataka were aware of European theories of earthquakes that featured electricity, and the long-standing association in Japan of lightning and earthquakes undoubtedly gave credence to the rumored loss of magnetism in the spectacle shop. As with so many other alleged precursory phenomena from "historical documents," the 1855 case makes sense only within the context of its day.

A variation on this basic idea, one that continues even today to receive serious attention, is that certain fish, especially catfish, can predict earthquakes because they are unusually sensitive to the electrical signals given off just before an earthquake. Some writers claim a long history for the idea of catfish predicting earthquakes, but Hashimoto Manpei correctly points out that it was only after 1855 that some writers credited catfish with earthquake prediction.[82] The apparent locus of this idea is the anonymous 1856 *Ansei Chronicle*. It contains an account of a fisherman named Shinozaki who noticed catfish were unusually active. He caught three catfish and recalled that when catfish are agitated and active, an earthquake will soon strike. Shinozaki returned home, spread a mat outside, put all his possessions on it, and otherwise made emergency preparations. The earthquake struck that night. The passage concludes by moralizing about the virtue of Shinozaki's perception and states that people who knew of the story realized "that negligence is one's own fault." *Ansei Chronicle* characterizes the agitation of catfish in connection with the earth starting to move as "a natural principle."[83]

The Ansei Edo earthquake cast serious doubt on the prevailing theory of earthquake mechanics. The reason was water wells. The previous large earthquake shook Edo in 1703, when there were few water wells in the city. Instead, people relied on a system of wooden pipes to bring water in from rivers. By 1855, however, nearly every city neighborhood had its own water well.[84] There were so many wells that townspeople commonly assumed the city was immune to large earthquakes because the wells would vent yang energy harmlessly to the surface. *Ansei Record* (*Ansei kenmonroku*), for example, after explaining the basic mechanism of earthquakes that we have already examined, adds, "However, in Edo earthquakes are few, just some occasional small ones that do not even shake off roof tiles. People have been reassured because they say that in Edo, wells are so numerous that yang ether is constantly dissipated. Therefore, large earthquakes are very rare."[85] Anyone who gave serious thought to the Ansei Edo earthquake's physical causes, therefore, would have had to question the theory of trapped yang energy as the cause of earthquakes.

Dutch sources provided explosive theories that were similar to the yang ether explanation but sufficiently different to fit the known facts. Especially popular was the idea that accumulations of electricity within the earth sometimes exploded and caused earthquakes. Utagawa Kōsai's 1856 *Earthquake Prevention Theory* (*Jishin yobōsetsu*), relying on this model, imagined placing giant lightning rods into the earth someday to prevent earthquakes by dissipating the buildup.[86] Somewhat less popular were theories proposing scenarios whereby the ingredients for gunpowder would combine under the earth and explode. Kawamoto Kōmin's *Lectures on Natural Science* (*Kikaikanran kōgi*) and Hirose Genkyō's *Essentials of Natural Science* (*Rigaku teiyō*) advanced variations on this idea.[87] These new theories of earthquakes were not highly influential, but their appearance in 1856 and 1857 indicates that the Ansei Edo earthquake encouraged a questioning of received knowledge in academic circles.[88]

I revisit some of the topics developed here in the later chapters. At this point, I would stress that in the late 1850s, European theories of earthquakes were beginning to dominate Japanese intellectual discourse. These theories were sufficiently similar to the idea of explosive yang ether that they caused no major paradigm shift. Moreover, at the popular level and even among scholars, the rich variety of earthquake lore that had developed in the context of the old yang ether theory carried over into the Meiji era. Japan's long history of earthquakes, earthquake records, and earthquake literature bequeathed to the emerging science of seismology a large body of raw source material. This material was in some ways as much of a burden as a benefit, however, because it led to research dead ends. Moreover, old lore continues to insinuate itself into the present, as mass media routinely give credence to tales of strange animal behavior or other "precursors" of early modern vintage. The inability of mainstream science to predict earthquakes provides a context that permits the recycling of this folklore.

USE AND ABUSE OF THE ANSEI EDO EARTHQUAKE

The Ansei Edo earthquake was a complex event that took place in a society quite different from modern or contemporary Japan. Drawing reasonable lessons from it that are relevant to contemporary society is no easy task. This earthquake has been especially prominent in the modern era, often as a benchmark against which to measure progress in understanding and dealing with earthquakes. As such, Ansei Edo has taken on a variety of guises, changing character to suit the argument at hand. Typically, the modern writer's goal is to press the earthquake into a mold such that it becomes characteristic of a longer-term pattern. I have discussed this phenomenon at length elsewhere, so I will highlight only one additional example here.[89]

A striking misreading of the Ansei Edo earthquake in the context of 3/11 appears in an otherwise superb book by Richard J. Samuels, *3.11: Disaster and Change in Japan*. Samuels claims that the catfish prints from Ansei Edo "clearly presented a class-based narrative of inequality and corruption in which incompetent officials, greedy tradesmen eager to rebuild (presumably at extortionate rates), and prostitutes were set against the suffering masses who had lost everything."[90] Later, Samuels characterized Ansei Edo (or all the Ansei earthquakes—it is unclear), along with the 1891 Nōbi earthquake, as "plagued by civil unrest and high levels of distrust."[91] These statements are all problematic. First, there was no civil unrest in Ansei Edo. Indeed, the immediate postearthquake period was a time when otherwise disparate groups within society came together to assist victims. Many catfish prints portray the earthquake as a joyous event, in part because so few of "the masses" lost very much and many of them had the brief opportunity to work for high wages in rebuilding the city. Moreover, townspeople genuinely praised the response of the *bakufu*, which was indeed exemplary by the standards of the day. In short, Samuels has twisted Ansei Edo badly out of shape to provide historical "guidance" in support of his otherwise convincing arguments about 3/11 and the possibilities for change as it plays out. There is no need for such contortions. Ansei Edo, or at least the actual Ansei Edo earthquake that took place in 1855, is not even a remote fit for a narrative of social unrest and distrust of the state. Indeed, the response of the city magistrate's offices to the earthquake was probably the *bakufu*'s last competent response to a crisis prior to its demise in 1867.

To find post-3/11 guidance from Ansei Edo and other early modern earthquakes, we must look elsewhere. One of the points Samuels makes is that effective responses to 3/11 and effective responses to future catastrophes depend in large part on local governments, especially local governments collaborating with one another and with NGOs.[92] In the early modern era, there was no central government in the modern sense. Nearly all disaster relief, therefore, was a local affair, often with local governments cooperating with one another and with certain nongovernment segments of society in a position to provide assistance. In some cases, the *bakufu* supplemented local efforts, but such aid was of secondary importance and late to arrive. Let us briefly consider two cases: the 1847 M7.4 Zenkōji earthquake in Shinano (Nagano Prefecture) and Ansei Edo.

According to one account, Zenkōji was "a disaster of shaking, fire, and water all at once."[93] The shaking, the fires that ravaged the densely populated area around Zenkōji (a temple), and massive flooding caused by the blockage of the Sai River from a collapsed mountain resulted in as many as twelve thousand dead and widespread physical destruction.[94] The death toll and overall situation could have been much worse, but the Matsushiro domain and other domain governments (the affected area crossed several political boundaries) provided effective leadership and relief. For example, to deal with the danger of a tsunami-like rush of floodwater from the lake created by the collapsed mountain, the Matsushiro domain mobilized thousands of retainers. They began work on an embankment to help channel the water. The domain also sent messengers to downstream areas, urging villagers to flee to higher ground, and to mountainous areas, ordering villagers to assist any strangers who might show up. Domain officials established a watch over the dammed area on a nearby mountain and floated unoccupied boats on the growing lake to serve as an early indication of the earth dam starting to give way. When the dam showed evidence of collapsing, those on duty were to light a signal fire.[95] Eventually, twenty days' accumulation of water burst onto the Zenkōji Plain. At Koichi, a town along the river at the edge of the plain, the water level briefly reached twenty meters.

The wild rush of water lasted about four hours, washing away over eight hundred dwellings and inundating more than two thousand more with sand and mud. Only about one hundred people perished, however, thanks to the domain's emergency measures.[96] The official response to the disaster encompassed much more than encouraging flood safety measures. In some areas, the earthquake wiped out sources of food, drinking water, and shelter all at once. Domain relief efforts included establishing temporary shelters and providing basic food and supplies, cash grants, and emergency loans for rebuilding. The Matsushiro domain, for example, provided some 1,268,000 meals as of the ninth day of the seventh lunar month and had distributed 13,429 *ryō* in cash.[97] Eight years later, the *bakufu*'s Machigaisho undertook many of these same steps in dealing with the aftermath of the Ansei Edo earthquake.

Although the Ansei Edo earthquake shook Japan's de facto capital, it is an oversimplification to say that "the *bakufu*" provided emergency relief. As a whole, the *bakufu* was a military organization, and governance of Edo was a relatively minor function handled by the city magistrate's (Machibugyō's) offices. There was also a specific disaster relief agency, the Machigaisho (or Machikaisho), partly supervised by the city magistrates. Because a relatively small part of the *bakufu* mobilized to provide short-term disaster relief, the situation was analogous to the response of a local government. The city magistrate offices leveraged and multiplied their limited resources by working closely with wealthy businesses (functioning in some ways like modern NGOs), domain lords in relatively good shape (damage to domain lord dwellings varied widely), temples and shrines, and other entities. A close examination of patterns of relief spending indicates tight, efficient coordination of resources. Local neighborhood heads quickly surveyed the actual damage and reported it to the city magistrate offices. Next, working with those offices, neighborhood officials spearheaded the successful campaign to provide food, shelter, and medical care to those in need.[98]

I am not suggesting that all early modern earthquakes were examples of effective relief by local governments. The large disasters of 1847 and 1855, however, did have these characteristics. Moreover, the coordination of resources between the city magistrate's offices and other local entities was analogous to recent and contemporary efforts by networked local governments to support one another and provide effective disaster relief and to coordinate with NGOs. Indeed, one tentative lesson from major early modern earthquakes is that networks of local governments with adequate resources and the power to make their own decisions in a flexible manner may well be the best model for disaster relief. This point is even clearer in light of the problems associated with the slow central government response to the 1995 Kōbe earthquake that Samuels discusses.[99]

That well-equipped local governments working in cooperation with one another and relevant nongovernment groups are in a position to provide the best emergency response makes intuitive sense, whether in Japan or elsewhere. The problematic response of a cumbersome, centralized system in 1995, the more effective local responses in the wake of 3/11, and the lessons from early modern earthquakes, in which local governments, essentially the only ones available, coordinated relief efforts that were often quite effective, provide strong empirical support for this approach to disaster relief.

EARLY MODERN AND MODERN EARTHQUAKES COMPARED

In his recent book on the 1923 Great Kantō Earthquake, J. Charles Schencking observes:

> Politicians and bureaucratic elites across cultures and from diverse political systems regularly make opportunistic and idealistic calls for reconstruction and renewal following major natural disasters. Frequently they attempt to use these events for larger political and ideological ends. . . . Rarely is the optimism and opportunism that is unleashed by natural disasters translated into fundamental, lasting, and transformative changes in society. Japan's experience calls into question the universality of claims that postdisaster utopias invariably emerge after calamitous occurrences, endure, and contribute to lasting transformations within society.[100]

Writing about the nature and degree of change to Japan's politics that 3/11 has caused and might yet cause, Samuels states that two years out, "a 3.11 master narrative was still under construction."[101] Nevertheless, it does not seem likely that 3/11 will result in any thoroughgoing or radical change. We will see that although the rhetoric of rebuilding "better than before" was relatively more muted after the 1896 and 1933 Sanriku tsunamis, in these cases, too, funding and other resources were never sufficient to match overly optimistic local expectations for beneficial change.

It seems almost a requirement of modern societies to declare major disasters to be opportunities for reconstructing a society even better than before the catastrophe struck. It is as if the catastrophe must be presented as something beneficial or at least potentially beneficial in the long run. By contrast, disasters in the early modern era did not bring forth a better-than-before rhetoric. Expectations of government responses were relatively modest, and restoration of social infrastructure to predisaster levels was always the ideal. Even popular characterization of the Ansei Edo earthquake as "world renewal" (*yonaoshi*) or as medicine typically referred only to the potential for short-term windfall profits by skilled and unskilled laborers toiling during the immediate cleanup and rebuilding phase. Soon, higher wage levels enticed workers to journey to Edo, bringing wages back down to usual levels. There was a typical rhetoric associated with many early modern disasters, with an emphasis on reassurances that society was fundamentally stable and would thus recover.[102] Compared with the modern era, early modern expectations for postdisaster recovery were more modest in scope.

A final point concerns the portrayal of early modern earthquakes in the modern era. By the late eighteenth century, mass media had become a major force in Japanese society. Despite claims that the 1891 Nōbi earthquake was the first Japanese natural disaster to receive nationwide media attention, such coverage had in fact become the norm roughly a century earlier.[103] As we have seen in connection with the 1830 Kyoto earthquake, one feature of mass media coverage was sensationalism, exaggeration of the death and destruction, and the repetition of rumors and unverified tales. We should be skeptical of claims from 1830 or 1855, which appeared in the rough equivalent of today's tabloid newspapers in grocery-store checkout aisles. There is an unfortunate propensity among some modern and contemporary authors to regard the age of a document as an emblem of its veracity. This tendency is particularly apparent in modern works touting earthquake-related folk wisdom. It also results in a penchant for portraying premodern earthquakes as much deadlier and destructive than they really were.

When Samuels conjured up an image of "suffering masses who had lost everything" in Ansei Edo, he was adding his voice to a long line of modern commentators who exaggerated the destructiveness of this event. Although the death toll for military and civilian personnel came to about eight thousand, less than 1 percent of the city's population, rumors of one hundred thousand or even two hundred thousand emerged from the event and have been repeated ever since. Extrapolating backward from the Great Kantō Earthquake, which certainly produced vast destruction and suffering masses, may be one factor. However, the exaggeration of Ansei Edo had begun much earlier. H. Tennant, writing in 1891 just after the Nōbi earthquake, said of Ansei Edo, "Its horrors still live in the recollection of the people, and they fear nothing more than a repetition of the occurrence." After the main shock, "Yedo [Edo] was turned into a rubbish heap" and "104,000 persons are said to have perished."[104] Tennant was indeed correct that by 1891 the Ansei Edo earthquake had become perceived as a catastrophe on this scale—much worse than it really had been.[105] Elsewhere in his brief summary of major earthquakes in Japan, Tennant claimed that thirty thousand perished in the 1828 Sanjō (Echigo) earthquake. We have seen, however, that the actual figure was about 1,450. Indeed, the tabloid press of the time sometimes reported a death toll as high as thirty thousand, and Tennant was somehow tapping into that exaggerated information.

My point here is not to try to lessen the significance of early modern earthquakes but simply to add a note of caution when encountering descriptions of early modern natural disasters, either in primary or secondary sources. Despite many superficial resemblances to our own time, early modern Japan was a vastly different society. One implication is that the social and intellectual context of early modern earthquakes should be understood in its own terms, a point I have made repeatedly in criticizing the ahistorical treatment of early modern earthquake lore by modern and contemporary writers. Moreover, sorting through the vast documentary record that early modern earthquakes have produced is fraught with difficulties, even for something as basic as determining reasonably accurate casualty figures. We can learn much from early modern earthquakes, but the lessons are rarely obvious or easy to grasp.

NOTES

1. Usami Tatsuo, *Nihon higai jishin sōran [416]–2001, Saishinpan* (*Materials for a Comprehensive List of Destructive Earthquakes in Japan, [416]–2001 [Latest Edition]*) (Tōkyō daigaku shuppankai, 2003), 53.

2. Watanabe Hideo, *Nihon higai tsunami sōran, dai-2 han* (*Comprehensive List of Tsunamis to Hit the Japanese Islands*) (Tōkyō daigaku shuppankai, 1998), 72. See also Koshimura Shun'ichi, "Sanriku chihō no tsunami saigai gaiyō," in *1896 Meiji Sanriku jishin*

tsunami hōkokusho (Chūō bōsai kaigi, 2005), 3–4; and Itō Kazuaki, *Jishin to funka no Nihonshi* (Iwanami shoten, 2002), 107.

3. Regarding the 1611 event as a slow earthquake, see Yamashita Fumio, *Tsunami no kyōfu: Sanriku tsunami denshōroku* (Sendai, Japan: Tōhoku daigaku shuppankai, 2005), 48.

4. "Iwate-ken tsunami shi 1," in *Shinshū Nihon jishin shiryō*, vol. 2, ed. Tōkyō daigaku jishin kenkyūjo (Nihon denki kyōkai, 1982), 101; and "Karakuwa-chō shi," in ibid., 98.

5. Yamashita, *Tsunami no kyōfu*, 13.

6. "Iwate-ken tsunami shi 1," 100.

7. "Karakuwa-chō shi," 98.

8. José Holguín-Veras, "Japan's 1,000-Year-Old-Warning," *Los Angeles Times*, March 11, 2012. I thank Ruth Ludwin for bringing this item to my attention.

9. "Higashi Nihon daishinsai: Senjin wa shitteita 'rekishi gaidō' shinsui sezu," *Mainichi shinbun*, April 19, 2011.

10. "Date jika kiroku," in *Shinshū Nihon jishin shiryō*, vol. 2, ed. Tōkyō daigaku jishin kenkyūjo (Nihon denki kyōkai, 1982), 98–99.

11. "Iwate-ken tsunami shi 1," 101; Usami, *Nihon higai jishin*, 53; and Koshimura, "Sanriku chihō no tsunami," 4.

12. Koshimura, "Sanriku chihō no tsunami," 6.

13. "Ika no toresugi wa daijishin no zenchō? Tokushima de 4-bai mo," *Yomiuri Online*, May 1, 2011. http://www.yomiuri.co.jp/national/news/20110501-OYT1T00194. htm.

14. Usami, *Nihon higai jishin*, 118–19; and Watanabe, *Nihon higai tsunami*, 88. For a detailed study of wave heights based on inundation patterns in eleven places, see Namegaya Yūichi, Tsuji Yoshinobu, and Ueda Kazue, "Kansei go-nen (1793) Miyagi-ken-oki ni hasseishita jishin no shōsai shindo bunpu to tsunami no jōkyō" ("Detailed Distributions of Seismic Intensity and Tsunami Heights of the Kansei off Miyagi Prefecture Earthquake of February 17, 1793"), *Rekishi jishin*, no. 11 (2003): 75–106.

15. Koshimura, "Sanriku chihō no tsunami," 5.

16. For a good example from 1793, see "Shirosawa-son shi, shiryōhen," in *"Nihon no rekishi jishin shiryō" shūi*, ed. Usami Tatsuo (Nihon denki kyōkai, 1998), 177–78.

17. See, for example, Tsukuda Tameshige, *Jishin yochi no saishin kagaku: Hassei no mekanizumu to yochi kenkyū no saizensen* (SoftBank Creative, 2007), 174–76; and the articles in Saumitra Mukherjee, ed., *Earthquake Prediction* (Leiden: Brill, 2006), esp. 21–51, 61–68.

18. Usami, *Nihon higai jishin*, 182–83; Watanabe, *Nihon higai tsunami*, 97–98; and Koshimura, "Sanriku chihō no tsunami," 5.

19. Yamashita, *Tsunami no kyōfu*, 31–33; and Yamashita Fumio, *Tsunami tendenko: Kindai Nihon no tsunamishi* (Shin Nihon shuppansha, 2008), 34–35.

20. Usami, *Nihon higai jishin*, 130–31; Okada Yoshimitsu, *Saishin Nihon no jishin chizu* (Tōkyō shoseki, 2006), 56; Sangawa Akira, *Jishin no Nihonshi: Daichi wa nani o kataru no ka?* (Chūōkōron shinsha, 2007), 158–62; and Hashimoto Manpei, *Jishingaku no kotohajime: Kaituakusha Sekiya Seikei no shōgai* (Asahi shinbunsha, 1983), 40.

21. Koizumi Kinmei, "Chōshin hiroku," in *"Nihon no rekishi jishin shiryo" shūi, Saiko 2-nen yori Shōwa 21-nen ni itaru*, vol. 3, ed. Usami Tatsuo (Watanabe tansa gijutsu kenkyūjo, 2005), 211.

22. Quoted in "Kekko no yamakoshie nikki," in http://bvd97629.niiblo.jp/e5571. html (accessed November 13, 2010). See also Sangawa, *Jishin no Nihonshi*, 158.

23. "Echigo jishin kudoki" (blog), accessed October 28, 2010, http://blogs.yahoo.co.jp/gojukara11/2937035.html; and Saitō Masachi, *Goze kudoki jishin no mi no ue* (1829). See also Hashimoto, *Jishingaku,* 40–41; and Sangawa, *Jishin no Nihonshi,* 162.

24. For a thorough analysis of the Great Kantō Earthquake interpreted as divine punishment, see J. Charles Schencking, *The Great Kantō Earthquake and the Chimera of National Reconstruction in Japan* (New York: Columbia University Press, 2013), 116–52.

25. Koizumi, "Chōshin hiroku," 213.

26. Koizumi, "Chōshin hiroku," 213–18.

27. Takashi Ito, "Were There Precursors of March 11 Quake?" *Daily Yomiuri Online,* July 25, 2011.

28. Chris Rowan, "Earthquake 'Precursors' and the Curse of the False Positive," *Highly Allochthonous: News & Commentary from the World of Geology and Earth Science* (blog), May 21, 2011, http://all-geo.org/highlyallochthonous/2011/05/earthquake-precursors-and-the-curse-of-the-false-positive.

29. For a detailed study of early modern conceptions of earthquakes, see Gregory Smits, *Seismic Japan: The Long History and Continuing Legacy of the Ansei Edo Earthquake* (Honolulu: University of Hawaii Press, 2013), 37–70.

30. Among the most vociferous advocates of earthquake clouds is Zhongshao Shou. See "Earthquake Vapor, a Reliable Precursor," in Mukherjee, *Earthquake Prediction,* 21–51. For another example, see Motoji Ikeya, *Earthquakes and Animals: From Folk Legends to Science* (River Edge, NJ: World Scientific, 2004), front matter photos, 4–6, 22–23, 170–79.

31. Tsukuda, *Jishin yochi no saishin kagaku,* 174–76. He describes earthquake clouds within the subsection "Strange Weather Phenomena" ("Ijō kishō genshō").

32. Ikeya, *Earthquakes and Animals,* 6–7.

33. Sangawa, *Jishin no Nihonshi,* 162; Itō, *Jishin to funka no Nihonshi,* 187–90; and Miki Haruo, *Kyōto daijishin* (Shibunkaku shuppan, 1979), 4–48, 115–250. Miki argues that an accurate count of the dead is impossible. See also Shinsai yobō chōsakai, eds., *Dai-Nihon jishin shiryō,* vol. 1 (kō) (Shibunkaku, 1973), 533–89.

34. Musha Kinkichi, *Jishin namazu* (Meiseki shoten, 1957; repr., 1995), 55.

35. "Mitsuhisa Kyūki," in Shinsai yobō chōsakai, *Dai-Nihon jishin shiryō,* vol. 1 (kō), 533–35.

36. "Kyōto jishin kenmonki," in Shinsai yobō chōsakai, *Dai-Nihon jishin shiryō,* vol. 1 (kō), 569.

37. Quoted in Miki, *Kyōto daijishin,* 111.

38. *Ukiyō no arisama,* quoted in Miki, *Kyōto daijishin,* 74, 105.

39. Miki, *Kyōto daijishin,* 75–88.

40. Quoted in Harold Bolitho, "The Tempō Crisis," in *The Cambridge History of Japan: Volume 5, The Nineteenth Century,* ed. Marius B. Jansen (New York, 1989), 117.

41. Kojima Tōzan and Tōrōan-shujin, *Jishinkō* (Kyoto: Saiseikan, 1830), first two page faces in the second section of the book; and Hashimoto, *Jishingaku,* 22–24.

42. Kojima, *Jishinkō,* page faces 1–3 after the heading "Jishinkō" describe the 1830 earthquake, and printed page faces 3–8 describe past earthquakes. "Jishinkō," in Shinsai yobō chōsakai, *Dai-Nihon jishin shiryō,* vol. 1 (kō), 589–90. See also Hashimoto, *Jishingaku,* 23–24; and Nihon gakushiin, eds., *Meiji-zen Nihon butsuri kagakushi* (Nihon gakjutsu shinkōkai, 1964), 562–63.

43. The Chinese text is *Astronomy Questions Answered* (J. *Tenkei wakumon;* Ch. *Tianjing huowen,* 1597). Kojima, *Jishinkō,* page faces 1–4 after the heading "Jishin no setsu" and "Jishinkō," in Shinsai yobō chōsakai, *Dai-Nihon jishin shiryō,* vol. 1 (kō), 590.

44. Kojima, *Jishinkō*, page faces 2–5 in the second section. The third page face consists of an illustration of the earthquake center. See also "Jishinkō," in Shinsai yobō chōsakai, *Dai-Nihon jishin shiryō*, vol. 1 (kō), 592 (no illustration); Hashimoto, *Jishingaku*, 24–25; and Nihon gakushiin, *Butsuri kagakushi*, 563. To view the earthquake center illustration, see Waseda University Library, http://archive.wul.waseda.ac.jp/kosho/i04/i04_00600/i04_00600_0175/i04_00600_0175_p0013.jpg.

45. Kojima, *Jishinkō*, first page face in the section "Jishin no shirushi"; "Jishinkō," in Shinsai yobō chōsakai, *Dai-Nihon jishin shiryō*, vol. 1 (kō), 590–91. See also Hashimoto, *Jishingaku*, 24.

46. Kojima, *Jishinkō*, page faces 6–10 in the second section; and "Jishinkō," in Shinsai yobō chōsakai, *Dai-Nihon jishin shiryō*, vol. 1 (kō), 592. See also Hashimoto, *Jishingaku*, 25; and Miki, *Kyōto daijishin*, 60–66.

47. Ikeya, *Earthquakes and Animals*, 5.

48. "Yobu karasu, sunahama ni kujira . . . shinsai mae ni dōbutsu ihen," *Yomiuri shinbun* (*Yomiuri Online*), July 2, 2011, 2:41 p.m. http://www.yomiuri.co.jp/science/news/20110702-OYT1T00504.htm.

49. "Japanese City to Watch Animal Behaviour for Disaster Signs," *Tokyo Times*, 2012; and "City Looks to Base Tsunami Warnings on Animal Behavior," *Japan Times*, June 3, 2012.

50. Joshua Hammer, *Yokohama Burning: The Deadly 1923 Earthquake and Fire That Helped Forge the Path to World War II* (New York: Free Press, 2006), 62.

51. Noel Fairchild Busch, *Two Minutes to Noon: The Story of the Great Tokyo Earthquake and Fire* (New York: Simon and Schuster, 1962), 43.

52. Musha, *Jishin namazu*, 16.

53. Musha, *Jishin namazu*, 16.

54. Gregory Smits, "Conduits of Power: What the Origins of Japan's Earthquake Catfish Reveal about Religious Geography," *Japan Review* 24 (2012): 41–65.

55. Okada, *Jishin chizu*, 119–20; Itō, *Jishin to funka no Nihonshi*, 91–96; Sangawa, *Jishin no Nihonshi*, 173; Watanabe, *Nihon higai tsunami*, 91–94; Usami, *Nihon higai jishin*, 151–64; and Tsuji Yoshinobu, "Ansei tōkai jishin, Ansei nankai jishin no jitsuzō to sonjin no saigai kyōkun," in *1854 Ansei tōkai jishin, Ansei nankai jishin*, ed. Chūō bōsai kaigi (2005), 1–2. See also 132.

56. Quoted in Sangawa, *Jishin no Nihonshi*, 173.

57. Ishibashi Katsuhiko, *Daijishinran no jidai* (Iwanami shoten, 1994), 20.

58. Sangawa, *Jishin no Nihonshi*, 173–77; and Sangawa Akira, *Nihonjin wa donna daijishin o keikenshitekita no ka: Jishin kōkogaku nyūmon* (Heibonsha, 2011), 84–95. See also Itō, *Jishin to funka no Nihonshi*, 97–99; and Ishibashi, *Daijishinran no jidai*, 16–20, 29–30, 35. For a detailed account of the damage to Shimoda, see Kitahara Itoko, "Shimoda-kō no higai to fukkō," in Chūō bōsai kaigi, *1854 Ansei tōkai jishin*, 20–42. See also "Zoku jishin zassan," in Shinsai yobō chōsakai, *Dai-Nihon jishin shiryō*, vol. 2 (otsu), 440–45. Regarding the claim of the *Heda* as Japan's first Western-style ship, Ishibashi points out that two or three such ships had been built earlier, but the *Heda* was a major advancement in skill and knowledge owing to assistance from the Russian sailors.

59. Okada, *Jishin chizu*, 119; Itō, *Jishin to funka no Nihonshi*, 99–100; Sangawa, *Jishin no Nihonshi*, 180–81; Watanabe, *Nihon higai tsunami*, 94–96; Usami, *Nihon higai jishin*, 164–68; Tsuji, "Ansei tōkai, nankai jishin"; and Kitahara Itoko, "Ansei tōkai, nankai jishin no higai jōhō ni tsuite: kawaraban o chūshin ni," in Chūō bōsai kaigi, *1854 Ansei tōkai jishin*, 1–2, 84–85, 132.

60. Ishibashi, *Daijishinran no jidai*, 25–26.

61. Sangawa, *Donna daijishin*, 98. See 95–104 for the complete account.

62. Karatani Tomoka, "Kii-koku Hiromura ni tsuite," in Chūō bōsai kaigi, *1854 Ansei tōkai jishin*, 68.

63. Karatani, "Hiromura," 68–71; Itō, *Jishin to funka no Nihonshi*, 102–4; Sangawa, *Jishin no Nihonshi*, 185–87; Sangawa, *Donna daijishin*, 95–104; Toishi Shirō, *Tsunami o tatakatta hito: Hamamura Goryō den* (Shin-Nihon shuppansha, 2005), 53–78; and many other sources.

64. Karatani, "Hiromura," in Chūō bōsai kaigi, *1854 Ansei tōkai jishin*, 3; Tsuji, "Ansei tōkai, nankai jishin," in Chūō bōsai kaigi, *1854 Ansei tōkai jishin*, 74–76; Itō, *Jishin to funka no Nihonshi*, 105–6; Sangawa, *Jishin no Nihonshi*, 185–87; and Hirakawa Sukehiro, *Koizumi Yakumo: Seiyō dasshutsu no yume* (Shinchōsha, 1981), 157–73.

65. *Hamaguchi Goryō shuki*, quoted in Hirakawa, *Koizumi Yakumo*, 164–65.

66. For the Japan-based website, see http://www.inamuranohi.jp. For copies of the tale in various languages, see the page "Tsunami Education Booklet 'Rice Bale Fire,'" accessed October 15, 2013, http://www.adrc.asia/publications/inamura/top.html, part of the Asian Disaster Reduction Center's website.

67. Toishi, *Tsunami to tatakatta hito*; and Sangawa, *Donna daijishin*, 95.

68. Yamashita, *Tsunami no kyōfu*, 127–34; and Hatamura Yōtarō, "Higashi Nihon daishinsai ni omō," in *Kyodai jishin, kyodai tsunami: Higashi Nihon daishinsai no kenshō*, ed. Hirata Naoshi, Satake Kenji, Meguro Kimirō, and Hatakemura Yōtarō (Asakura shoten, 2011), 151–55.

69. Quoted in Yamashita, *Tsunami no kyōfu*, 122.

70. "Zoku jishin zassan," in Shinsai yobō chōsakai, *Dai-Nihon jishin shiryō*, vol. 2 (otsu), 419, 420, 423, 462. The name of the village in the first quoted passage is not clear. For more examples of villagers fleeing to high ground in advance of tsunamis, see "Zoku jishin zassan" and "Jishin nikki," in Shinsai yobō chōsakai, *Dai-Nihon jishin shiryō*, vol. 2 (otsu), 462, 467, 469–71, 482–83.

71. Nishiyama Shōjin, "Ansei nankai jishin ni okeru Ōsaka de no shinsai taiō," in Chūō bōsai kaigi, *1854 Ansei tōkai jishin, Ansei nankai jishin hōkokusho*, 51, 55–59, 62. See also Tsuji, "Ansei tōkai, nankai jishin," in Chūō bōsai kaigi, *1854 Ansei tōkai jishin, Ansei nankai jishin hōkokusho*, 2; and "Ōya Hiroyoshi nikki," "Kaei kinoetora shokoku jishinki," "Zoku jishin zassan," and "Jishin nikki," in Shinsai yobō chōsakai, *Dai-Nihon jishin shiryō*, vol. 2 (otsu), 380, 392–95, 415–20, 427–28, 518–19. For an image of the carnage from the mass media, see http://gazo.dl.itc.u-tokyo.ac.jp/ishimoto/1/01-035/00001.jpg (upper left image).

72. Usami, *Nihon higai jishin*, 168.

73. Tsuji Yoshinobu, *Sennen shinsai: Kurikaesu jishin to tsunami no rekishi ni manabu* (Daiyamondo sha, 2011), 132–34.

74. See, for example, "Ōya Hiroyoshi nikki," in Shinsai yobō chōsakai, *Dai-Nihon jishin shiryō*, vol. 2 (otsu), 380.

75. "Jishin nikki," in Shinsai yobō chōsakai, *Dai-Nihon jishin shiryō*, vol. 2 (otsu), 488.

76. The details of this earthquake are summarized in many sources. A thorough yet relatively concise listing of damage and other essential parameters is in Usami, *Nihon higai jishin*, 171–82.

77. Smits, *Seismic Japan*.

78. Ikeya, *Earthquakes and Animals*, 15–16; and Chihiro Yamanaka, Hiroshi Asahara, Yutaka Emoto, and Yuko Esaki, "Earthquake Precursors—From Legends to Science and a Possible Early Warning System," in *Future Systems for Earthquake Early Warning*,

ed. Ülkü Ulusoy and Himansu Kumar Kundu (New York: Nova Science, 2008), 204, 205.

79. Suzuki Tōzō and Koike Shōtarō, eds., *Fujiokaya nikki*, Kinsei shomin seikatsu shiryō, vol. 15 (San'ichi shobō, 1995), 556; and *Ansei kenmonshi*, 3 vols., illustrations by Utagawa Kuniyoshi et al. (Authors and publisher unknown, 1856), 3:19–20. To view this device, see http://archive.wul.waseda.ac.jp/kosho/wo01/wo01_04209/wo01_04209_0003/wo01_04209_0003_p0019.jpg. See also Arakawa Hidetoshi, ed., *Jitsuroku, Ō-Edo kaimetsu no hi: Ansei kenmonroku, Ansei kenmonshi, Ansei fūbunshū* (Kyōikusha, 1982), 191–92; Hashimoto, *Jishingaku*, 30–31; Usami, "Kaisetsu," 43–45; Gregory Clancey, *Earthquake Nation: The Cultural Politics of Japanese Seismicity, 1868–1930* (Berkeley: University of California Press, 2006), 153; and Tsuji Yoshinobu, *Sennen shinsai: Kurikaesu jishin to tsunami no rekishi ni manabu* (Daiyamondo sha, 2011), 93–95.

80. According to Ikeya, the loss of magnetism in the stone "led to the immediate construction of an earthquake prediction apparatus." He claims to have constructed a working replica in his laboratory based on the drawing in *Ansei kenmonshi*. Ikeya, *Earthquakes and Animals*, 15. See also Yamanaka et al., "Earthquake Precursors," 204, 205.

81. Murayama Masataka, *Shinden kōsetsu* [1856], Edo josei bunko, vol. 49 (Ōzorasha, 1994) (no pagination). See also Tōkyō kagaku hakubutsukan, ed., *Edo jidai no kagaku* (1934; repr. Meicho kankōkai, 1980), 268.

82. Hashimoto, *Jishingaku*, 20–21.

83. *Ansei kenmonshi*, vol. 1, approximately full page 15 of text after the table of contents. See also Arakawa, *Jitsuroku, Ō-Edo kaimetsu no hi*, 121.

84. Jun Hatano, "Edo's Water Supply," in *Edo and Paris: Urban Life and the State in the Early Modern Era*, ed. James L. McClain, John W. Merriman, and Ugawa Kaoru (Ithaca, NY: Cornell University Press, 1994), 247–48.

85. *Ansei kenmonshi*, vol. 1, page ue-no-1 and next page face in "Jishin no ben." See also Arakawa, *Jitsuroku, Ō-Edo kaimetsu no hi*, 25.

86. Udagawa Kōsai, *Jishin yobōsetsu* (Edo: Suhara Yaihachi, 1856), 2 (quoted passage), 16 (illustration of the rods). See also Hashimoto, *Jishingaku*, 35–36. To view the illustration, see http://archive.wul.waseda.ac.jp/kosho/bunko08/bunko08_c0090/bunko08_c0090_p0019.jpg.

87. Hashimoto, *Jishingaku*, 36–38.

88. Explosive theories of earthquakes had a long history in Europe. In *Principia philosophiae* (1644), for example, René Descartes advanced a theory of earthquakes whereby fumes from inside the earth might combine to form combustible mixtures. Soon after the Ansei Edo earthquake, Irish engineer Robert Mallet began important work on seismic waves. Mallet thought that explosive forces of volcanic origin caused earthquakes. See Emanuela Guidoboni and John E. Ebel, *Earthquakes and Tsunamis in the Past: A Guide to Techniques in Historical Seismology* (New York: Cambridge University Press, 2009), 167, 170–72, 184.

89. For a comprehensive survey of the legacies of the Ansei Edo earthquake, see Smits, *Seismic Japan*, 174–88.

90. Richard J. Samuels, *3.11: Disaster and Change in Japan* (Ithaca, NY: Cornell University Press, 2013), 49.

91. Samuels, *Disaster and Change*, 191–92.

92. See, for example, Samuels, *Disaster and Change*, 151–79, 187–88.

93. "Tokutake-shi jishin kiji," in Shinsai yobō chōsakai, *Dai-Nihon jishin shiryō*, vol. 2 (otsu), 156.

94. For an authoritative study of the death and destruction, see Akabane Sadayuki and Inoue Kimio, "Saigai no jōkyō," in Chūō bōsai kaigi, *1847 Zenkōji jishin hōkokusho* (Nihon shisutemu kaihatsu kenkyūsho, 2007), 22–42, 222.

95. "Kenshūroku," in Shinsai yobō chōsakai, *Dai-Nihon jishin shiryō*, vol. 2 (otsu), 105–107, 109–111; Harada Kazuhiko, "Matsushiro-han de sakusei sareta jishinzuerui ni tsuite," in Chūō bōsai kaigi, *1847 Zenkōji jishin hōkokusho*, 110–11; Shinano mainichi shinbunsha kaihatsukyoku shuppanbu, ed., *Kōka yonen Zenkōji daijishin* (Nagano-shi: Shinano mainichi shinbunsha, 1977), 138–50; and Kitō Yasuyuki and Nagase Satoshi, "Saigai to kyūsai: Machi to mura," in *Zenkōji jishin ni manabu*, ed. Akahane Sadayuki and Kitahara Itoko (Nagano-shi, Japan: Shinano mainichi shinbunsha, 2003), 75–94.

96. "Kenshūroku," in Shinsai yobō chōsakai, *Dai-Nihon jishin shiryō*, vol. 2 (otsu), 107, 109–11; Itō, *Jishin to funka no Nihonshi*, 139–41; and Shinano mainichi shinbunsha kaihatsukyoku shuppanbu, *Zenkōji daijishin*, 150–80.

97. Harada, "Matsushiro-han," 111. For a comprehensive study of emergency response, relief, and rebuilding efforts, see 71–121. See also Shinano mainichi shinbunsha kaihatsukyoku shuppanbu, *Zenkōji daijishin*, 180–204. For a sample of relevant documents concerning specific relief efforts and proposals, see "Kamahara Dōzan jishin kiji," 51–52, 83–85, 90–91; "Nogisono zakki," 139; "Daijishin kōzui saigai kiroku," 212–32; and "Sinkōkan," in Shinsai yobō chōsakai, *Dai-Nihon jishin shiryō*, vol. 2 (otsu), 317–18.

98. For a detailed discussion of this process, see Smits, *Seismic Japan*, 112–14, 126–35.

99. Samuels, *Disaster and Change*, esp. 57–63.

100. Schencking, *Great Kantō Earthquake*, 8.

101. Samuels, *Disaster and Change*, 200.

102. For more on these aspects of the Ansei Edo earthquake, see Smits, *Seismic Japan*, esp. 95–100, 121–25, 139–44.

103. Samuels, following Clancey, characterizes Nōbi as "the first large-scale disaster to receive sustained nationwide news coverage." See *Disaster and Change*, 50. Nōbi probably did receive more sustained media attention than any previous disaster, but this additional attention was an incremental change in a well-established pattern, not a radically new phenomenon. For an excellent summary of the history of disaster journalism from the late eighteenth century through the Nōbi earthquake, see Kitahara Itoko, *Saigai jaanarizumu, mukashi hen* (Sakura, Japan: Rekishi minzoku hakubutsukan shinkōkai, 2001).

104. H. Tennant, *The Great Earthquake in Japan, October 28, 1891: Being a Full Description of the Disasters Resulting from the Recent Terrible Catastrophe* (1892; repr. Kessinger, 2007), 3.

105. For details on the Ansei Edo earthquake in modern memory, see Smits, *Seismic Japan*, 176–81.

THREE
Nōbi and Great Kantō

This chapter examines two influential and well-studied earthquakes in prewar Japan, the 1891 Nōbi earthquake and the 1923 Great Kantō Earthquake. As natural disasters, these events differed in significant ways. In terms of social significance, the Nōbi earthquake served as a catalyst for the development of modern national consciousness, and the Great Kantō Earthquake highlighted prevailing social anxieties of the time—among other things. These two modern earthquakes shared some social characteristics with early modern earthquakes, but they also differed significantly. Both earthquakes also contributed to the advancement of seismological knowledge in Japan and throughout the world, and both contributed to early forms of antiseismic engineering.

NŌBI AND MODERN EARTHQUAKES

The M8.0 Nōbi earthquake was the strongest intraplate earthquake in Japan's known history. Also called the Mino-Owari earthquake, it was felt in almost every part of Japan and occurred at 6:38 a.m. on October 28, 1891. The strongest shaking was in the Neodani (Neo Valley) area of Gifu Prefecture, a rural area then and now. The event did considerable damage to the city of Nagoya, but had it occurred under a large city, Nōbi might have been deadlier than the 1923 Great Kantō Earthquake (a tsunamigenic offshore earthquake). The fatality toll from Nōbi was 7,273, putting it in approximately the same class as the 1855 Ansei Edo earthquake or the 1995 Kōbe earthquake in terms of deadliness. The Nōbi

71

earthquake engendered debates about the future of architecture—brick (Western) versus wood (native)—and was an opportunity for the emperor and top government officials to appear in public at the head of a national relief effort.[1]

Although major early modern earthquakes from the early nineteenth century onward received nationwide coverage in urban areas, dealing with them was mainly a local matter. As I stated in the previous chapter, even Ansei Edo was a de facto local relief and recovery effort. A small quantity in donations and other aid came into Edo from areas unaffected by the earthquake, and domain lords sometimes imported labor or resources from their territories. Nevertheless, the majority of the recovery effort was local. Nōbi was different. Although the event took place far from the capital, the central government took the lead in orchestrating relief. A parade of top officials, one after another, visited the stricken areas. Military units played a key role in the relief, as they would in many future earthquakes. A variety of volunteers also traveled to the region. For example, fifteen medical students traveled in the area to help the wounded, and hospitals as far away as Kyūshū dispatched doctors and nurses to the afflicted areas. On the thirty-first, an emergency cabinet meeting to allocate funds and decide on emergency measures took place, which was great speed, even by contemporary standards. Insofar as the earthquake crippled vital infrastructure, the Nōbi earthquake generated unprecedentedly high expectations that the state would move quickly to limit the scope of damage and provide relief.[2]

Another new aspect of the Nōbi earthquake was the involvement of foreigners. Some foreigners provided direct assistance, and several traveled through the devastated areas and wrote reports. Foreigners also organized charity and relief organizations. The German community acted with particular speed to raise funds and distribute aid. The Kōbe Relief Fund raised money from all over the world.[3] Japanese entities began relief funds, often with newspapers sponsoring funds or serving as the major vehicle for publicizing them. For example, two days after the earthquake, the newspaper *Jiji shinpō* collected ten sen from each of its employees and publicized the names in its pages. The prefectural offices (*kenchō*) in Aichi and Gifu sent funds to the paper, which in turn publicized these donations. Thus began a prominent mode of raising disaster relief funds in the modern era. At the same time, the emperor and empress donated twenty-six thousand yen to the two most severely affected prefectures.[4]

A similar pattern of fundraising and relief support followed the earthquakes of 1896, 1923, and 1933, and it represents a significant change from the early modern era. In modern Japan, newspapers not only reported on natural disasters, they actively intervened in the recovery efforts.

Experts were quick to offer advice and point out the significance or lessons from the Nōbi earthquake. The ailing seismology pioneer, Sekiya Seikei, for example, expressed his view in letters. In one, he stated that because earthquakes cannot be prevented, it is imperative that carpenters, masons, plasterers, bricklayers, and other construction workers study the aftermath of the earthquake and determine ways to construct buildings that withstand earthquake shocks. In a different letter, Sekiya cited Spain and Italy as examples of countries with building codes for withstanding seismic shocks. Japan too, he argued, should enact such codes. Alternatively, the government should construct model buildings in the Mino-Owari area so that others could imitate the design features.[5] Those today who advocate putting public resources into reducing the damage from earthquakes, not into trying to forecast them, echo Sekiya's basic point.

Comparing aspects of the social history of the Nōbi earthquake and that of the Ansei Edo earthquake reveals some of the major changes in society over the course of a generation. The emperor, for example, was a key figure in both events, but the nature of these two emperors was quite different. In the 1855 event, it was not so much the emperor as an actual person but the imperial institution as an abstraction that helped impart meaning to the earthquake. The deity Amaterasu, sometimes represented as a male warrior, sometimes as the sun, and sometimes as beams of light, was the main manifestation of the imperial institution.[6] In 1891, the Meiji emperor was a prominent public figure, whose wife was also active in public affairs. The imperial couple were the benevolent face of the state and intervened in a concrete way via a large cash donation. Moreover, their actions might serve as exemplars for all the citizens of the nation to contribute what they could to the common good. Newspapers reached even into small villages and served as a convenient means for channeling this participation in benevolent national work. Although donations from common people were a significant part of the relief effort in the Ansei Edo earthquake, with local media often publishing the names of donors, the scale was much larger in 1891. By the time of the Nōbi earthquake,

Japan as a whole had become a more tightly organized and mobilized society compared with a generation earlier.

This new, modern situation had implications for the relationship between the state and natural disasters. It is common, though not entirely accurate, for commentators on early modern disasters to claim that existence of a disaster cast moral suspicion on the state. Strong antigovernment interpretations of early modern earthquakes were uncommon. One pragmatic reason is that it was not always clear what "the government" was. In any case, in the modern era, major natural disasters became the de facto property of the central government. In this very important sense, natural disasters were a greater challenge to the state's moral authority than early modern catastrophes ever were.

IMPACT OF NŌBI ON SCIENCE

The Nōbi earthquake led to what is arguably the earliest manifestation of an official earthquake bureaucracy, the Imperial Earthquake Investigation Committee (IEIC). Created in 1892, this agency resided within the Ministry of Education, with Kikuchi Dairoku as its chair. A year after the committee's establishment, Kikuchi wrote to the education minister explaining the goals of the committee. "One aspect of our work is to ascertain whether or not there is a method for predicting earthquakes. The other aspect is to devise plans for minimizing the damage from earthquakes when they do occur. Therefore one part of our work focusses on science and the other part on engineering."[7] This view was common in the wake of the Nōbi earthquake. Notice the strong link between "science" and "prediction" at this time as well as the classic division between science as an abstract intellectual discipline (knowledge) separated from ordinary experience and a practical application of technology to real-world problems (know-how) by people such as engineers. In theory at least, the IEIC sought to bridge this division.

The Imperial Earthquake Investigation Committee came into existence owing to widespread sentiment for the need to shine the light of science on the phenomenon of earthquakes and tsunamis. Nōbi was bad, but something similar located near Tokyo would be much worse. Perhaps the most dramatic feature of the Nōbi earthquake, besides the extensive damage, was a long fault scarp resulting from roughly six meters of vertical offset cutting through the village of Midori. Still visible today, this massive rupture of the land came to broader attention in 1893, when geologist Kotō Bunjirō published a photo, sketches, and a detailed analysis of the fault in a lengthy English-language article speculating on the causes of the earthquake. In it, Kotō first describes in detail the geology of the region before moving to a discussion of death and destruction. He considers one published theory, positing "the downfall of a superincumbent mass of rock into some subterranean hollow." Next was a theory proposed by a foreign physician who lived through the earthquake and regarded it as "an electric storm in the earth." Interestingly, the theory of electricity as a cause of earthquakes that first received attention in Japan in the 1850s was still in circulation.[8] In Kotō's view, however, neither theory adequately explains the cause.

Throughout his article, Kotō stresses the key role of volcanic activity in causing earthquakes. He explains that when he surveyed an earthquake in Kumamoto in 1889, he concluded that the cause was "a combined process of dislocation and an unsuccessful approach to a volcanic explosion." Moreover, "a violent earthquake often manifests its activity along some narrow line or fissure within the earth's crust."[9] He then

Figure 3.1. The Neodani Fault, Cause of the 1891 Nōbi Earthquake, Cutting Diagonally across a Built-Up Road. The white sign to the left of the road is at the point where the fault and road intersect. *Source*: **Wikimedia Commons, Tomomarusan.**

speculates that "seismic lines" are a widespread phenomenon in the Japanese islands, accounting for the uneven patterns of destruction so commonly observed in strong earthquakes. This point segues to the "earthrent" in the Neo Valley, which "resembles the pathway of a gigantic mole more than anything else," a metaphor he repeats several times. Indeed, the sight reminded Kotō of the old folklore of a giant "earthquake-insect."[10] His conclusion is that movement along the fault was the cause of the earthquake: "This vertical movement and horizontal shifting seem to me to have been the sole cause of the late catastrophe."[11]

For Kotō, the situation in Neodani was atypical. He writes, "The formation of such a colossal fault on the surface, as this in Midori, is exceptionally rare, and finds its equal only in the 'Ullah-bund,' or God's dam at the Runn of Cutch, in the lower course of the Indus."[12] Moreover, shifts and tears in the earth "are usually considered as the effects rather than the cause of subterranean commotions; but in my opinion it can be confidently asserted that the sudden formation of the 'great fault of Neo' was the actual cause of the great earthquake of the 28th of October, 1891." He describes such seismic events as "tectonic" earthquakes and distinguishes them from those caused by depressions or volcanic explosions.[13] Kotō's observations were, potentially, an important step forward in understanding earthquake mechanics.

LATE MEIJI CONCEPTIONS OF EARTHQUAKES

Even after the Nōbi earthquake, the proximate cause or causes of earthquakes remained unclear. Faulting was part of seismicity, but was it the cause of earthquakes or the result—or perhaps sometimes one and sometimes the other? Until plate tectonics became widely accepted during the 1960s, a grand theory of earthquake causality remained elusive. Consider the following passage, written just before the prominence of plate tectonics:

> As to the widely entertained theory that all earthquakes are caused by shifts or slides along well-defined splits or "faults" on the earth's surface, this is, at best, a plausible half-truth. It owes its prevalence, in the United States especially, to the fact that the great San Francisco quake of 1906 did indeed occur along the renowned San Andreas fault and that a good many other quakes have occurred along fault lines also. In fact, earthquakes are of two kinds: those that occur along fault lines

and those that don't. Both kinds are numerous; and even in the case of the ones that do occur on faults, no one can be sure whether it was the fault that caused the commotion or the other way around. In Japan, both sorts of earthquakes abound.[14]

Appearing in 1962, these words echo Kotō's discussion of the Nōbi earthquake: "Geologists are altogether silent as to whether the formation of faults and chasms should be considered as the direct cause, or only the outcome, of subterranean convulsions."[15] Kotō correctly insisted that the Neodani Fault caused the Nōbi earthquake, but more than six decades would pass before scientists were able to say with confidence that faults cause earthquakes.

Pioneering seismologist John Milne, who did much of his work in Japan, saw earthquakes as having several possible causes, though faulting was not one of them (Milne thought faults were a result of earthquakes). Writing in 1898, he summarized earthquake causes:

The majority of earthquakes, including all of any magnitude, are spasmodic accelerations in the secular [slow, long-term] folding or "creep" of rock masses; a certain number, particularly those originating off the mouths of large rivers like the Tonegawa in Japan, may result from the sudden yielding in the more or less horizontal flow of deeply seated material, the immediate cause of which is overloading by the deposition of sediments; whilst a few, which are comparatively feeble and shake limited areas, are due to explosions at volcanic foci.[16]

Milne's idea of creep resembles the contemporary view of strain accumulating in rocks as the tectonic plates of which they are a part move. Today we know that the movement of tectonic plates is the main source of the forces that fracture rock to create faults. As strain builds up along these faults, segments of them or the whole fault gives way, releasing energy.

JAPAN'S DEADLIEST SEISMIC DISASTER

The Great Kantō Earthquake (Kantō daishinsai) was a subduction zone earthquake, but not a product of the Japan Trench. It occurred along the Sagami Trough, formed by the Philippine Sea Plate pushing under the North American Plate. The Great Kantō Earthquake was a multifaceted event of such broad scope that even book-length studies usually focus only on certain dimensions of the disaster. The account here, therefore, is

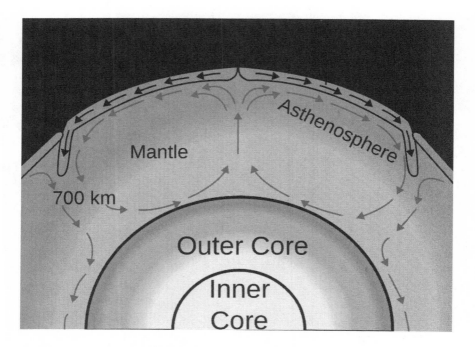

Figure 3.2.   Ocean Spreading and Subduction of Tectonic Plates. *Source*: Wikimedia Commons, Surachit.

highly selective, focusing only on points of direct relevance to the larger themes of this book.

The shaking began at 11:58:32 a.m. on September 1, 1923, as the flames in gas stoves and other cooking devices all over the Tokyo metropolitan area flickered amid routine lunch preparations. As fate would have it, the weather was windy. Seismometers around the world recorded the seismic waves. There is some variance in the estimated magnitude owing to data from different locations, but it falls within the 7.9–8.1 range. The shaking itself, a tsunami (that did not hit Tokyo directly), widespread violence owing to the breakdown of social order, and especially fires and firestorms killed well over one hundred thousand.[17] The fifty-nine thousand who died within Tokyo constituted just under 3 percent of the city's population of two million.[18] In other words, within Tokyo, the Great Kantō Earthquake was approximately three times deadlier than the Ansei Edo earthquake.

In historical earthquake documents, the term "unprecedented" (*mizō* or *zendai-mimon*) frequently occurs, even though major earthquakes were not, in fact, unparalleled events. Unlike its predecessors, however, the Great Kantō Earthquake might deserve that appellation. Major earthquakes had shaken Edo in 1855 and 1703, but never had a seismic event been so deadly, so destructive, and so conducive to violence in the social realm. In the Great Kantō Earthquake, violent natural hazards wiped out many components of modern urban infrastructure, which facilitated the carnage.

Major earthquakes of the Tokugawa period, especially during the latter half of that period, tended to follow a predictable rhetorical pattern. Because in most cases the survivors had never experienced a major earthquake, the initial reaction was to characterize the event as "unprecedented." A truly unprecedented natural disaster carried ominous implications about the possible breakdown of society. Therefore, a counter discourse soon arose to normalize the event. Using mass-produced books and prints to get their message out, writers would explain that Japan had a long history of earthquakes, often adding that deadly earthquakes also arose in China under the rule of ancient sage kings. Some writers would further endeavor to explain earthquakes in a logical manner. Although social critics and moralizers often seized on the fact of an earthquake's occurrence to imply cosmic sanction for their agendas, such voices were distinctly in the minority in the aftermath of most early modern earthquakes. Much more prominent were dramatic or fantastic tales from the catastrophe with entertainment value. Sometimes these tales advanced a moral message, but often they did not.

The rhetorical pattern following the Great Kantō Earthquake was similar, but with some important differences in emphasis. Just as in the past, the 1923 event brought forth accounts of Japan's long history of earthquake disasters. Experts in a variety of disciplines speculated about the cause, lessons, or significance of the event. Among seismologists, Imamura Akitsune's commentary was in particularly high demand for reasons we will see. Dramatic tales from the 1923 earthquake were, if anything, even more numerous and widely accessible than in past catastrophes. There was a strong tendency in 1923, however, to produce morally uplifting tales of virtuous and heroic conduct. Indeed, the aftermath of the disaster became an occasion to display the alleged national character of Japan.[19]

As one might expect, Japanese writers tended to overlook events such as the massacre of resident Koreans, "Reds" (leftists), or anyone suspected of being such, sometimes including Japanese from outlying areas who spoke with strong accents.[20] Many foreign authors tended to focus on precisely those and other ignoble events, such as the reports of Japanese officials refusing foreign aid out of arrogance or paranoia.[21] A related contrast with earthquakes of the Tokugawa period was that in 1923, the state played a significant role in guiding or manipulating interpretations of the disaster. During the early modern era, the various governments that held sway over Japan lacked both the means and the ambition even to try to impose official interpretations of disasters onto the populace.

An especially prominent and distinctive feature of the rhetoric in 1923 was characterization of the catastrophe as "heavenly punishment."[22] In nearly every early modern earthquake, critics of social morality claimed the earthquake was divine retribution for social ills, most commonly greed and excessive luxury. With the possible exception of the 1828 Sanjō earthquake, however, such voices were usually peripheral. Moreover, we do not find this theme prominent in the Nōbi earthquake or the major Tōhoku earthquakes of 1896 and 1933. Why, then, was the theme of divine retribution so prominent in interpretations of the 1923 event?

There is probably no single answer. One factor was surely the deadliness of the Great Kantō Earthquake. Tokyo in 1923 was much more vulnerable than was Edo in 1855. Because the soil base is a major consideration in determining damage levels in Tokyo, the 1923 earthquake, like the Ansei Edo earthquake, devastated some areas and left others in much better shape. In other words, the damage could appear to have been selective and purposeful. For example, the earthquake and fires destroyed the entertainment district of Asakusa, which many moralists regarded as a blight on society. The most commonly cited reason for the divine retribution interpretation is that the earthquake struck at a time in Japan's history of extreme anxiety concerning such phenomena as urbanization, consumerism, changing gender roles, an expanding middle class, and other changes associated with rapid modernization.

Schencking provides detailed statistics about changes in spending between 1912 and 1925 on phonographs and records, cosmetics, sake, and tobacco, as well as crime statistics. He points out, however, that statistical "reality" was not really the point:

> Statistics aside, what we are dealing with here are perceptions about the state of Japanese society during a transformative period in its histo-

ry. The decline, degeneration, or "destruction of civilization," as Nonomura and others described the post–First World War era, was not an objective social, political, ideological, or economic fact. Rather it was a perceived phenomenon constructed by concerned elites, journalists, reform-minded bureaucrats, and government officials. Images of a degenerate society were products primarily of their casual observations, though sometimes supported by more thorough investigations and analysis. All, however, were heavily influenced by prejudices and preconceived notions about people and society at large.[23]

Early modern social critics typically also railed against imagined social degeneration. One difference in 1923 was the sheer number of prominent members of government, the military, and other social institutions who embraced the idea of urban Japan as a degenerate society. A telling statistic about the influence of such rhetoric on the population is that after the earthquake, sales of romance books fell by roughly half, whereas sales of religious and ideological books, including books about war heroes, increased.[24]

GREAT KANTŌ AS PORTRAYED IN *THE GREAT TAISHŌ EARTHQUAKE AND FIRE DISASTER*

In this section, I analyze one of those popular postearthquake books, one that incorporates many of the themes of this book and reveals specific features of the Great Kantō Earthquake. Kōdansha is Japan's largest publisher today, and in 1923, its prewar iteration quickly compiled a volume of articles on the earthquake. It released this volume exactly one month after the main shock, that is, on October 1, 1923. Titled *The Great Taishō Earthquake and Fire Disaster* (*Taishō daishinsai daikasai*), it begins with a brief introduction by philosopher and social commentator Miyake Setsurei, who wrote in part:

> The current earthquake is not without precedent, and even in our Japan, as well as in other lands, there have been larger ones. The catastrophe that accompanied the earthquake, however, can be regarded not only as unprecedented in Japan, but also in most of the world. . . . One person professed this [earthquake] in advance. Generally, however, nobody thought much of it, and a seismologist warned that revealing knowledge to the public that a fault would eventually cause danger would alarm society.[25]

The unnamed forecaster of the current earthquake in this account was Imamura Akitsune, and there is a backstory to Miyake's ambiguous sentences.

In 1905, the magazine *Taiyō* (*The Sun*) published an article featuring Imamura's forecast that Tokyo would suffer a great earthquake in the relatively near future and that based on historical records, it is likely that fire would be a severe problem. This article appeared in the September issue, coinciding with the Hibiya Incendiary Incident, in which angry crowds rioted in protest over perceived government weakness in agreeing to the Treaty of Portsmouth to end the Russo-Japanese War. In other words, Imamura's potentially incendiary article came out at a time when government authorities were very much concerned with maintaining calm and order among the public. The *Taiyō* article did not make waves, but the following year, the daily newspaper *Tōkyō niroku shinbun* published a more sensational version of Imamura's unpleasant forecast.

Imamura, with the encouragement of his superior, seismologist Ōmori Fusakichi, published a clarification in the *Tōkyō niroku shinbun* saying that his main point was that Tokyo should switch from petroleum lanterns to electric lights as soon as possible. However, Imamura did not disavow his basic idea that a large earthquake shaking Tokyo was likely in the near future and that it would create the danger of catastrophic fires. In 1907, an earthquake shook Tokyo and surrounding areas, causing light damage and great anxiety. It sparked sufficient commotion to require police intervention.

At that point, Ōmori's attitude changed. He rebuked Imamura in the pages of the March issue of *Taiyō*, saying: "Based on an assessment using fundamentally incomplete statistics, there is no doubt that it is impossible to predict the day and time of a future [seismic] event. Because theories like [Imamura's] future big Tokyo earthquake are ultimately the creation of the average yearly occurrences of earthquakes, they are without academic value." In this context, at least, Ōmori denied the ability to predict earthquakes and implicitly criticized the idea of characteristic earthquakes. He went on to say that because the 1703 Genroku earthquake mainly shook Odawara, not Edo, Tokyo itself had experienced only one severe earthquake in historical times, the 1855 Ansei Edo earthquake. A sample size of one is hardly a sufficient basis for Imamura's predictions. Ōmori disagreed with other aspects of Imamura's forecasts, though he did agree with Imamura's point that petroleum lanterns would be dangerous in a major earthquake.[26]

The Imamura-Ōmori feud, which had been simmering for years, burst forth in 1907. Ōmori's critique of characteristic earthquakes and his call for caution in relying too heavily on historical documents was reasonable, but neither man possessed the knowledge to say that a major earthquake would or would not strike in the near future. In this dispute, the earth itself intervened in a way that made Ōmori look like a villain for suppressing his rival and subordinate and Imamura appear as the long-suffering hero who persevered and was vindicated.[27]

Returning to *The Great Taishō Earthquake and Fire Disaster*, historian Mikami Sanji next points out that many have characterized the present disaster as "truly a divine punishment," owing to greed and widespread poverty. He calls on the citizens of Japan to honor the sacrifices of the victims by building a greater society. Imamura also takes up the theme of divine chastisement in an introduction to the volume, writing:

> Heaven has never inflicted such a punishment on the Yamato race in the past, and surely will not do so to our progeny. I think there must be some kind of moral lesson in the fact that we in particular have incurred such a thing. . . . At the least, our fellow countrymen (*dōhō*) have not believed in science and have not valued the academic study of earthquakes. Even considering only this point, might it not be possible to say that it is only natural that there is such a reckoning?[28]

Notice how malleable the rhetoric of divine punishment and moral failing can be in promoting agendas. Here it is not greed or hedonism, but lack of attention to science, that is the takeaway moral point of the earthquake—according to a scientist. In any case, Imamura's allegations that the Japanese people had rejected science in general and seismology in particular did strike a chord, as we will see.

The Great Taishō Earthquake and Fire Disaster contains sections on death and destruction caused by the shaking, the subsequent fires and firestorms, the gruesome problem of disposing of corpses, and the destruction in Yokohama and other nearby areas. Next is a chapter on the formation of the cabinet of Prime Minister Yamamoto Gonbei (a.k.a. Gonnohyōe), whom many observers at the time and later viewed as having benefited politically from the disaster. Following this discussion are several sections about recovery efforts and damage to various types of infrastructure.

This relatively dry material is followed by a lengthy series of horrific tales from the earthquake and firestorms, starting with the Benten Pond in the Yoshiwara brothel district. Flames forced the prostitutes and other workers into the pond, causing a horrific scene in which some drowned, others were crushed to death, and others were cooked by the flames, which raged for hours. "When at last the flames subsided and the next day dawned, 200 fortunately were saved, but over 630 drowned or otherwise died."[29] These mainly tragic tales no doubt served both to document the horrors of the event and to appeal to a sense of disaster voyeurism.

The following section consists of tales representing "beautiful outpouring of human feelings," the "beautiful tales" so prominent in the aftermath of this earthquake. Examples of titles include "Maid Rescues Her Master's Precious Items," "A Youth's Sense of Duty That Puts Adults to Shame," "Manifestation of Beautiful Humanity," "Nurse Who Carried a Seriously Ill Patient on Her Back and Did Not Eat or Drink for Two Days," and "Rescuing an Elephant from a Raging Fire."[30] The tales in this volume anticipate formal attempts to gather and compile such beautiful tales for use in school reading books and other edifying purposes. These tales stand in stark contrast to the actual conditions in the days after the earthquake, when gangs of young men armed with crude weapons went on murderous rampages in areas of the city ravaged by fires.

The longest section of the volume is titled "True Tales That Seem to Be Lies! Strange Stories from the Earthquake." Selecting two titles at random, they include "The Foreign Woman Who Encountered an Earthquake on Mt. Fuji" and "77 Babies Born in One Night on a Mountain in Ueno."[31] Such tales of the strange and sometimes supernatural were a staple product of early modern earthquakes.

Perhaps with these strange tales as a transition, the focus shifts to past earthquake legends and earthquake history. Especially interesting among this later material is a section written by Imamura, "Discussion of Earthquakes." It begins by pointing out that although the present earthquake is not the largest to have struck Japan in terms of physical power or breadth of area affected, it is the most deadly and destructive. Next Imamura points out, correctly, that he had long warned of such a catastrophe, especially the possibility of massive fire danger. He then pursues the topic further, stating that that great scholar of earthquakes Ōmori also worried about the connection between earthquakes and firefighting capabilities. Their calls for better firefighting capabilities went unheeded, and in this era of widespread petroleum use, the inadequacies of the current system are now tragically obvious.

Next Imamura discusses the two "earthquake zones" capable of producing destructive events in the capital. One runs from Edogawa to Tokyo Bay, and the other from the coast of the Bōsō Peninsula to the ocean bottom near the southern tip of the Izu Peninsula. This first earthquake zone has produced a series of events in the recent past, including the 1855 Ansei Edo earthquake. For the time being, its energy is spent. Rather generously, Imamura points out that when Ōmori stated that there would be no large earthquake in the near future, he was referring to events from this zone. Moreover, Imamura states that he had always been in complete agreement with Ōmori on that point.

Imamura then explains that the present earthquake came from the offshore zone, and, awful as it is, at least the residents of Tokyo need not worry about another large earthquake for decades if not hundreds of years to come. Imamura bases this point on the idea that characteristic earthquakes recur semiregularly, and he concludes that when the next big one does roll around, the capital will be fully recovered and ready to deal with it.[32] The experience of 3/11 suggested that Imamura's forecast for Tokyo was at least partially accurate in that advanced building design and antiseismic safety systems appeared to have worked well, albeit in the context of a glancing blow. The shortages of food and other necessities that plagued the capital area for days and even weeks after 3/11, however, suggest at least one possible vulnerability.

The next section of *The Great Taishō Earthquake and Fire Disaster* explains the use of seismometers to pinpoint the origin point of earthquakes in general and the current one in particular. Toward the end of this discussion, Imamura points out that seismic activity in the offshore earthquake zone creates faults and causes uplift or subsidence of the land on either side.[33] Notice the assumption here, perfectly reasonable for the time, that the violence of the earthquake creates a fault in the process of pushing some pieces of land upward and others downward.

Imamura wraps up his discussion with "Future Warnings." Starting with the lessons of the 1908 Messina earthquake in Italy, one lesson is that roads must be wider, parks more numerous, and new buildings limited to no more than three stories, preferably two. He claimed that three years after the 1906 San Francisco earthquake, the city had been rebuilt better than before. As for the specific lessons the denizens of Tokyo should learn, improvement in firefighting is indispensable. A more reliable water supply is essential, as is an increase in parks (which can function as firebreaks). Above all, the new Tokyo should consist of anti-seismic, fire-resistant structures. Imamura provides examples of problematic areas such as heavy roof tiles on homes or glass skylight features in roofs and proposes that research into antiseismic building techniques is of the utmost importance for protecting the country.[34] He provides valuable advice about antiseismic goals in the realms of engineering, construction, urban planning, and infrastructure. However, Imamura and the other commentators in *The Great Taishō Earthquake and Fire Disaster* ignore one major dimension of what made the 1923 earthquake so awful: the breakdown of social order.

HUMAN VIOLENCE IN THE GREAT KANTŌ

The fires and tornado-like firestorms were the result of timing. Severe ground motion occurred when open cooking fires had been lit all over the city and the weather was windy. Moreover, the shaking and mass confusion greatly degraded the city's limited firefighting capability.[35] These are the reasons large parts of Tokyo and Yokohama burned in the wake of the earthquake. During the early modern era, many governments quite correctly recognized the harm that rumors could do in the wake of a disaster and ineffectively tried to ban them and punish those who spread them. No major early modern earthquake in Japan generated large-scale human violence such as rioting, looting, or murder. In 1923, however, the rumors that spread through the devastation of the Tokyo area in September proved to be at least as dangerous as the flames for certain groups within society.

During the first few days of September 1923, anarchy or near anarchy prevailed in the shattered areas of the city. Food and water were scarce. Few people understood the broader picture of what had happened, and communication in the days just before commercial radio was largely limited to word of mouth. In this atmosphere, rumors swirled that Korean residents of Tokyo had taken advantage of the earthquake to set fires and poison wells. Moreover, "Reds" (socialists and Marxists) had similarly taken advantage of the situation. Amid the horrors of raging bubonic plague in Europe in the fourteenth century, Jewish communities became scapegoats. In September 1923 in Tokyo, it was Koreans, "Reds," and miscellaneous others on the margins of society.

Vigilante groups of young men—street gangs—quickly formed, and the police typically ignored them or actively worked with them.[36] Some police and military units seemed convinced that an armed rebellion of the Korean population (about 12 percent at that time in Tokyo) was imminent. A broader context for these fears was Korean independence uprisings in Korea (at the time a Japanese colony) and the recent birth of the Soviet Union. The earthquake served as a catalyst for bringing forth the worst aspects of human nature. Speech became a proxy for Koreanness in many instances:

> Since Koreans in Japan—unlike victims of race prejudice in most other countries—are likely to be more or less indistinguishable in appearance from their persecutors, confusion characterized these atrocities. Many of the victims were undoubtedly not Koreans at all but Japanese in such a state of shock or terror that their replies to interrogation were sufficiently tongue-tied to suit the purposes of the vigilantes—whose main objective was often simply to find victims. Others qualified on even more dubious ground. The most distressing case of all was perhaps that of two teen-age children skewered on homemade bamboo spears, who were later identified as members of the first graduating class of Japan's aural school for the deaf. Halting enunciation of their native tongue, combined with inability to comprehend the questions shouted at them by the vigilantes, understandably failed to satisfy the latter, who had found these victims searching for their parents in the Tokyo ruins.[37]

This lawless, brutal violence is well known, especially outside of Japan, and it is not my intention here to add anything new. I bring it up, however, because it points to what may be an underappreciated potential danger of major earthquakes in the modern era.

Commenting on these events, geophysicist and scholar of historical earthquakes Amos Nur points out:

> Much of the chaos and violence might have been avoided with better preparedness. Had it been publicly known that fires commonly occur after earthquakes, the Japanese might have been less quick to blame the Koreans for starting the fires. Had there been an emergency plan in place before the earthquake, there might have been less panic in the aftermath.[38]

Nur may have overstated the power of education and public ignorance of fire hazards, but his general point that knowledge of likely problems in the wake of an earthquake and a viable plan to deal with them makes sense. In 1923, the imposition of martial law, backed up by soldiers, was the proximate move that restored order.

Earthquakes or other disasters do not inevitably cause lawlessness or a breakdown of the social fabric, as the relatively violence-free early modern earthquakes suggest. In the early modern era, however, society was much more self-regulating, and the state was less instrumental in maintaining order. Moreover, early modern social and physical infrastructure was less susceptible to earthquake damage. I am not arguing that future earthquakes in Japan will inevitably cause social mayhem. In the aftermath of 3/11, a dominant motif echoed by the world media was that of orderly, stoic, well-behaved Japanese standing in lines. That 3/11 was largely free of social violence does not necessarily mean that 1923 was an isolated phenomenon. Its causes deserve close study. In Schencking's summary, in addition to infrastructure vulnerability owing to rapid growth of the capital area,

> few government officials . . . believed that the acts of criminal behavior and murderous violence exhibited by residents of eastern Japan following the disaster were within the realm of possibility in 1923. Put simply, Japanese officials were unprepared and ill equipped to deal with the anarchy, pandemonium, and murder that transpired following the catastrophe. No detailed or coordinated plans had been put in place to deal with these contingencies. In this regard, Japanese leaders could be blamed for suffering from a failure of imagination. Japan's leaders also ignored the all too obvious social, economic, political, and geographic vulnerabilities that emerged in Tokyo from the turn of the century onward.[39]

There is a long history in many societies of finding scapegoats in the wake of major earthquakes.[40] Moreover, the shortages of necessities in Tokyo during the weeks after 3/11 point to potential problems should a major earthquake directly strike Tokyo, Osaka, or another large urban area. Given contemporary dependence on communications, transportation, and other infrastructure that a serious earthquake might disable, any disaster planning should include steps to deal with a possible breakdown of social order on a large scale.

SEISMOLOGY AND ENGINEERING AFTER GREAT KANTŌ

Recall the comments by Sekiya in the wake of the Nōbi earthquake, urging that the disaster serve as means for advancing antiseismic building construction. Moreover, recall Imamura's concern with infrastructure better suited to seismic hazards, both before and after the great Kantō Earthquake. One relatively underappreciated effect of the 1923 disaster is its contribution to better building design. Here is a summary of the results of an exhaustive postearthquake survey of the damage to structures:

> Of reinforced concrete and steel structures, about 40 percent were heavily damaged, with only 1–2 percent of each type collapsing wholly or in part. Brick and masonry buildings fared worse, with 60–70 percent sustaining heavy damage. About 7 percent of brick buildings collapsed wholly or in part; 4–5 percent (one out of 20–25) of other masonry (dressed-stone) structures met the same fate. Only 10–20 percent of buildings escaped unscathed.[41]

Moreover, wooden structures generally do well in earthquakes, but not if they have heavy tiled roofs, as is common in Japan. Of the thirty-four thousand structures destroyed by the shaking (not fires), the vast majority, thirty-two thousand, were wooden structures. Of the 375,000 structures destroyed in the catastrophe, fire was responsible for 90 percent, and wood was the worst material for fire resistance.[42] As might be expected, advocates of different types of construction rushed to claim that their type was superior to others. In any case, however, the earthquake served to highlight the importance of construction type and quality for the purposes of seismic and fire resistance. The famous case of Frank Lloyd Wright's Imperial Hotel surviving the earthquake with only modest damage even presaged what would later become the foundation of antiseismic engineering, base isolation (also called seismic isolation).[43]

The Great Kantō Earthquake did not lead directly to any new theoretical breakthroughs in science, but it did shift the focus of mainstream seismology, a field dominated until then by Ōmori. The Nōbi earthquake precipitated a turn toward "science" in the investigation of earthquakes, and Great Kantō prompted a turn toward the geophysical approach of Imamura. According to Clancey:

> Ōmori's failure to correctly predict Tokyo's destruction was taken by many to be a failure of his research program. In "A Historical Sketch of the Development of Seismology in Japan," written by physicists Terada

Torahiko and Matazawa Takeo for an international scientific audience in 1926, Ōmori is diplomatically credited with having had "some kind of presentiment [of the earthquake], though he did his best to avoid exciting useless and pernicious commotion among the public by giving expression to too positive warnings of the coming catastrophe." But turning to Ōmori's research, the physicists conclude that "the results are not quite [as] decisive as they might have been well expected [*sic*]." The work of the IEIC [Imperial Earthquake Investigation Committee] had "taken a somewhat one-sided course of development" under his stewardship. Such verdicts would only strengthen as seismology became more mathematical and experimental, and Ōmori's statistical and cartographic accounts of seismicity . . . came to be seen as increasingly old-fashioned. "Ōmori seismology" continues even today as a shorthand for the dark ages of their science among some Japanese practitioners.[44]

The diplomatically stated reference to "a somewhat one-sided course of development" in the Terada and Matazawa paper refers to the situation toward the end of Ōmori's life.

The cooperation between engineering and science that the Imperial Earthquake Investigation Committee under Kikuchi had tried to foster gradually broke down. Ōmori was able to use this rift to chair the committee and eventually take complete control of it. He spent the committee's funds on whatever projects he liked, and he wrote the majority of the committee's reports in its last years. Ōmori gradually alienated his potential colleagues, and he never made an effort to cultivate graduate students or otherwise groom a successor.[45] Perhaps fitting as a sign of the turn away from Ōmori seismology, the Imperial Earthquake Investigation Committee dissolved in 1924. Imamura, in effect, became Ōmori's successor and assumed the mantle of Japan's foremost seismologist. Ōmori seismology, however, did not entirely die out after 1923.

The mathematical and experimental turn in Japanese seismology after 1923 was significant, but there is more to the story. Even an event as traumatic as the Great Kantō Earthquake would not cause all working scientists rapidly to change course. A variety of what we might call Ōmori seismology continued to flourish and remains active to this day. With some modification, I adopt Robert Geller's label and call this group the "catfish school" (*namazu-ha*).[46] The catfish school includes earthquake researchers who advocate exploration of realms such as abnormal animal behavior or atmospheric abnormalities as a beneficial use of time, effort, and funds. The stated goal for such research is often that it might someday contribute to earthquake prediction. Essentially, the catfish school consists of those who take seriously earthquake lore inherited from the Tokugawa period, even if they are unaware of the full extent of that lore's provenance.

It is helpful to briefly take stock of trends in Japanese seismology during the early twentieth century. Perhaps the best summary can be found in a 1904 report by Kikuchi, outlining the future work of the Imperial Earthquake Investigation Committee. Kikuchi listed five areas of work: (1) compiling old records of earthquake and tsunami damage as the material for statistical analysis of past seismic activity; (2) refining methods and tools for measuring earthquake motion; (3) illuminating the mechanics of what goes on under the earth's surface by observing changes in topography and geology after earthquakes and volcanic eruptions; (4) examining phenomena that seem to accompany or change in connection with earthquakes, such as magnetism of the earth, changes in latitude, gravity, subterranean temperature, seiches (standing waves) in bays and lakes, and changes in well-water levels and rock elasticity, determining whether they are real and determining whether they might assist in earthquake prediction; and (5) measuring and observing the movement of the earth's surface and built structures during an earthquake as a basis for better antiseismic construction of chimneys, bridge beams, bridge columns, and so forth. The various committee members set to work on these areas, publishing a vast quantity of papers and reports. The Imperial Earthquake Investigation Committee set the agenda for seismology in Japan during the Meiji and Taishō periods.[47]

Of these five areas of academic investigation, the first and fourth are especially relevant to the emergence of the catfish school. The project to compile historical records led eventually in the early Shōwa era to Musha Kinkichi's (1891–1962) three-volume *Revised Great Japan Historical Earthquake Documents* (*Zōtei Dai-Nihon jishin shiryō*), an invaluable resource that in its 1970s iteration has informed parts of this book. Ōmori and Imamura were both thoroughly familiar with this collection, and Imamura sometimes impressed others with his ability to recall obscure historical earthquake details from memory. A potential problem with massive compilations of historical documents, however, is that they require interpretation. The fourth item is concerned with possible precursory phenomena. Notice that the agenda sets the first goal as determining whether these phenomena really exist as earthquake precursors. If so, then there is a possibility that they could assist in earthquake prediction. It was a reasonable research agenda item in 1904. The postwar tendency to pursue earthquake prediction by compiling more data is in part a legacy of the prewar catfish school. The continued interest in strange animal behavior, well-water levels, earthquake weather, earthquake clouds, earthquake lights, and so forth is another aspect of this legacy.

I revisit some of these topics in the context of earthquake prediction in postwar Japan in chapter 5. Next I turn to the Tōhoku region and its Sanriku coast, the place where the 3/11 disaster unfolded. As we have seen, tsunamigenic earthquakes are common in this region. The large earthquake/tsunami combinations that occurred there in 1896 and 1933 have not attracted the historical spotlight to the degree that Nōbi and Great Kantō have, but these Sanriku earthquakes are even more important for contextualizing 3/11. Moreover, the 1896 event in particular contributed to the advancement of science because it prompted a massive academic debate over the cause of tsunamis. Kotō Bunjirō, of Nōbi fame, made an appearance in that debate via a student. In retrospect, however, the standout scholar was a young seismologist named Imamura Akitsune, at the time laboring in relative obscurity.

NOTES

1. On the politics of the Nōbi earthquake, see Gregory Clancey, *Earthquake Nation: The Cultural Politics of Japanese Seismicity, 1868–1930* (Berkeley: University of California Press, 2006).

2. Kitahara Itoko, *Saigai jaanarizumu, mukashi hen* (Sakura, Japan: Rekishi minzoku hakubutsukan shinkōkai, 2001), 105–8.

3. For a detailed breakdown of the donations, see H. Tennant, *The Great Earthquake in Japan, October 28, 1891: Being a Full Description of the Disasters Resulting from the Recent Terrible Catastrophe* (1892; Kessinger, 2007), 43–58.

4. Kitahara, *Saigai jaanarizumu*, 108–10.

5. Tennant, *Great Earthquake in Japan*, 30. See also Hashimoto Manpei, *Jishingaku no kotohajime: Kaituakusha Sekiya Seikei no shōgai* (Asahi shinbunsha, 1983), 190.

6. For details, see Gregory Smits, *Seismic Japan: The Long History and Continuing Legacy of the Ansei Edo Earthquake* (Honolulu: University of Hawaii Press, 2013), 143–61.

7. Quoted in Hagiwara Takahiro, *Jishingaku hyakunen* (Tōkyō daigaku shuppankai, 1982), 43.

8. Bundjiro Kotô [Kotō Bunjirō], "On the Cause of the Great Earthquake in Central Japan, 1891," *Tōkyō teikoku daigaku kiyō, rika* 5, no. 10 (1893): 322–23.

9. Kotô, "On the Cause," 325–26.

10. Kotô, "On the Cause," 326–28.

11. Kotô, "On the Cause," 329.

12. Kotô, "On the Cause," 339.

13. Kotô, "On the Cause," 352–53. See also Amos Nur with Dawn Burgess, *Apocalypse: Earthquakes, Archaeology, and the Wrath of God* (Princeton, NJ: Princeton University Press, 2008), 39–40.

14. Noel Fairchild Busch, *Two Minutes to Noon: The Story of the Great Tokyo Earthquake and Fire* (New York: Simon and Schuster, 1962), 43–44.

15. Koto, "On the Cause," 297.

16. John Milne, *Seismology* (London: Kegan Paul, Trench, Trübner and Co., 1898), 38.

17. Basic statistics, analysis, and summaries of the damage are available from a variety of sources. See, for example, Usami Tatsuo, *Nihon higai jishin sōran [416]–2001, Saishinpan (Materials for a Comprehensive List of Destructive Earthquakes in Japan, [416]–2001 [Latest Edition])* (Tōkyō daigaku shuppankai, 2003), 272–78; Okada Yoshimitsu, *Saishin Nihon no jishin chizu* (Tōkyō shoseki, 2006), 88–91; and Chūō bōsai kaigi, *1923 Kantō daishinsai hōkokusho, dai ippen* (Nihon shisutemu kaihatsu kenkyūsho, 2006).

18. Susan Elizabeth Hough and Roger G. Bilham, *After the Earth Quakes: Elastic Rebound in an Urban Planet* (New York: Oxford University Press, 2006), 182–83.

19. Janet Borland, "Capitalising on Catastrophe: Reinvigorating the Japanese State with Moral Values through Education following the 1923 Great Kantô Earthquake," *Modern Asian Studies* 40, no. 4 (October 2006): 875–907; and Janet Borland, "Stories of Ideal Japanese Subjects from the Great Kanto Earthquake of 1923," *Japanese Studies* 25, no. 1 (May 2005): 21–34.

20. On the massacre of Koreans, see Michael A. Weiner, *The Origins of the Korean Community in Japan, 1910–1923* (Manchester, UK: Manchester University Press, 1989), 164–200; Borland, "Capitalising on Catastrophe," 882; and Nur, *Apocalypse*, 267–69.

21. For a sampling of these kinds of incidents, see Joshua Hammer, *Yokohama Burning: The Deadly 1923 Earthquake and Fire That Helped Forge the Path to World War II* (New York: Free Press, 2006). This book relies only on English sources, but it provides a good sense of how many non-Japanese perceived the event.

22. For a fine analysis of the political discourse following the earthquake, see J. Charles Schencking, *The Great Kantō Earthquake and the Chimera of National Reconstruction in Japan* (New York: Columbia University Press, 2013), 116–52. See also see Gennifer Weisenfeld, *Imaging Disaster: Tokyo and the Visual Culture of Japan's Great Earthquake of 1923* (Berkeley: University of California Press, 2012), 178–89.

23. Schencking, *Great Kantō Earthquake*, 151.

24. Schencking, *Great Kantō Earthquake*, 121.

25. Miyake Yūjirō [Setsurei], "Jo," in *Taishō daishinsai, daikasai*, comp. Dai-Nippon yūbenkai Kōdansha (Dai-Nippon yūbenkai Kōdansha, 1923), unpaginated front matter.

26. Quoted in Hagiwara, *Jishingaku hyakunen*, 57.

27. For an analysis of the Ōmori-Imamura rivalry, see Hagiwara, *Jishingaku hyakunen*, 51–61. See also Andrew Robinson, *Earthquake: Nature and Culture* (London: Reaktion, 2012), 78–83.

28. Mikami Sanjin, "Jo," and Imamura Akitsune, "Jo," in, *Taishō daishinsai, daikasai*, comp. Dai-Nippon yūbenkai Kōdansha, unpaginated front matter.

29. Dai-Nippon yūbenkai Kōdansha, *Taishō daishinsai, daikasai*, 109. See also Robinson, *Earthquake*, 87–88, for a vivid description.

30. Dai-Nippon yūbenkai Kōdansha, *Taishō daishinsai, daikasai*, 140–67.

31. Dai-Nippon yūbenkai Kōdansha, *Taishō daishinsai, daikasai*, 170–98.

32. Dai-Nippon yūbenkai Kōdansha, *Taishō daishinsai, daikasai*, 246–50.

33. Dai-Nippon yūbenkai Kōdansha, *Taishō daishinsai, daikasai*, 251–52.

34. Dai-Nippon yūbenkai Kōdansha, *Taishō daishinsai, daikasai*, 253–54.

35. On firefighting in Edo and Tokyo and the causes and dynamics of the fires in 1923, see Busch, *Two Minutes to Noon*, 73–104.

36. For an analysis of visual images of these gangs, see Weisenfeld, *Imaging Disaster*, 167–78.

37. Busch, *Two Minutes to Noon*, 109–10. For the whole discussion of this aspect of the disaster, see 105–13.

38. Nur, *Apocalypse*, 269.

39. Schencking, *Great Kantō Earthquake*, 56.

40. See Nur, *Apocalypse*, 83–84, including a chilling example from the 1960 Chile earthquake.

41. Hough and Bilham, *After the Earth Quakes*, 175. See also Clancey, *Earthquake Nation*, 222–30.

42. Hough and Bilham, *After the Earth Quakes*, 176.

43. Hough and Bilham, *After the Earth Quakes*, 176–79. Clancey discusses debates over building materials extensively. See *Earthquake Nation*, esp. 222–33.

44. Clancey, *Earthquake Nation*, 226.

45. Hagiwara, *Jishingaku hyakunen*, 46–47.

46. Robert Geller (Robaato Geraa), *Nihonjin wa shiranai "jishin yochi" no shōtai* (Futa-basha, 2011), 113.

47. Hagiwara, *Jishingaku hyakunen*, 43–44.

FOUR

Prewar Tsunamigenic Earthquakes in the Northeast

Despite its awesome force, vast devastation, and the cries of "unimaginable" that it elicited from politicians, bureaucrats, and TEPCO officials, 3/11 was not unprecedented except, of course, for the presence of nuclear power plants. As we saw in chapter 2, Japan's Sanriku coast has been subject to medium and severe earthquake/tsunami combinations since humans have been residing there. The event of 1611 may well have been roughly on a par with 3/11 in terms of several parameters. Moreover, the event of 1896 retains the morbid title of Japan's deadliest tsunami disaster. 3/11 has prompted an interest in the history of tsunamigenic earthquakes off the Sanriku coast. Nevertheless, details of the earthquake/tsunami combinations of 1896 and 1933 remain relatively unknown compared with the Nōbi and Great Kantō earthquakes. This chapter constitutes a close study of these seismic events.

As with previous chapters, the approach here is to consider these disasters both as agents of social history and as agents of change in the history of science and technology. Arguably, the 1896 event had the greater impact on the advancement of science because it stimulated intense debate over the cause of tsunamis. Within this debate, we now know that the theory advanced by Imamura Akitsune was correct, and it foreshadowed the work on "slow" or "tsunami" earthquakes by Hiroo Kanamori and others. The 1933 event had a particularly large impact on society as a whole because as an apparent repeat of the 1896 tsunami, it became impossible to regard large tsunamis as rare events that would not recur for hundreds of years. Moreover, a close study of both events reveals a range of possibilities for how seismic disasters play out in society. Particularly in light of the dilemmas posed by 3/11, it is useful to examine social changes in the wake of the 1896 disaster and their impact in 1933.

MEIJI SANRIKU EARTHQUAKE AND TSUNAMI, 1896

One report on the 1896 Meiji Sanriku earthquake and tsunami by the Imperial Earthquake Investigation Committee (IEIC, Shinsai yobō chōsakai) for 1896 begins:

> The tsunami of the evening of the fifteenth of this month was a massive seismic sea wave unprecedented since the Ansei era [1856]. The eastern coast of Miyagi Prefecture and the coastal areas of adjacent prefectures have suffered considerable destruction. The status of the bays and inlets of Miyagi Prefecture is cruelly tragic in the extreme. Several thousand are dead and injured and the homes and vessels washed away or destroyed are too numerous to count. There is no town or village along the coast that has not suffered severe damage. In the worst cases, entire villages have been washed away or destroyed.
>
> Forty years previously, on Ansei three, seventh month, twenty-third day (in the lunar calendar), around noon, the earthquake was very strong, and elderly people reported that the tsunami waves, while numerous, came to shore at a crawling pace. The basic circumstances of the present tsunami are that the weather the previous day was gloomy, with rain and fog. Barometric pressure and humidity were higher than in a typical year. At 7:32:30 p.m., there was weak shaking of the earth for a duration of five minutes, the extremely slack waves moving in an east-northeast to west-southwest direction. Next, at the same hour, 53 minutes, 30 seconds, there was weak shaking, as well as at 8:02:35, 8:23:15, 8:33:10, and 8:59:00. Later, there was weak shaking four times between the hours of 9 and 10 p.m., one time around 11 p.m., and twice before midnight. Shaking occurred a total of thirteen times, and the start of the tsunami (the time when the water began to recede) was at night and difficult to determine precisely.[1]

Despite the availability of some precise data, the mechanism of this deadly tsunami was unclear to investigators.

The June 15, 1896, Meiji Sanriku earthquake occurred during the evening hours of the fifth day of the fifth month in the old lunar calendar. Villages in the area had been celebrating the Boys' Festival, and military organizations were celebrating Japan's recent victory in the First Sino-

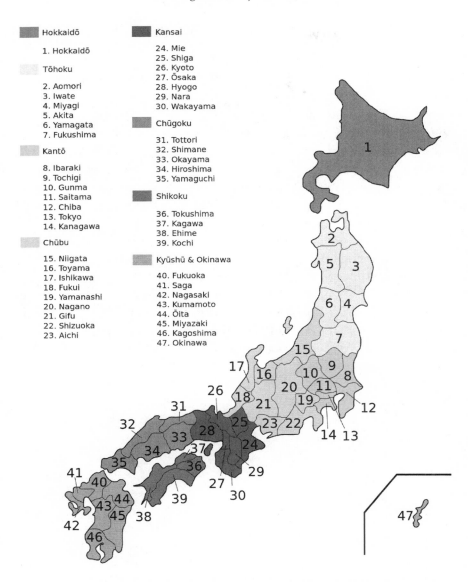

Figure 4.1. Regions and Prefectures of Japan. *Source*: **Wikimedia Commons, TheOtherJesse.**

Japanese War. As the report emphasizes, the ground motion was mild. There was no damage from the earthquake itself, but there was a maximum wave run-up height of 38.2 meters at the village of Ryōri in Iwate Prefecture. Modern estimates posit approximately ten meters of slip at the plate boundary. For comparison, the slip in 3/11 was approximately forty-five meters. Nevertheless, the maximum wave height in 2011 was 38.9 meters, a negligible difference.[2] Had settlement patterns in 2011 reflected a serious consideration of the 1896 tsunami, 3/11 would have been much less destructive.

The tsunami waves in 1896 arrived while celebrations were still under way, and the first indication of them for many was a sound like thunder or the roar of cannon. "Suddenly there was a roar that sounded like many clasps of thunder descending all at once" or "A sound like the roar of cannon continued for about three times" were typical recollections of survivors.[3] It is unlikely that the momentary warning such sounds may have provided would have made much difference. Given the circumstances of that day and the broader context of there being no living experience of a comparably large, deadly tsunami, it is unlikely that many, if any, coastal residents correctly identified the sound.

Estimates of the death toll vary because conditions made a precise count impossible. According to the report of the IEIC, 26,360 perished, but for reasons that need not concern us, a figure of around 22,000 is probably more accurate.[4] Even using this lower figure, the 1896 event was the deadliest tsunami in Japan's history in absolute terms. The 1923 Great Kantō Earthquake, of course, killed many more people, but there is a rough way to calculate population-adjusted death rates. The procedure is to calculate the death rate as a ratio of houses damaged or destroyed, and the result is 0.2 for 1923 and 2.6 for 1896. In other words, by this method, 1896 was thirteen times deadlier per capita. Another instructive statistic is to calculate the percentage of those injured to those killed, with a larger number indicating a relatively less deadly event. In that case, the Meiji and Shōwa (1933) Sanriku tsunami events were 16.2 percent and 30.3 percent, respectively (Iwate Prefecture data), and the 1923 earthquake and the 1995 Kōbe earthquake were 70.5 percent and 68.1 percent, respectively. In other words, major tsunamis tend to be deadlier than earthquakes.[5]

SLOW EARTHQUAKES, DANGEROUS TSUNAMIS

Today we know that the Meiji Sanriku earthquake and tsunami event was especially deadly because it was a tsunami earthquake, also known as a slow earthquake. To understand this phenomenon, we need briefly to consider tsunami magnitude and some aspects of tsunami mechanics. Modern earthquake magnitude is a measure of quantity of energy released when the fault slips. As we have seen, it is actually a measurement called seismic moment, converted via a formula to match the older Richter scale, which becomes increasingly inaccurate from about 8.0 on up. It is important to note that magnitude is not the same thing as intensity (shaking, ground motion) because there are many mediating factors at any point on the earth's surface, such as distance from the epicenter, distance from the hypocenter (or focus), and the characteristics of various materials that constitute local geology. An M7-class earthquake located directly under the surface often does more damage than an M8-class megathrust earthquake originating deep within an offshore subduction zone. The basic reason is that some of the energy from the megathrust earthquake attenuates before reaching the surface in a populated area. Seismic intensity, or ground motion, is a measure of the actual shaking a person or structure might experience. Instruments can measure acceleration, and there is a variety of scales for seismic intensity based on the effect of the shaking on humans and structures.

What about seismic sea waves? Usually, the extent (wave height and area affected) of a tsunami scales up or down in proportion to the magnitude of the earthquake causing it. Starting with Imamura, scientists in Japan have created a variety of ways to measure either the intensity or the magnitude of tsunamis. Tsunami magnitude formulas dating from the late 1960s transpose the major metrics of a tsunami into a numerical scale that matches earthquake magnitude. Notice the basic difference. Earthquake magnitude is a measure of sheer quantity of energy released, but tsunami magnitude is a measure of results of that energy in the form of waves of water. Unlike earthquake magnitude calculations, therefore, tsunami magnitude formulas often require adjustments for local conditions. In most formulas, the key variables are wave amplitude (height) and distance from the epicenter.[6]

As a technical term, a "tsunami earthquake" (*tsunami jishin*) is an event in which there is a major discrepancy between earthquake magnitude and tsunami magnitude. A looser, pragmatic definition would be an earthquake whose seismic land waves result in only mild shaking but which generates a large, deadly tsunami. Because the main cause of such events is abnormally slow movement when the fault ruptures, such events are often called "slow earthquakes" (*surō jishin* or *nuru-nuru* [creeping] *jishin*). Other terms in Japanese include *yukkuri jishin* (slow earthquake), *teishūha jishin* (low-frequency-wave earthquake), *nendansei jishin* (viscoelastic earthquake), and *kuriipu jishin* (creeping earthquake). Caltech seismologist Hiroo Kanamori coined the term "tsunami earthquake" and proposed its mechanism in 1972.[7] As we will see, however, the general idea had its roots in the work of Imamura, who proposed in 1897 that a slow rupture of the earth caused the Meiji Sanriku tsunami.

Low-frequency waves have a longer wavelength. The result is a more gentle undulation of the ground instead of a jolting or chopping sensation. It is for this reason that tsunami earthquakes are so dangerous. Even people well accustomed to the link between the shaking earth and the arrival of tsunami waves will be unprepared for the devastating waves arriving after mild ground motion. According to Watanabe Hideo, the 1896 earthquake was M6.8. However, the magnitude of the tsunami was 8.3—a striking difference. At a distance of roughly four hundred kilometers from the epicenter, the shaking in 1896 was approximately 2 (barely perceptible) on the current JMA seismic intensity scale. In the 1933 Shōwa Sanriku earthquake, which generated a smaller, though still large and destructive, tsunami, the seismic intensity level was 5 (strong shaking).[8]

What causes the slow rupture speed? Current thinking holds that there are two basic types of tsunami earthquakes, only one of which is directly relevant for our purposes. The 1896 event was type one, caused by an accretion of sediments in the trench formed at the plate boundary. The 1611 Keichō Sanriku tsunami was probably also a type one tsunami earthquake, and as explained in chapter 2, it may have been even deadlier than the 1896 event on a per capita basis. On the basis of these two earthquakes, Watanabe has suggested that this region may be subject to tsunami earthquakes with an average recurrence interval of less than three hundred years.[9] Regardless of whether it is possible to state a recurrence interval with accuracy, there can be no doubt that the possibility of a tsunami earthquake in this region is a genuine danger.

SHORT-TERM IMPACT ON SOCIETY

> A dragon suddenly rears up from the sea floor
> The headlong flood of a massive tide
> Ten thousand cries of suffering, no time to flee
> Rows of villages swept away in an instant, silent

The air full of bitterness, cruel rains fall from heaven
Cries blanket the earth, an apprehensive wind blows
What is the crime of these countless souls?
The dead go unattended, the living starve
Corpses strewn along the roads
No smoke from the stoves, no jackets to wear
The utmost bitterness—a child has lost its mother
The solitary cries of those rendered unknown
Among the world's catastrophes, can anything compare?
I want to shed tears of blood
Our emperor, most benevolent, has bestowed vast treasure
The people weep tears of gratitude.[10]

A local newspaper serving Miyagi Prefecture, the *Ōu nichinichi shinbun*, published this and other retrospective compositions in classical Chinese verse. Two to three weeks after the killer wave struck, local newspapers began to devote space to literary works inspired by the disaster. Perhaps a combination of the solemnity of the event and the almost surreal level of destruction made it ideally suited to classical Chinese verse, a genre still familiar to many educated Japanese at the end of the nineteenth century. The lines quoted here summarize the vast extent of the destruction and its emotional toll. Reminiscent of early modern seismic disasters, the imperial institution serves as a source of stability and at least partial succor in the final two lines. The major difference is that by the 1890s, the emperor was no longer an abstraction but a specific person, a source providing concrete financial relief as well as general psychological encouragement. The emperor served as an emotional counterbalance to the seemingly capricious, cruel forces of nature.

The Meiji Sanriku tsunami fit the classic definition of a natural disaster, in which a natural hazard meets a vulnerable society with catastrophic effects. The scope of the disaster in 1896 was overwhelming at first. Without warning, mud and sand buried about seventy coastal communities, bodies mixing with debris from smashed houses. The extensive devastation often extended to police stations, medical facilities, and local government offices. Several days passed, therefore, before local newspapers could begin printing reliable estimates of the destruction and basic relief efforts could begin. The total monetary cost of the 1896 disaster was between 7,100,000 and 8,700,000 yen, approximately 10 percent of the national budget for that year. For comparison, the total cost of the 1995 Kōbe earthquake was just over 10 percent of the national budget, so the financial impact of both events was comparable.[11] Only the military was in a position to rush large quantities of material aid to the stricken region, but even that aid was slow to arrive. For example, an Iwate Prefecture newspaper report six days after the tsunami explained that owing to a request by the governor, the 867-ton naval vessel *Tatsuta* had set sail from Yokosuka two days earlier.[12]

Demographic patterns to the destruction reflected underlying social conditions. A newspaper article appearing four days after the Shōwa Sanriku earthquake pointed out that the very old, the very young, and women died in disproportionate numbers in the tsunamis of 1896 and 1933.[13] In Iwate Prefecture, 125 women died for every 100 men in 1896. One reason was that men often set out in the evening for night fishing. In one village, for example, about forty fishermen in five or six boats went out the evening of the tsunami. At sea, they experienced nothing unusual and were shocked to see their demolished village as they approached shore. Many such returning fishermen heard voices calling out for help in the dark as they returned. Local lore regarded voices in the water as those of ghosts. Moreover, answering the calls of such ghosts would result in their pulling the responder into the water. Such beliefs resulted in delays in the fishing boats mounting rescue operations.[14]

Although being out at sea saved a few men, that factor alone could not account for the relatively higher number of female deaths. Other key factors would have been sheer physical strength and the ability to flee quickly. Women were more likely to be encumbered by children or elderly relatives in 1896 and 1933. By contrast, fifty years later in the 1983 M7.7 Japan Sea Central earthquake and tsunami (off the coast of Aomori Prefecture), a disproportionate number of deaths were male. That tsunami struck in the middle of the day, when most men were away from home at work. Most homes in the affected areas were located on relatively high ground and unharmed.[15] In 3/11, women died in much greater numbers than men, but the population of the region was elderly, and elderly women were more numerous than elderly men. The very old and the very young also perished in higher numbers relative to the overall population in the disasters of 1896, 1933, and 2011.[16]

In the hardest-hit villages, the tsunami killed the majority of residents who were present. Tarō Village, for example, lost 83 percent of its residents. Only thirty-six of its population of two thousand survived. The waves washed away all public infrastructure plus 285 of 336 houses, and because the village faced the Pacific Ocean directly, the water swept most bodies out to sea. In the days following the tsunami, many of these bodies washed up onshore.[17] Owing to warm summer conditions, a lack of people, and a lack of infrastructure, identification and disposal of the many bodies were major problems. Sometimes debris became a funeral pyre for unclaimed bodies. Hirota Village used fishing nets to recover bodies at sea. As many as fifty came up in one sweep, so many that only half could be brought to shore at a time. Marine life soon started coating bodies in the ocean, and starving dogs set on corpses on land, sometimes biting people who tried to restrain them. Many bodies could not be identified because they were too badly mangled. Bodies from one village often floated to other areas, further complicating identification. In Iwate Prefecture, 10,200 of the 18,158 bodies recovered went into mass graves.[18] This gruesome aftermath would have made a strong psychological impression on survivors and people entering the area.

Newspapers became a forum for the notification and possible identification of corpses. The following ad in a local Miyagi Prefecture newspaper is a typical example. It appeared on July 2, roughly two weeks after the tsunami:

> Corpse of a drowned, unidentified woman, approximately thirty. Entire body decayed. Long hair and breasts identify her as female. There is flesh from the upper abdomen to the head. Lower body is completely decayed, with only bone fragments remaining. The flesh of the four limbs has decayed, with only some bone remaining. Drifted in and found June 27, off the southern shore of Nagato Beach, Sakegawa Village, Oshika District. Will be interred in that village's common graveyard upon completion of the coroner's inspection. Relatives or other concerned persons should proceed with haste to the local administrative office. Meiji 29, June 29.[19]

Such gruesome notices appeared in local newspapers until at least the end of July, some six weeks after the tsunami.

Throughout this disaster, prefectural governors played major roles in leading and coordinating recovery and relief. For example, governor of Iwate Prefecture Hattori Kazumi issued general instructions published on June 19 and 20 in the local newspaper, the *Iwate kōhō*:

> The present tsunami that struck sixty *ri* off the Tōhoku coast is an unprecedented catastrophe, and it is essential to be alert to maintain hygiene in the affected areas to the best of our ability. Especially after a

> disaster, fearsome outbreaks of epidemic and contagious disease oc-
> cur. . . . It is especially necessary for us to attend to steps such as setting
> up evacuation centers, treating the wounded and sick, properly dispos-
> ing of corpses, potable water, and cleaning up the debris widely strewn
> about the disaster area.[20]

This almost obsessive concern with "hygiene" (*eisei*) appears frequently in documents related to this earthquake, and it was typical of the times.[21] Governor Hattori's general directive became a detailed set of instructions for cleansing, burning, disinfecting, and taking other measures thought to prevent the spread of disease. For example, "Periodically open the windows and light a fire to maintain dryness in houses. In particular, this should be done before sleeping."[22]

The dissemination of these instructions was an example of the key role that newspaper companies played in the immediate aftermath of the disaster, a phenomenon that emerged after the Nōbi earthquake some five years earlier. As the primary means of mass communication, news-papers helped coordinate relief efforts, raised aid, and circulated official directives. Newspaper reporters were among the first responders. For example, on June 20, the *Ōu nichinichi shinbun* announced that it had dispatched Imazumi Torajirō from its staff to visit the town of Shizu-gawa—located in a hard-hit area north of Sendai in Motoyoshi District at the end of Shizugawa Bay—and issue detailed reports on the situation there. The first article from Imazumi appeared on June 21, with others following in the days after.[23] Referring to the same area, an article under the headline "Method for Aiding Victims" explained that the tsunami had rendered communication and travel within Motyoshi District diffi-cult. Therefore, locally prominent people (*jinshi*) were to make the rounds of their neighborhoods and communicate the details of their situations to the paper, which would publish them.[24] Reports from special correspon-dents dispatched to other districts in the disaster area also began to ap-pear within a week of the disaster.

On the day of the tsunami, the *Ōu nichinichi shinbun* published a list of donors from its own staff, most of whom contributed one yen. Two days later, the paper published a formal call for donations and explained that the funds collected would go to district (*gun*) government offices for distribution to disaster victims.[25] The newspaper repeated its call for donations and extended the deadline several times. Through July 31, it listed the names of thousands of donors, most giving modest cash contributions, some contributing food, clothing, or other supplies. A July 28 announcement of a deadline extension noted that the campaign had thus far raised "the giant sum of eight hundred yen."[26] To put this figure in perspective, the typical yearly income for a newspaper reporter at about this time ranged from 145 to 300 yen. All major newspapers serving the Sanriku coast launched relief campaigns that followed a similar pattern: high rates of response, but a modest total collected, especially compared with the immense scale of the destruction. This situation reflected the general poverty of this part of Japan.

The destruction hindered transportation, especially in the immediate aftermath of the tsunami. Ships were the only practical means of moving large quantities of supplies or people to the disaster area, and until food shipments began to arrive, starvation was a serious threat to survivors. A June 21 newspaper article announcing a shipment of 400 *koku* of rice from Hakodate bound for Miyako in Iwate Prefecture also estimated that more than sixty thousand survivors were currently enduring starvation.[27] Even after the immediate threat of starvation lessened, there was a severe shortage of basic foods other than rice, such as salt, miso, soy sauce, and pickles. Moreover, a lack of basic nutrients such as protein became an acute problem in hospitals and a potential longer-term threat to general health. Some two weeks after the disaster, hospitals appealed for donations of condensed milk. An acute shortage of cooking pots exacerbated problems with food and nutrition.[28] Scarcities of food, clothing, and shelter, destruction of infrastructure, and shortages of skilled personnel hindered short-term relief and recovery.

Other steps in dealing with the immediate aftermath of the tsunami included dispatching medical personnel and gangs of laborers to the area, steps to control theft and looting, and attempts to control hoarding and price gouging. In one case, the police investigated a rice dealer in Miyako claiming his shelves were empty and found that he had enough rice in stock for twenty days. They lectured him on the evils of price gouging during this unprecedented emergency and forced him to sell his stock at a moderate price. In general, the price of necessities and the wages charged by laborers shot up in the aftermath of the tsunami.[29] There was a desperate need for medical personnel, and newspaper reports appealed for doctors and nurses from outside the stricken region to come and treat their wounded compatriots (*dōhō*, an emotive term common in the disaster discourse). "Above all," stated an article under the headline "Urging Physicians to Reflect," nearly ten days after the tsunami, "physicians or those with medical skills are desperately needed to take charge of the treatment of the many wounded." The piece ends with an emotional appeal: "Ah, the tens of thousands who without warning are agonizing in the wild with broken limbs and smashed skulls. Doctors, search your souls, for surely you are not without blood and tears!"[30] Agencies of the central government and the military eventually dispatched a variety of specialists to the region, but urgent shortages plagued the region for weeks.

Within days of the tsunami, local newspapers printed frequent reports of the dispatch of various officials to survey damage and assess relief and recovery needs. The article cited above, on the need for physicians, stated that Her Majesty the Empress was so moved by the people's suffering that she dispatched chamberlains to the region. Perhaps most important, home minister Itagaki Taisuke left Tokyo for a tour of the region on June 22. Each of the affected prefectures established relief centers. Miyagi Prefecture, for example, created the Temporary Tsunami Bureau (Kaishō rinjibu). It operated for sixty-seven days, from June 20 to August 25. People from Iwate, Miyagi, and Aomori Prefectures living in Tokyo established an agency to coordinate the solicitation, collection, and shipping of aid to the afflicted regions.[31] One key point to bear in mind is that in the immediate aftermath of the tsunami, local communities received almost no assistance beyond the prefectural level. Locally prominent citizens, surviving police officers, and reporters from local newspapers typically spearheaded the initial damage assessments and relief efforts in towns and villages along the Sanriku coast. In many respects, Meiji Sanriku more closely resembled early modern earthquakes in terms of the patterns of relief response. Technological and other limitations meant that this relatively remote area initially had to rely on its own human and material resources.

BEAUTIFUL AND UGLY DISASTER STORIES

One product of the 1896 disaster was stories of individual experiences. Newspapers published many of these tales, often as a series of bulleted short paragraphs. Typically, in sparse language they stressed the tragic qualities of the disaster. An example from Iwate Prefecture that appeared ten days after the tsunami reads:

In Ōtana District, several households were swept away, with only one man escaping. His wife's face was torn away owing to her being struck by a savage wave, and nobody knew who she was. The man was able to identify the body as that of his wife by a few strands of hair that remained on her head. Weeping, he removed his wife's corpse and buried her.[32]

Other reports, however, stressed kindness, heroism, generosity, or other virtuous behavior. A typical example, after mentioning cases of disaster victims giving away their clothes or other items to those in even greater need, exclaims, "The depth and richness of displays of mutual aid and righteous assistance by our compatriots (*dōhō*) is nothing short of awesome." Similarly, "In hearing the tales of the vast virtue and deep benevolence of the citizens of our prefecture [Miyagi], it can indeed be said that such is the face of our noble Tōhoku residents (*Tōhoku jinshi*)."[33] Here the "compatriots" are not "Japanese" but a subset of them, northeasterners. In other contexts, the term *dōhō* (brethren, compatriots) might well mean Japanese. That it sometimes did not in 1896 points in part to the cultural distinctiveness and relative isolation of the Sanriku coast vis-à-vis the center of national affairs. More important were the circumstances of the relief and recovery operation. The vast majority of those who provided aid were local inhabitants, many of whom were fellow victims of the disaster.

From at least as early as the 1662 Kanbun earthquake (near Kyoto), one effect of earthquakes was to transform affected areas into de facto stages for the enactment of personal dramas. The vast majority of the dramatic tales from Tokugawa-period earthquakes are unverifiable, and many are difficult to believe.[34] The ostensible point of most of these Tokugawa-period tales was moral edification, although the real point was entertainment. Entrepreneurs gathered or created earthquake tales and sold them in the form of broadside prints or cheap books. This tradition continued into the modern era almost unchanged. However, owing to a more robust censorship apparatus and state interest in the dissemination of certain types of messages, the discourse connected with modern earthquakes stressed moral edification more than ever before. As we saw in the previous chapter, a genre of "beautiful tales" (*bidan*) developed in the modern era that contributed to self-images of Japanese as a national group. These beautiful tales were especially noticeable in the wake of twentieth-century disasters, but they have older roots.

The 1896 tsunami produced a modest quantity of apocryphal stories at least roughly in the "beautiful tales" genre. For example, there was "Reservist Neguchi Manjirō," filled with patriotic zeal and ever wary of the possibility of a foreign invasion of Japan. Because the roar of the tsunami waves sounded like the roar of cannon from a ship offshore, he charged out to the ocean, rifle and sword in hand. Later, his body was found with his hand still clutching his sword. That was the essence of the popular story. In fact, however, there was no such soldier, and even his surname is suspicious, sounding much like that of Kiguchi Kohei, the celebrated Sino-Japanese War bugler of school textbooks, who supposedly used his last breath to blow his bugle for the emperor. Neguchi, too, died clutching his military tools.[35] A version of the Neguchi tale even appeared in a *National Geographic* article on the tsunami:

> One loyal schoolmaster carried the emperor's portrait to a place of safety before seeking out his own family. A half-demented soldier, retired since the late war and continually brooding on a possible attack by the enemy, became convinced that the first cannonading sound was from a hostile fleet, and, seizing his sword, ran down to meet the foe.[36]

A beautiful tale with a higher level of veracity involved prisoners. Guards at a local prison freed all 195 prisoners as the water rushed in, but only about 31 ultimately survived. In one case, likely a true story, a fleeing prisoner stopped to rescue a young woman about to drown and later received formal recognition for his "sense of righteousness."[37] In short, the genre of beautiful tales so prominent after the Great Kantō Earthquake was apparent as early as 1896, and its distant roots go even farther back in time.

SOCIAL CHALLENGES OF MEIJI SANRIKU

The Meiji Sanriku tsunami presented several interrelated social challenges, especially because of the relative isolation of the region. Basic infrastructure had to be rebuilt, along with homes and fishing boats, as a foundation for reviving the local economy. Ideally, the reconstruction process would also make the area more resilient to future earthquakes and tsunamis. When considering this point, however, it is important to keep the perspective of the times in mind. Today we can look back at the tsunamis of 1933 and 2011 and see the value in preparing for future events of the magnitude of the Meiji Sanriku disaster. From the standpoint of the summer of 1896, however, the previous giant tsunami had taken place way back in 1611. We know from reactions to the 1933 event that in 1896 many local residents believed that the next giant tsunami was hundreds of years away. The earth is unpredictable, but this point has been, and remains, difficult for many people fully to appreciate.

The coast of northeastern Japan was an impoverished region dependent on the fishing industry. While nearly all of the short-term disaster relief came from local sources and military aid, restoring the region to its pre-tsunami socioeconomic level within a reasonably short time would require assistance from agencies of the central government. As we have seen in the previous chapter, for better or worse, the central government "owned" major modern natural disasters in the popular imagination. This phenomenon is an indication of the extent to which the idea of Japan as a modern nation had taken root and the increasing extent to which modern Japanese identified with this entity.

As early as June 18, newspaper articles began to point out that the national treasury was the key to full recovery.[38] In this context, comparisons with the 1891 Nōbi earthquake were common. An article in the *Ōu nichinichi shinbun*, for example, begins by stating that the home minister and all his officials, as well as the prime minister and most local officials, are affiliated with the Liberal Party (Jiyūtō). The recent disaster, therefore, serves as a "litmus test" (*shikinseki*) of the party's ability to govern. Moreover, after the Nōbi earthquake of 1891, Prime Minister Matsukata inspected the disaster area right away. Immediately upon his return, he arranged for the disbursement of two million yen as aid, followed later by a separate disbursement of four million yen. "Now that Home Minister Itagaki has completed his tour of the Tōhoku area, we will soon see whether he and the Liberal Party are of the same caliber as Matsukata's government during Japan's previous major earthquake."[39] This sort of rhetoric would have made no sense in the early modern era, and it is a good example of how much the Nōbi earthquake changed the focus and scope of natural disaster expectations. Not only was the national government responsible for any disaster that happened in Japan, its ability to restore the afflicted area was an emblematic test of its legitimacy. Similar rhetoric has accompanied many other modern disasters, including 3/11. In reality, few, if any, modern governments have been able to meet these idealistic expectations.

Indeed, the Tōhoku region did not receive the vast outlays from the central government many of its residents expected. An article appearing on July 14 on a relief bill taken up at a special Diet session reported plans to allocate approximately 450,000 yen to be divided among the three affected prefectures. It ended by contrasting the "indifference" (*reitan*) of the central government with the earnest sincerity of prefectural officials and the generosity of citizens from far and near who contributed to disaster relief.[40] The next day, in an "appeal to benevolent people of the sea," the *Ōu nichinichi shinbun* pointed out that Miyagi Prefecture's share of the relief funds, if distributed to each of the destroyed households, would amount to forty-five yen each. Next, in a detailed comparison with the farmers who suffered damage from the Nōbi earthquake, the article pointed out that the central government supported all aspects of agricultural recovery (harvest loss, seeds, tools, etc.). Fisherfolk, similarly, farm "the vast ocean," but the proposed aid did not even come close to providing for new boats, nets, and other fishing necessities.[41] Several days later, a two-part article appeared, attacking the Liberal Party in strong terms and urging the people of the region to work for its demise while supporting the Progressive Party (Shinpotō—which in 1898 would merge with the Liberal Party).[42] Soon afterward, an article appeared explicitly lamenting the dire condition of the region, which lacked the power of Russia, Germany, and France to influence the government.[43] This comparison was a reference to the April 1895 intervention of these three countries to force Japan to modify its peace treaty with China and give up the Liaodong Peninsula.

This so-called Triple Intervention (*sankoku kanshō*) and subsequent Russian development of railroads in the Liaodong Peninsula helped divert considerable resources into a Japanese military buildup in anticipation of eventual war between Russia and Japan. These larger developments were surely a background factor contributing to the relative dearth of central government support for rebuilding in 1896. The frequent comparisons with the Nōbi earthquake in the local press highlighted the importance of geography. The 1891 event did considerable damage to Nagoya, a major city in what might be regarded as Japan's heartland. Moreover, the plight of farmers might well have attracted more concern than that of fisherfolk. Another factor may simply have been timing. The Nōbi earthquake happened first, and as Gregory Clancey points out, the 1891 event functioned as "a dress rehearsal" for the major "nationalizing" event of the era, the First Sino-Japanese War.[44] Occurring after both the dress rehearsal, the event itself, and a shocking aspect of the aftermath (the Triple Intervention), the Meiji Sanriku tsunami resulted in putting its victims at a cultural, geographic, and temporal disadvantage in garnering central government support. The empress ended up contributing seven hundred yen to the relief effort, and the names of literally tens of thousands of contributors appeared in the pages of local newspapers.[45] Nevertheless, the region faced the task of long-term recovery with relatively modest outside assistance.

The 1896 disaster generated a variety of proposals for reviving or improving the region, also an important aspect of the 1923, 1933, and 2011 disasters. Because the fishing industry was the economic foundation of the region, discussions about recovery frequently focused on the replacement of fishing boats, most of which were destroyed or badly damaged. The two basic issues were cost and speed. One multipart discussion in late July, for example, points out that at the time, the ordinary cost of constructing a bonito fishing boat was around three hundred yen. The typical crew size for such a vessel ranged from six to twelve, so one boat would employ about seven to eight fishing households. Owing to the recent disaster, however, raw materials and labor were both in short supply and therefore much more expensive than normal. Moreover, the payout from the central government to each household for economic recovery amounted to only about twenty yen. Furthermore, fishing communities typically used a variety of small vessels for different purposes at different times of the year. Adding in the cost of netting and other necessary equipment, central government funding amounted to a drop in the bucket (translated literally, "one hair of nine cows"). After analyzing other expenses and obstacles to recovery, one conclusion was that local governments should construct a road running up and down the coast, connecting fishing communities.[46] One effect of the disaster was to bring into focus the relative isolation of many coastal fishing communities.

Another relevant aspect of infrastructure was seawalls, typically earth embankments, often augmented by protective groves such as those constructed to protect Hiro Village after the tsunamis of 1854. Compared with 1933, the 1896 tsunami stimulated only modest attempts to construct defensive barriers.[47] One contributing factor to this lack of interest was surely funding priorities. Building boats was more important than seawalls, especially considering the widespread belief that the region was unlikely to experience another major disaster for hundreds of years. Moreover, Hiro benefited from Hamaguchi Goryō's wealth and leadership skills, but no community along the Sanriku coast was similarly fortunate. It was mainly the tsunami of 1933 that focused resources on protective barriers.

One might assume that there would have been a rush to relocate after the harrowing experience of the tsunami. Indeed, one June 28 newspaper article encouraged people of the region to "escape cold and hunger" by moving to Taiwan, Japan's newly acquired colony. Taiwan would be ideal for fishing. If several thousand fishing families were to relocate there, it would it would be a win-win situation for the households making the move, the Sanriku coast, and Japan as a whole.[48] Such escapist scenarios notwithstanding, in 1896 there was considerable local resistance to relocation in many areas, including public demonstrations of opposition. Local newspapers sometimes framed relocation as an attempt to get fishing households to change occupations.

Tarō, for example, originally planned to relocate. One common theory for explaining why it did not is that because so few villagers survived, new residents who moved in lacked direct tsunami experience. While this demographic situation may have been a contributing factor, the mind-set of people all along the Sanriku coast carried much weight. As we have seen, many residents were under the impression that great tsunamis occurred once every few hundred years. Since one had just occurred, many thought the region would be free of such disasters for generations to come.[49] A mere thirty-seven years later, however, the next great tsunami smashed into the coast. Here again we see a problem with assuming that the historical record provides a pattern of "characteristic" events. The prominence of rhetoric about "thousand-year earthquakes" in the wake of 3/11, discussed in chapter 6, reflects a similar mode of thinking to that which prevailed in 1896.

In examining all of the communities that made plans to relocate after the 1896 disaster, a majority were either unable to put their plan into action or gradually moved back to low-lying areas. Communities that relocated to higher ground and remained there usually suffered little or no damage in 1933. Some specific examples illustrate the range of possibilities. Funakoshi, in Iwate, relocated to higher ground by extending a road up a mountain and building houses on either side of it. Tanohama, which had been wiped out, planned to merge with Funakoshi and redistributed land at the same location. New Tanohama residents, however, unaware of the danger, gradually relocated closer to the coast. In 1933, Tanohama was destroyed again, but Funakoshi escaped with no damage. Yoshihama escaped damage in 1933 by similarly extending a lowland road up a mountain and relocating there. Ryōri moved several residences to high ground, but over the years, they returned to the original location. The village was devastated again in 1933. Hashikami, in Miyagi, entirely relocated to high ground, assisted by the prefecture's building a new road. Damage in 1933 was light.[50]

Notice the key role of infrastructure in the form of roads to support communities that successfully relocated. In the wake of the 1896 disaster, the central and local governments funded short-term aid but invested little in long-term solutions and undertook no active initiative to promote change. After the 1933 tsunami, however, the state took a greater interest in long-term disaster mitigation. For example, within a year, three thousand households relocated to higher ground with state support and encouragement.[51]

In the case of Tōni, a devastated village (now part of Kamaishi, Iwate Prefecture), locally prominent residents raised three thousand yen to finance relocation to the foot of the mountains behind the original village. There was a source of water, and one hundred households moved to the higher location. Finding the new location inconvenient, however, some fishermen established temporary dwellings in the old lowland location, and other people took up residence there. Soon a formal fishing settlement was in place, and the upland location became a commercial area of shops. The appeal of locating near their customer base then drew shopkeepers back to the old village location. Another important factor was that the upland location was subject to a greater danger from wildfires. Moreover, water in the upland location was not as readily available as in the old location, where most households had their own wells. The tsunami danger was an abstract future possibility, but the fire danger and lack of water were ever-present problems. Households gradually relocated to lower areas, and the 1933 tsunami swept away about half of the houses in the village.[52]

In analyzing settlement patterns in parts of the Middle East, Amos Nur explains several factors that contributed to a tendency to settle in seismically dangerous areas. One is also relevant to Japan's Sanriku coast, namely mountainous topography and its effect on precipitation:

Most of the precipitation falls in the mountains and collects in streams that flow down to the lower areas, where they deposit sediments eroded from the higher elevations. Over time, this creates great wedges of loose sediment, called *alluvial fans*, which in many ways are ideal sites for settlements. The sediments are loose and easily worked, slopes are gentle, and fresh-water springs are common where water percolates down from the mountains. The mountains themselves, however, are the result of activity on faults that often are still active. Indirectly and directly, then, earthquakes entice people to build in the region and repeatedly destroy their handiwork.[53]

For Japan's Sanriku coast, an additional contributor to this broad cycle of creation and destruction was the sheltered bays and inlets, which appealed to fishing communities. Such inlets provided a degree of protection from the open ocean, especially during storms, even though they amplified tsunami wave run-ups.

The trend to return to original locations or otherwise to abandon relatively safe venues and move lower and closer to the coast accelerated after the passing of ten years. It is as if historical memory, or at least the sense of danger, greatly diminished after a tsunami-free decade. Other reasons for remaining in or returning to low-lying areas included convenience for those in the fishing industry, a lack of potable water after moving, inconvenient road networks, the main part of the community remaining where it had been, attachment to ancestral land, a tendency to gradually turn temporary huts used for work into permanent dwellings, and an influx of people without knowledge or experience of tsunamis into the area.[54] Some similar issues are likely to play a role in the future of the region.

In looking at the broad picture of the post-1896 recovery and adaptation, one key point that stands out is greater local government involvement relative to central government involvement, especially at the prefectural level. Governors issued emergency guidelines almost immediately, and prefectures set up disaster relief centers. Insofar as local communities received beneficial help with infrastructure, the funds usually came from the prefectural government. As discussed in chapter 2 in connection with the work of Richard J. Samuels, cooperative networks of local governments were also instrumental in the 3/11 relief effort.[55]

One final point is that the disaster of 1896 did not involve any major cultural issue. The Nōbi earthquake highlighted and intensified ongoing debates about architecture, which was itself in part a proxy for broader debates about Japan's role in the world, alleged Japanese cultural distinctiveness, and the influence of Western cultures. After Nōbi, and to some extent after Great Kantō, a hotly debated question was whether to build Japan's cities with bricks and mortar or by using native (real or imagined) construction materials and techniques centered on wood and skilled joinery. Although the emperor and empress received occasional mention in public discourse in the wake of the 1896 disaster, compared with Nōbi and Great Kantō, the sovereign and his wife remained relatively remote figures from the standpoint of the Tōhoku survivors. Indeed, the relative lack of imperial presence along the Sanriku coast in 1896 and the relative lack of funds from the national treasury compared with the Nobi earthquake underscores the degree of isolation of the region in relation to the national center.

SCIENTIFIC CHALLENGE: THEORIES OF TSUNAMIS

As we have seen, the precise relationship between the mild earthquake and the massive tsunami was a mystery to the experts of the day. This inexplicable element soon prompted a major scientific debate on the subject of tsunamis and their causes. In retrospect, we can say that one of the several proposed theories was correct. However, at the time and for decades thereafter, a dominant, widely accepted theory remained elusive. As with so much else in seismology, it was only after the acceptance of plate tectonics that the basic causal mechanism of tsunamis became reasonably clear. Let us begin our survey of the debates with the scientist who correctly stated that a rupture of the Neodani Fault caused the Nōbi earthquake, Kotō Bunjirō.

In 1896, Kotō posited that undersea volcanic activity was the cause of the great tsunami.[56] The undersea volcano theory found its main advocate in one of Kotō's students, Iki Tsunenaka, who visited the stricken region and published a detailed report for the IEIC. Its fourth chapter, "Discussing the Cause of the Recent Tsunami," begins with two possibilities. Either an earthquake or undersea volcanic activity caused the tsunami. Summarizing the evidence that an earthquake caused the tsunami, Iki lists four peculiarities of the event that made it atypical of earthquake-generated tsunamis, one of which was "extremely weak ground motion." Therefore, he concludes, the more likely cause was undersea volcanic activity.

How is it, though, that large-scale volcanic activity would be located on the sea floor off Japan's Sanriku coast? The report posits, "Indeed there exists a weak point in the earth in this area" because grooves in the earth's crust at this location are aligned in a northeast to southwest orientation. Therefore, volcanic activity could break through the crust in this weakened area and displace enough seawater to cause a tsunami. Moreover, anecdotal reports, for example, by people who were washed into the sea and rescued, indicate that the water temperature was warmer than usual, adding further support to the volcanic activity theory.[57] Seismologists of the time could measure ground motion, wave heights, and other metrics with considerable precision. Teams of investigators carefully surveyed and documented the damage. Nevertheless, causal explanations remained speculative.

The report cited at the start of this chapter lists no author and was probably a consensus of the IEIC. Its description of the cause was as follows:

> There are two types of causes of tsunamis, violent winds and earthquakes. Observing the weather at the time of the tsunami, the high atmospheric pressure that had been in effect for several days running met low pressure in the Pacific that was expanding toward the Japan Sea. This small difference in pressure would not have caused violent winds. Shaking of the earth was observed at the time of the event, so clearly it was not winds but an earthquake tsunami originating out at sea or along the coast. The strong shaking movement would have agitated the water, generating a water disturbance (a so-called tsunami), causing severe damage along the coast. In other words, the phenomenon that produced this event was without a doubt a great shaking in the sea.[58]

The weak shaking on land, however, remained difficult to explain. Speculation about possibilities continued without a firm conclusion, and the report raised the possibility of earth slippage and involvement of the Tuscarora Deep (the Japan Trench).[59] When *National Geographic* reported on the event, it mentioned both theories as possible causes:

> The plainest inference has been that the great wave was the result of an eruption, explosion, or other disturbance in the bed of the sea, 500 or 600 miles off the San-Riku coast. The most popular theory is that it resulted from the caving-in of some part of the wall or bed of the great "Tuscarora Deep," one of the greatest depressions of the ocean bed in the world, discovered in 1874 by the present Rear-Admiral Belknap,

U.S.N., while in command of the U.S.S. *Tuscarora*, engaged in deep-sea surveys.[60]

Explaining the 1896 tsunami was a major challenge for science. Imamura Akitsune took up the challenge, as both an intellectual endeavor and because the social tragedy moved him. Throughout his career, Imamura argued that earthquakes are inevitable, but disasters (*shinsai*) are not.[61] In two papers in 1897, he argues that earth slippage, in other words, movement along faults, was the cause of the disaster.

Imamura considers a wide range of observations, data, and recent advances in knowledge, such as those surrounding the faulting observed in connection with the Nōbi earthquake. He considers varying speeds of waves and local differences in wave heights with respect to models using recorded wave heights of the tsunami to calculate average sea floor depths. He specifically rejects Iki's undersea volcanic activity theory and refutes it in detail. Imamura even anticipates Kanamori's idea of a slow tsunami earthquake. For example:

> Consider the theory by Mr. Iki, who surveyed the disaster area, that an eruption of an undersea volcano caused the great Sanriku tsunami, not earth slippage. His main reason is that the tsunami was much larger relative to the weak shaking of the earthquake. I have considered this point, and it is not sufficient to reject earth slippage as the cause. If the slippage occurred slowly, then it would not be accompanied by a large earthquake, but it could produce a large tsunami. . . . The cause of the current Sanriku tsunami consists in the slow slippage of the earth.[62]

There is much more to this rich article than I have conveyed here, and in the same journal issue, Imamura follows up with a refinement of his ideas, in part prompted by criticism.[63]

Imamura further developed his initial assessment with papers in 1899 and 1900 that advanced knowledge of destructive tsunamis in several key respects. First, he argues that tsunami waves are a special type of periodic wave. The extent of their propagation depends on both the origin of the waves and the depth of the ocean. As tsunami waves approach the shore they become larger, but far out at sea they cause hardly any disturbance. Moreover, ocean floor earthquakes cause tsunami waves, which arrive shortly after the land shakes, but not all ocean floor earthquakes produce tsunamis. Imamura bases his conclusions in part on the analysis of many historical earthquakes from around the world between 1088 and 1897.[64]

In his second paper, Imamura hits the nail on the head with respect to the cause and basic mechanism of tsunami waves:

> Owing to earth slippage that occurs at the ocean floor, in an instant, a large part of a layer of the earth (for example, the radius of its surface area may be ten times greater than its depth) slightly uplifts or slightly subsides. Thereupon the placid surface of the water changes its level in precise accordance with this occurrence.[65]

According to Imamura, tsunami wave generation is a function of depth changes caused by uplift and subsidence of the sea floor. The upward thrusting of large portions of the sea bottom can displace water, forming tsunami waves whose long wavelength causes a gentle undulation in the open ocean but can produce destructive waves as local topography compresses this volume of water into an ever-smaller volume as the waves approach the shore.

Throughout the paper, Imamura argues against Iki's volcanic origin theory and refines points he has made in earlier papers. For example, Imamura presents mathematical arguments to support his idea that time is the key variable whereby it is possible to produce large seismic sea waves despite weak seismic land waves.[66] Moreover:

> In considering the origins of the [Meiji Sanriku] tsunami in light of Iki's theory, we find that phenomena like the following all have close analogs in earth-slip tsunamis of the past: (1) the extent and range of the waves; (2) the very weak shaking from the earthquake; (3) the extremely large tsunami waves; and (4) the relatively small degree of withdrawal of the tide.[67]

By the turn of the twentieth century, Imamura had made available a sophisticated and largely accurate theoretical framework for understanding tsunamis. There was no immediate rush, however, to embrace his conclusions.

Ōmori Fusakichi, who later became a fierce rival of Imamura, as we have seen, also weighed in on the debate about the causes of the 1896 tsunami. In 1900, Ōmori proposed a theory completely different from that of anyone else. He hypothesized several divisions of the world's oceans, with each region oscillating in a characteristic way, like a "fluid pendulum." This idea derived in part from seiches, standing waves in enclosed or partially enclosed bodies of water. Typically, these bodies of water oscillate at a regular frequency, and agitation by storms or seismic waves, even when the earthquake originated thousands of miles away, can create sudden destructive seiches. Ōmori pointed out, for example, that the Lisbon earthquake of 1755 caused a sudden wave to arise in Scotland's Loch Lomond.

Ōmori argued the key element in this process is that the seismic waves have the same period as the "characteristic period" (*koyū naru shindōki*) in that body of water, thus amplifying the water's oscillations. In his two lengthy papers published on this subject, Ōmori provides extensive evidence from around the world. Among other things, his theory delivers an explanation of discrepancies between the size of tsunami waves and the strength of earthquakes. Ōmori rejects both Iki's theory of volcanic activity and Imamura's theory of uplift and subsidence of the sea floor (that is, water displacement) as causes of the 1896 tsunami. He also rejects a theory that had been recently presented by a scientist named Forster, who posited the severing of conduits of electricity at the sea floor as the cause, and the theory that wind and rainstorms caused that event.[68]

We know today that seiches can occur because of seismic activity, and lakes in seismically active areas are prone to destructive seiches. Moreover, in rare cases, incoming tsunami wave trains with the same period as a bay or other enclosed body of water can actually cause a seiche, thus amplifying the potential damage. Ōmori's theory, therefore, was not as strange as it may seem. Indeed, most tsunami damage occurred in bays and inlets, and Ōmori's theory explained the weak ground motion. Even though now we know that seiches and tsunamis are quite different phenomena, it made sense in 1900 to regard them as cases of the same basic process. Close observation of actual tsunami activity, however, presented two problems that derailed Ōmori's fluid pendulum theory.

Imamura responded to Ōmori's theory in 1905, pointing out in a published lecture that if it were accurate, tsunamis would occur at the same time as earthquakes, not thirty to forty minutes later, as was the case in 1896. An even stronger refutation focused on topography. Tsunami wave heights varied as a function of the specific shape of bays and inlets. Those with a V-shaped opening to the sea experienced high tsunami waves, whereas the waves in nearby round bays were shorter. If Ōmori's theory were correct, these factors would not matter. Clearly, Imamura argues, what caused the tsunami was not the water in the bays and inlets but something originating at the ocean floor offshore. Ōmori never responded.[69]

THE SHŌWA SANRIKU EARTHQUAKE AND TSUNAMI, 1933

As a segment of Japan's scientific community was debating the nature and causes of tsunamis, the Sanriku coast gradually recovered from the 1896 disaster. It never became a prosperous region, and the urbanization and industrialization that followed World War I had little direct effect on the area. Although Japan did enjoy a postwar economic boost during the late 1910s and early 1920s, by the late 1920s, the national economy had begun a long-term period of recession. Poverty in the Tōhoku region was a major political issue, at least in the realm of political party rhetoric, throughout the 1920s and into the 1930s. In short, the region was in a state of economic depression when the Shōwa Sanriku earthquake violently shook the area's residents awake in the wee hours of a cold morning.

At 2:31 a.m. on March 3, 1933, the earth in northeast Japan shook violently. Unlike 1896, the earthquake magnitude of 8.1 was similar to the tsunami magnitude of 8.2. The tsunami waves arrived in various locations between thirty and sixty minutes after the earth shook. Also unlike 1896, the cause of this earthquake was probably the rupture of an intraplate fault near the Japan Trench. In other words, it was geologically different from the 1896 event, although the destructive interaction with human society was the same: a powerful train of tsunami waves. The maximum wave height at Ryōri Bay was 28.7 meters. Although not as high as the 1896 event, the 1933 tsunami was still powerful enough nearly to wipe out entire villages, as we have seen in previous discussion.[70]

This tsunami killed 3,064. To put this figure and other damage in perspective, let us assign the value of one hundred to the 1896 tsunami destruction in each major category. In terms of the number of structures destroyed, the Shōwa Sanriku event was seventy-two. Maximum wave heights varied from place to place, and the range in 1933 was sixty to eighty. Most important, the value assigned to tsunami fatalities in 1933 would be fifteen. Notice that the property damage was directly proportional to the wave height, but the death toll was much lower. The main reasons were the living memory and remaining physical reminders of 1896 and the presence of severe shaking.[71] The difference in the death toll between these two events is a striking reminder that following simple rules such as fleeing to high ground immediately after an earthquake greatly reduces fatalities in coastal areas.

Recall that there was little sustained attention by the central or local governments to infrastructure improvements after 1896 and that many communities failed to relocate permanently. One reason was a general sense that major destructive tsunamis are so rare that the next event would be hundreds of years in the future. The 1933 tsunami changed that attitude. Another factor in the mix was that the Tōhoku region in general at this time was in serious economic difficulty, and the plight of farmers there had become an issue in national politics. Moreover, because a military career was one possible way out of poverty, the region had close ties with the armed forces at a time when military influence was increasing. More broadly, unemployment was a severe problem throughout Japan in the early 1930s. A newspaper report from April 2, 1933, estimates that nine million Japanese received unemployment relief.[72] The total population at that time was sixty-seven million. This distressing economic situation played a role in Japan's foreign policy, and it limited the resources the central government could send to the disaster area.

Much more so than in 1896, the 1933 tsunami stimulated ideas and concrete steps to mitigate future tsunami risk. These steps included infrastructure improvement, seawall construction, and the planting of groves of trees to enhance seawalls. These barriers failed in 3/11, but many of them afforded good protection from less severe tsunamis. Although the 1896 tsunami was not an impetus for large-scale construction of defensive barriers, protective groves were in place in a few locations by 1933. A March 11 *Kahoku shinpō* article conveyed a message from the head of the forestry office in Sendai who had inspected tsunami damage in areas protected by raised groves. He declared these barriers to have been a success in attenuating the force and damage of the waves. Of course, such a conclusion would be especially appealing to the head of the local forestry office. A report issued by Tokyo Imperial University's Earthquake Research Institute was generally sanguine about the potential for barriers, but it also pointed out shortcomings. For example, the tsunami swept away a 420-meter embankment at Yoshihama and an embankment at Okkirai. Moreover, although trees might serve to attenuate the force of incoming waves, they could also become damaging projectiles when waves broke them off.[73]

The March 11 *Kahoku shinpō* also carried a short piece about a proposal to install an ultra-shortwave wireless phone (*chō-tanpa musen denwa*) system on the island of Enoshima or in its vicinity to serve as a tsunami warning system. Enoshima is eight nautical miles from Onagawa in Oshika District (Miyagi Prefecture).[74] This conception of an automated tsunami warning system was some seventy years ahead of its time. Such warning systems are now a smartphone reality.

A somewhat more realistic proposal by Tōhoku Imperial University professor Tanakadate Hidezō appeared in a March 25 issue of the *Mainichi shinbun*. He proposed that the creation of a wide tsunami escape road leading to high ground be part of the rebuilding of each coastal community. Moreover, each road should lead to a wide plaza, where the school, administrative offices, hospital, and other key public facilities should be built. Eventually, all residents would know the route well because they traveled it daily to school. Moreover, two or so times a year, for example, on the anniversary of recent deadly tsunamis, the village or town should hold a practice evacuation. Moving the whole village to high ground, as in the case of Funakoshi Village, is desirable but not practical for many fishing communities. The proposed "tsunami road" would be a viable alternative.[75] There is much to be said for the basic ideas in this proposal, even now, in the wake of 3/11.

The 1933 disaster generated a range of ideas for enhancing the safety and resiliency of the Sanriku coast. A newspaper summary of the preliminary conclusions of the Miyagi Prefectural Assembly concerning tsunami safety and awareness listed several points. First, with the 1896 event also in mind, coastal communities should resolutely decide never to face such a tragedy again, either by relocating to higher ground or by constructing defensive barriers. Second, people must be aware that whenever an earthquake occurs, they should immediately flee to high ground. Third, complacency regarding tsunami danger invites tragedy. Fourth, if fleeing to distant high ground is not possible, measures such as crawling on top of the roof can be very effective. Fifth, proper hygienic practices are essential to prevent the spread of disease in the wake of such a disaster. Finally, unlike farming households, fishing households do not usually have large stocks of food or other necessities at hand, so these items will quickly become scarce in a disaster.[76] In short, the wide dissemination of basic information and simple guidelines would greatly enhance public safety.

In this context, the erection of stone monuments and markers was another result of the Shōwa Sanriku tsunami. Most of these markers indicated both the 1896 and 1933 water levels and included basic tsunami advice. Imamura was a strong supporter of the need for these warning monuments and helped raise funds for them. Today there are approximately two hundred extant tsunami monuments along the Sanriku coast. The text on each one is unique. Examples include "If there is an earthquake, be alert for tsunamis; if a tsunami arrives rush to high ground" or "Be ever alert for an unexpected tsunami."[77]

The most famous of these markers is a tall stone monument in the former village of Omoi (Aneyoshi, now part of the city of Miyako), built with donated funds in 1933. It reads:

A dwelling on high ground — the happiness of descendants
Recalling the catastrophe of great tsunamis
Do not build houses below this point
Tsunamis in 1896 and 1933 reached this point
The village was destroyed and survivors numbered a mere two and four people respectively
No matter how many years pass, be on guard[78]

There is a small hamlet of ten homes just beyond and above this marker, and there are no homes (or remains of homes) below the marker. In other words, right up until 3/11, local residents heeded the warning. The 3/11 tsunami waves were approximately on a par with those of 1896, and none of the homes in this hamlet suffered any harm. According to observers in the wake of 3/11, the high-wave boundary near the marker is obvious, marked in part by a different coloration and appearance of the vegetation. Moreover, the area below the marker is now strewn with broken and uprooted trees.[79]

In retrospect, the strategy of avoidance appears as the better approach regarding an event like 3/11. We have seen, however, that some communities that moved to high ground after 1896 eventually gravitated back to more convenient but dangerous lowland areas by 1933. Another consequence of the 1933 tsunami was the inclusion several years later of *Rice Bale Fire* (*Inamura no hi*) in the standard elementary-school curriculum.[80] Of course, the defiant spirit of that tale was ineffective in the face of the 3/11 tsunami, and the dilemma of using technology to resist the fury of nature or yielding to it remains relevant today.

The Shōwa Sanriku disaster also raised concerns about possible adverse effects on the broader natural environment. An early newspaper report, for example, speculated that the churning up of the seafloor by the tsunami might have an adverse effect on fish catches in the short term and possibly interfere with seasonal fishing patterns for the coming summer.[81] Approximately two weeks after the tsunami, it became clear that the demand for lumber, to rebuild fishing boats and for other rebuilding needs, was putting a severe strain on state-owned forest lands. Other practical problems arose in addition to sheer quantities of certain species of wood. For example, only dry boards are useful in boat construction, thus putting a limit on the speed with which boats could be constructed using local resources. One possible expedient was to purchase materials from boatyards in places such as Hakodate, Nagoya, and Osaka.[82]

From the above discussion, it should be clear that although the 1933 tsunami was in some sense a repeat of the 1896 disaster, there were significant differences. The event itself was different in that the waves were not quite as high, the earth shook violently, and it took place in the middle of the night in winter. Though still deadly, far fewer people died in 1933, and the impact of the disaster on society played out differently in at least some respects. Particularly important was the psychological impact in 1933, which disabused local residents of the idea that major tsunamis were unlikely to strike the region in the reasonably near future. In some other respects, however, the reaction in 1933 was similar to that of 1896, even if not exactly the same.

The military, for example, was best poised to provide rapid relief. On March 7, for example, a naval ship arrived in Miyagi Prefecture from Yokosuka loaded with food, military clothing, blankets, and undershirts.[83] The next day, a government vessel from an experimental fish farm loaded aboard similar relief supplies from a navy destroyer and distributed them to the villages of Ōhara, Onagawa, and Jūsanhama in the districts of Oshika and Motoyoshi.[84] Military units were key early responders in 1896, 1933, and 2011. The same goes for newspapers, which solicited donations, coordinated communications, and dispatched teams of relief workers.[85]

Instances of hoarding, profiteering, and otherwise taking personal advantage of the situation, while not a major theme in the postdisaster discourse, did occasionally appear in the press. Some residents of the village of Jūgohama, for example, came under criticism for gathering sardines swept ashore by the tsunami, drying them, and selling them as fertilizer for an unfair profit.[86] By contrast, uplifting tales (*bidan*) were even more prominent in 1933 than in 1896. Indeed, the glorious deeds of local residents even extended into the international realm. Two brothers from the same village as the alleged sardine profiteers were frantically trying to save their family as their house washed out to sea. They were unsuccessful, but at risk to themselves they rescued a Chinese man in the process, thus epitomizing "the flower of Japanese manhood" (*Nippon danshi no hana*).[87] Uplifting tales of virtue amid the tragedy of natural disasters became a common feature in early-twentieth-century Japanese disasters. The Great Kantō Earthquake produced many such tales, and so did less famous disasters, such as the 1938 Kōbe flood. Whether in Kōbe in 1938 or Jūgohama Village in 1933, the inclusion of an international dimension involving Chinese and Japanese was especially significant. As Timothy Tsu points out in connection with the Kōbe flood, tales emerged that featured Japanese rescuing Chinese and vice versa. In one tale, several Chinese save the women and children in a household whose only male member is away fighting in China, an example of "beautiful Sino-Japanese cooperation," declared the *Kōbe shinbun*, the local daily newspaper.[88] Portrayals of natural disasters of the 1930s sometimes ended up reflecting Japan's official war aims in China, an example of the peculiar ways earthquakes can play out in society.

The emperor was also more prominent in the Shōwa Sanriku earthquake and tsunami compared with the 1896 event. The emperor and empress sent an envoy to the region and granted funds from the imperial household to assist the relief effort. On March 20, the governor of Miyagi Prefecture conducted a ceremony in which he conveyed the imperial largess to seventeen village heads from the "ever benevolent, ever merciful emperor and empress."[89] Similar ceremonies took place throughout the region. Similarly, speeches and other public events celebrated both the imperial benevolence and the generosity and virtuous spirit of the region's people.[90] In the larger picture, compared with 1896, the imperial institution had become even more central to Japanese society. It is not surprising, therefore, that the imperial presence was greater after the 1933 event.

A variety of plans and proposals for the region's economic recovery appeared in the press. One proposal, for example, was that fifteen villages coordinate financing and construction to build a large-scale hundred-ton fishing vessel. Other proposals called for the construction of large numbers of smaller boats. Yet another proposal offered oyster farming as a possible way for the region to recover.[91] In late March, detailed reports on proposals by the central government to allocate funds for recovery appeared. For example, a March 20 report stated that the Interior Ministry asked the treasury for 4,200,000 yen, to be divided between Miyagi, Iwate, and Aomori Prefectures, with a small amount going to Hokkaidō. A day later, the press reported that the cabinet had approved a sum of 6,308,000 yen, to be financed by issuing bonds. State support for the devastated region was somewhat greater in 1933 than in 1896, but neither the allocation of funds nor the various recovery schemes led to major changes, except perhaps in the case of seawall construction.

In the aftermath of the disasters of 1891, 1896, 1923, and 1933, we find that, at best, the afflicted regions returned to approximately the condition they were in before the disaster struck. The rates of recovery differed, and the extent of central government aid differed. The 1933 event changed attitudes about tsunami danger, as manifest in the erection of warning monuments and protective barriers. Even this enhanced sense of danger faded, having become greatly attenuated by 3/11. Although some of these great seismic disasters generated minor social changes, none of them functioned as agents of radical change, despite optimistic rhetoric about rebuilding better than before. As a rule, earthquakes and other natural disasters can serve as catalysts for changes already under way, but they rarely, if ever, cause sweeping social change.

Of course, soon after 1933, Japan marched ever more relentlessly into war, first in China and then on multiple fronts. Wartime exigencies took precedence over nearly everything else, and in the immediate postwar years, basic survival dominated society. As Japan recovered from the massive human-made disaster of war, earthquakes and earthquake danger gradually reemerged as social issues. It is to the postwar era that we turn next.

NOTES

1. Shinsai yobō chōsakai, eds., "Sanriku chihō tsunami ihō (sanshō dai-yon)," *Shinsai yobō chōsakai hōkoku*, no. 11 (1896): 41.

2. Satake Kenji, "Kyodai tsunami no mekanizumu," in *Kyodai jishin, kyodai tsunami: Higashi Nihon daishinsai no kenshō*, by Hirata Naoshi, Satake Kenji, Meguro Kimirō, and Hatakemura Yōtarō (Asakura shoten, 2011), 71–72, 82.

3. Yamashita Fumio, *Tsunami tendenko: Kindai Nihon no tsunamishi* (Shin Nihon shuppansha, 2008), 36–37.

4. For statistics and geophysical parameters of this event, see *Shinsai yobō chōsakai*, "Sanriku chihō tsunami," 44–48; Itō Kazuaki, *Jishin to funka no Nihonshi* (Iwanami shoten, 2002), 107–13; Okada Yoshimitsu, *Saishin Nihon no jishin chizu* (Tōkyō shoseki,

2006), 58; Usami Tatsuo, *Nihon higai jishin sōran [416]–2001, Saishinpan* (*Materials for a Comprehensive List of Destructive Earthquakes in Japan, [416]–2001 [latest edition]*) (Tōkyō daigaku shuppankai, 2003), 219–30; and Watanabe Hideo, *Nihon higai tsunami sōran, dai-2 han* (*Comprehensive List of Tsunamis to Hit the Japanese Islands*) (Tōkyō daigaku shuppankai, 1998), 100–104. For an analysis of the fatality statistics, see Yamashita, *Tsunami tendenko*, 27–28.

5. Yamashita Fumio, *Tsunami no kyōfu: Sanriku tsunami denshōroku* (Sendai, Japan: Tōhoku daigaku shuppankai, 2005), 69–73.

6. After the 1968 Tokachi Offshore tsunami, Abe Katsuyuki developed a pair of equations for calculating tsunami intensity. The variables are wave amplitude (in meters) as measured by a tide gauge and direct distance from the epicenter in one equation and the total crest-to-trough wave amplitude and distance to the epicenter in another. Watanabe Hideo has modified Abe's equations, creating one for use in measuring tsunami intensity in Pacific Ocean events, $M_{t0} = \log A + 0.86 \log R + 5.96$, and another for tsunamis originating in the Japan Sea, $M_{t0} = \log A + 0.52 \log R + 6.56$. In these equations, A is total crest-to-trough wave amplitude, and R is distance from the epicenter. Determining A can be complex, but scientists in Japan routinely use Abe's or Watanabe's equations. For a discussion of the details, see Watanabe, *Nihon higai tsunami*, 6–7; and Katsuyuki Abe, "Estimate of Tsunami Run-Up Heights from Earthquake Magnitudes," in *Tsunami: Progress in Prediction, Disaster Prevention, and Warning*, ed. Yoshihito Tsuchiya (Leiden: Kluwer Academic, 1995), 21–35. See also Yamashita, *Tsunami tendenko*, 31–32.

7. Watanabe, *Nihon higai tsunami*, 10.

8. Watanabe, *Nihon higai tsunami*, 11, 100.

9. Watanabe, *Nihon higai tsunami*, 12, 13. See also Yamashita, *Tsunami no kyōfu*, 17.

10. Takahashi Katsumine, "Bun'en: Daikaishō kiji (Sensha kadai)," *Ōu nichinichi shinbun*, July 22, 1896.

11. Shutō Nobuo and Koshimura Shun'ichi, "Meiji Sanriku jishin tsunami ni yoru higai," in *1896 Meiji Sanriku jishin tsunami hōkokusho*, ed. Chūō bōsai kaigi (2005), 45–46.

12. "Tatsuta-kan no kaken," *Iwate Kōhō*, June 21, 1896.

13. "Nigeashiosoi rōjin, kodomo ni gisei ga ōi," *Kahoku shinpō*, March 7, 1933.

14. Shutō and Koshimura, "Higai," 22–25. See also Yamashita, *Tsunami no kyōfu*, 50–68, 73–79.

15. Yamashita, *Tsunami no kyōfu*, 76–77.

16. For a demographic breakdown of 3/11 deaths, see Meguro Kimirō, "Higashi Nihon daishinsai no jinteki higai no tokuchō to tsunami ni yoru giseisha no tsuite," in *Kyodai jishin, kyodai tsunami: Higashi Nihon daishinsai no kenshō*, by Hirata Naoshi, Satake Kenji, Meguro Kimirō, and Hatakemura Yōtarō (Asakura shoten, 2011), 105–9, 116–99. See also Yamashita, *Tsunami no kyōfu*, 83–90.

17. Itō, *Jishin to funka*, 113; and Shutō and Koshimura, "Higai," 38.

18. Shutō and Koshimura, "Higai," 38–41; Yamashita, *Tsunami tendenko*, 38–52; and Yamashita, *Tsunami no kyōfu*, 111–13.

19. "Kōkoku," *Ōu nichinichi shinbun*, July 3, 1896.

20. "Higaichi to eisei," *Iwate kōhō*, June 19, 1896. See also Shutō Nobuo and Koshimura Shun'ichi, "Gyōsei no ōkyū taiō," in *1896 Meiji Sanriku jishin tsunami hōkokusho*, ed. Chūō bōsai kaigi (2005), 47.

21. For a discussion of the emerging concept of hygiene, including in Meiji Japan, see Ruth Rogaski, *Hygienic Modernity: Meanings of Health and Disease in Treaty-Port China* (Berkeley: University of California Press, 2004).

22. "Suisaigo eiseijō no chūi," *Iwate kōhō*, June 20, 1896. See also Shutō and Koshimura, "Gyōsei," 48.

23. "Kaishō jisshiroku ni Shizugawa-chō, honsha tokuha'in Imazumi Torajirō," *Ōu nichinichi shinbun*, June 20, 1896.

24. "Higaisha kyūjo no ippō," *Ōu nichinichi shinbun*, June 24, 1896.

25. "Kaishō no sangai gikin no boshū," *Ōu nichinichi shinbun*, June 17, 1896.

26. "Gisonkin boshū enki kōkoku," *Ōu nichinichi shinbun*, July 28, 1896.

27. "Hakodate yori beikoku o yunyū su," *Iwate kōhō*, June 21, 1896.

28. See, for example, "Fuku-tabemono oyobi jiyōhin no ketsubō," *Ōu nichinichi shinbun*, June 27, 1896; and "Nabe, tetsubin, kondensu miruku, kanzume rui," *Ōu nichinichi shinbun*, July 2, 1896.

29. Shutō and Koshimura, "Gyōsei," 49–50.

30. "Ishi mōsei wo unagasu," *Iwate kōhō*, June 24, 1896.

31. Shutō and Koshimura, "Gyōsei," 51–59.

32. "Sanshin hitotaba," *Iwate kōhō*, June 25, 1896.

33. "Gisonsha rikuzoku tari," *Ōu nichinichi shinbun*, June 23, 1896.

34. For details, see Gregory Smits, *Seismic Japan: The Long History and Continuing Legacy of the Ansei Edo Earthquake* (Honolulu: University of Hawaii Press, 2013). See also Gregory Smits, "Earthquakes as Social Drama in the Tokugawa Period," in *Environment and Society in the Japanese Islands*, ed. Philip Brown and Bruce Batten (Eugene: University of Oregon Press, forthcoming).

35. Yamashita, *Tsunami no kyōfu*, 184–88. Kiguchi Kohei was originally misidentified as Shirakami Genjirō, which is perhaps the origin of Neguchi Manjirō's given name.

36. Eliza Ruhamah Scidmore, "The Recent Earthquake Wave on the Coast of Japan," *National Geographic* 8, no. 9 (September 1896): 287.

37. Yamashita, *Tsunami tendenko*, 38.

38. "Kokka shōbi no kyūmu," *Iwate kōhō*, June 18, 1896.

39. "Kaishō no zengosaku to jiyūtō no kakaku reigan kyoshi," *Ōu nichinichi shinbun*, July 2, 1896.

40. "Kyūjohi no kafu," *Ōu nichinichi shinbun*, July 14, 1896.

41. "Futatabi, kainai no jinjin ni uttau," *Ōu nichinichi shinbun*, July 15, 1896.

42. "Jiyūtō no tame ni tsurushi, Shinpotō no tame ni keisu," *Ōu nichinichi shinbun*, July 18–19, 1896.

43. "Chōsakai no kyūsai hōhō," *Ōu nichinichi shinbun*, July 28, 1896.

44. Gregory Clancey, *Earthquake Nation: The Cultural Politics of Japanese Seismicity, 1868–1930* (Berkeley: University of California Press, 2006), 131.

45. Regarding the empress, see "Miyagi kenpō kokuji dai hachijūroku gō," *Ōu nichinichi shinbun*, July 9, 1896.

46. "Fujisawa gichō no kaishō higaichi saisatsudan (shōzen)," *Ōu nichinichi shinbun*, July 28–29, 1896.

47. For a discussion of seawalls and groves created in response to the 1896 disaster, see Haruo Matuo [Matsuo], "Estimation of Energy of Tsunami and Protection of Coasts," *Jishin kenkyūjo ihō bessatsu*, no. 1 (March 3, 1934): 55–64.

48. "Taiwan ijū o shōrei seyo," *Ōu nichinichi shinbun*, June 28, 1896.

49. Yamashita, *Tsunami no kyōfu*, 124–27.

50. Shutō Nobuo and Koshimura Shun'ichi, "Meiji Sanriku tsunami saigai kara no fukkō," in *1896 Meiji Sanriku jishin tsunami hōkokusho*, ed. Chūō bōsai kaigi (2005), 91–92.

51. Yamashita, *Tsunami no kyōfu*, 142.

52. Yamashita, *Tsunami no kyōfu*, 145–47.

53. Amos Nur with Dawn Burgess, *Apocalypse: Earthquakes, Archaeology, and the Wrath of God* (Princeton, NJ: Princeton University Press, 2008), 60–61.

54. Shutō and Koshimura, "Fukkō," 92–93.

55. Richard J. Samuels, *3.11: Disaster and Change in Japan* (Ithaca, NY: Cornell University Press, 2013).

56. See Kotō Bunjirō, "Takanami no yūin," *Tōyō gakugei zasshi* 13 (1896): 441–44. For a rebuttal, see Ochibe Chūshō, "Sanriku chihō tsunami ni tsuki chishitsugakujō no kōsetsu," in "furoku" (supplement), *Chigaku zasshi* 8 (1896): 1–17; and Watanabe, *Nihon higai tsunami*, 32–33. Ochibe argued in favor of slippage of the earth (*jisuberi*), which in the terminology of the time indicated the movement of faults.

57. Iki Tsunenaka, "Sanriku chihō tsunami jistujō torishirabe hōkoku," in *Shinsai yobō chōsakai hōkoku, dai 7 gō* (Shinsai yobō chōsakai, 1896), 30–33.

58. Shinsai yobō chōsakai, "Sanriku chihō tsunami ihō," 42.

59. Shinsai yobō chōsakai, "Sanriku chihō tsunami ihō," 43.

60. Scidmore, "The Recent Earthquake Wave," 289.

61. Yamashita, *Tsunami no kyōfu*, 193–94.

62. Imamura Akitsune, "Jisuberi ni tsuite ronji jinari oyobi tsunami no gen'in ni oyobu," *Chishitsugaku zasshi* 4 (1897): 68.

63. Imamura Akitsune, "Futatabi tsunami no gen'in ni tsuki," *Chishitsugaku zasshi* 4 (1897): 116–19.

64. Imamura Akitsune, "Sanriku tsunami ni tsuite," *Chigaku zasshi* 11 (1899): 801–10. See also Watanabe, *Nihon higai tsunami*, 33.

65. Imamura Akitsune, "Sanriku tsunami ni tsuite," *Chigaku zasshi* 12 (1900): 143; and Watanabe, *Nihon higai tsunami*, 33.

66. Imamura, "Sanriku tsunami" (1900), 146–47.

67. Imamura, "Sanriku tsunami" (1900), 151.

68. For the detailed version of Ōmori's theories and their application to a variety of events, see Ōmori Fusakichi, "Nihon ni okeru tsunami ni tsuite," *Shinsai ybō chōsakai hōkoku, dai 34 gō* (January 1901), 5–81. For analysis of the Meiji Sanriku earthquake and tsunami, sometimes in comparative perspective, see esp. 36–52. For a concise statement of his concept, see Ōmori Fusakichi, "Tsunami ni tsuite," *Tōyō gakugei zasshi* 18 (1901): 20–21. See also Watanabe, *Nihon higai tsunami*, 33.

69. Imamura Akitsune, "Jishin tsunami no gen'in ni tsuite," *Chigaku zasshi* 17 (1905): 792–801; and Watanabe, *Nihon higai tsunami*, 33–34.

70. For the basic statistics and facts, see Okada, *Jishin chizu*, 59–60; Usami, *Nihon higai jishin*, 302–6; and Watanabe, *Nihon higai tsunami*, 114–21.

71. Analysis based on Yamashita, *Tsunami no kyōfu*, 37–40. See also Tsuji Yoshinobu, *Sennen shinsai: Kurikaesu jishin to tsunami no rekishi ni manabu* (Daiyamondo sha, 2011), 168.

72. "Honnendo shitsugyō kyūsai shikō hōshin kettei," *Mainichi shinbun*, April 2, 1933.

73. Matuo, "Estimation of Energy of Tsunami," esp. 59–60, 62–63.

74. "Tsunami o fusegu yūkina mōza hoanrin no hitsuyō o toku Akabayashi Sendai eirinshō-chō," *Kahoku shinpō*, March 11, 1933; and "Tsunami sanjuppun mae ni SOS

tsūshin Onagawa Enoshima-kan no muden sōchi iyoiyo kōshōsaru," *Kahoku shinpō*, March 11, 1933.

75. Tanakadate Hidezō, "Sankakuten 'tsunami hinan dōro,'" *Mainichi shinbun*, March 25, 1933.

76. Fujita Hiroshige, "Kenkai giin ōjishin attara tsunami shūrai o kakugo," *Kahoku shinpō*, March 14, 1933.

77. Yamashita, *Tsunami tendenko*, 103–4.

78. Yamashita, *Tsunami no kyōfu*, 156–57; and Yamashita, *Tsunami tendenko*, 104–5.

79. Hatamura Yōtarō, "Higashi Nihon daishinsai ni omou," in *Kyodai jishin, kyodai tsunami: Higashi Nihon daishinsai no kenshō*, ed. Hirata Naoshi, Satake Kenji, Meguro Kimirō, and Hatamura Yōtarō (Asakura shoten, 2011), 154–57.

80. Yamashita, *Tsunami tendenko*, 105.

81. "Toreru sakana no henka ga arō jishin to Sendai akana ichiba, ichi, ni ryōshi no hanashi," *Kahoku shinpō*, March 4, 1933.

82. Fujita Hiroshige, "Kenkai giin kokuyūrin nai ni wa kanjin no yōzai ga kiwamete kinshō," *Kahoku shinpō*, March 20, 1933.

83. "Imonhin bunpai gunkan *Itsukushima* no tsundekita Yokosuka chinfu kizōhin," *Kahō shinpō*, March 7, 1933.

84. "Kaigun kyūjutsuhin *Yakaze* yori juryō tadachini risai mura e," *Kahō shinpō*, March 8, 1933.

85. See, for example, "Honsha imon dai-ni han, Sanriku higaichi no mukau torakku no Hitsujuhin o mansai shite hikitsuzuki dai-san han o soshiki," *Kahō shinpō*, March 6, 1933.

86. "Nagaretekita iwashi kasu o shūtoku kansōsasete baikyakusu," *Kahō shinpō*, April 26, 1933. Samuels provides much thoughtful analysis of the role of the military after 3/11 and in previous disasters. See Samuels, *3.11*, esp. 51–63, 185, 195–98.

87. "Hi to mizu no naka kara umareta kokusai bidan Sanriku shinsai aiwa no hitotsu," *Mainichi shinbun*, March 8, 1933.

88. Timothy Yun Hui Tsu, "Making Virtues of Disaster: 'Beautiful Tales' from the Kobe Flood of 1938," *Asian Studies Review* 32, no. 3 (June 2008): 207.

89. "Seishi o hōtai shite okashikin o yūkō ni saigai fukkō ni tsutomu beshi shingaichi jūshichi chōsonchō ni kokuyu o hassu," *Kahoku shinpō*, March 21, 1933.

90. See, for example, the summary of a speech by the priest of Tenyūji. "Kōen Sanriku kashō no ippashi o kataru ato roku no nigo Sendai kara," *Kahoku shinpō*, March 26, 1933.

91. "Fukkō wa kaki no yōshoku kara tanekaki haikyū no tairyō mōshikomi ni me o mawasu Watanoha shuishi," *Kahoku shinpō*, April 15, 1933.

FIVE

Prediction to Forecasting

Attempting to Outsmart the Earth in Postwar Japan

We live in an age of high expectations of science and technology. Robots perform surgery, our phones guide us to our destinations with pinpoint precision, and scholars interact in real time with students halfway across the world. It is easy to overlook the substantial limits to our knowledge of the physical world and our ability to intervene usefully in it. Natural disasters such as the Sumatra tsunami of late 2004, the Sichuan earthquake of 2008, and 3/11 dramatically remind us of the destructive power natural forces can bring to bear on human societies. Deriving the maximum benefit from science and technology requires intelligent policies that support the development of fruitful avenues of research, frank acknowledgment of risks and limits to what is possible, an awareness of opportunity costs, and the dissemination of clear and accurate information to the public about natural hazards and our capacity to deal with them.

Popular expectations have a tendency to exceed the bounds of what is reasonable or even possible. One reason is simply that scientific advances and the technologies resulting from them have altered human life in countless ways, most of which are beneficial. Although excessive faith in science is more common among nonscientists, scientists themselves sometimes display unwarranted optimism. Early-twentieth-century seismologist Musha Kinkichi, for example, anticipated a capability both to predict and to prevent earthquakes. He thought it difficult but someday possible to devise a way to release energy that had built up within the earth's crust and posed an earthquake danger.[1] Musha was active before the theory of plate tectonics became widely accepted, and his view of earthquakes as essentially explosive events caused by energy accumulations was a legacy of theories of earthquake mechanics with roots in the early modern era. Knowing the massive scale of the geophysical processes that produce crustal strain, the notion of preventing earthquakes from occurring is now inconceivable—at least among experts. On repeated occasions, however, I have participated in panels or roundtable discussions in which highly educated people asked seismologists about how scientists are working to prevent earthquakes.

During the 1960s and 1970s, there was considerable enthusiasm among seismologists in Japan and elsewhere that although earthquakes are unpreventable, they might soon become predictable. During the 1980s, this enthusiasm began to wane as the enormity of the task became apparent. Today, confidence that we will soon be able to predict earthquakes with short-term specificity is rare in mainstream seismology. Although nearly all experts acknowledge that specific prediction is currently impossible, especially in Japan, many scientists remain committed to the goal of eventually becoming able to predict earthquakes. This chapter explains the major reasons for this situation and some of the costs associated with legal and public financial support for what has been, in effect, a futile effort to outsmart the earth.

Science is not the only realm in which modern people tend to place excessive confidence. Legislation is another. The rule of law has undoubtedly brought about many social benefits, but as with science, there are inherent dangers and limitations in the modern affinity for attempting to solve complex problems through legislation. Earthquakes constitute both a social and a geophysical problem, and legislation specifying responsibility for emergency response preparations or requiring antiseismic construction for infrastructure often makes good sense. Legislation that assumes earthquakes are predictable, however, is problematic. Japan is the only country in the world with such legislation.

Strictly speaking, it is not *any* earthquake that is predictable, but a particular megathrust earthquake known as a Tōkai (eastern sea) earthquake to which the law applies. The 1854 Ansei Tōkai and Nankai earthquakes are examples of this type. These earthquakes are sometimes called Tōnankai (eastern-southern sea) earthquakes because the subduction

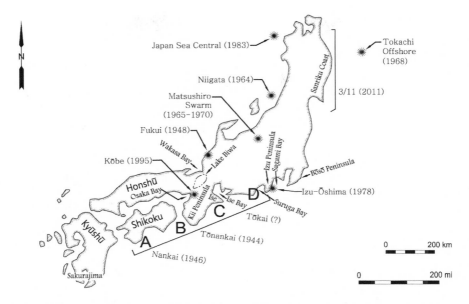

Figure 5.1. Selected Earthquakes, 1944–2011. *Source:* **Jeffrey Smits, Cherokee Drafting Specialists.**

zone that produces them extends from approximately the Izu Peninsula just south of Tokyo to the end of the island of Shikoku. Sometimes the eastern section of the zone ruptures, sometimes the southwestern section ruptures, and sometimes both rupture, if not at the same time, then within a few days or years. The possibility of these tsunamigenic earthquakes is undoubtedly a real and significant danger to heavily populated areas such as the Osaka area. Nevertheless, extreme fear of a Tōkai earthquake has produced some strange results.

One of these results is the 1978 Special Measures Law for Large-Scale Earthquakes (Daikibo jishin taisaku tokubetsu sochi hō). It is known by the abbreviated name Daishinhō in Japanese, and I call it the Special Measures Law in these pages. The law assumes the ability to predict a Tōkai earthquake as an unproblematic premise. The third item in article 2, for example, specifies that the Japan Meteorological Agency (JMA) will issue earthquake prediction reports, and article 4 specifies that the state will predict large-scale earthquakes within the zone likely to be affected by a Tōkai earthquake.[2] This law has serious implications for resource allocation and the nature of public information. One cost of the intense focus on a Tōkai earthquake, for example, is relative neglect of earthquakes or their possibility elsewhere in Japan.

The majority of state earthquake research funding goes toward prediction (now often called forecasting). This chapter examines major postwar earthquakes in the context of state support for prediction. My argument is that the combination of very few earthquake-related fatalities between 1948 and 1995, the lure of public funding for research, and the fear of a Tōkai earthquake from the late 1970s onward has resulted in a skewed allocation of resources and other obstacles to dealing with seismic hazards.

THE BLUEPRINT

In 1962, a group of Japanese seismologists interested in earthquake prediction led by Wadachi Kiyoo, Tsuboi Chūji, and Hagiwara Takahiro published a summary of their ideas and plans for the future. The document, *Prediction of Earthquakes: Progress to Date and Plans for Further Development (Jishin yochi, genjō to sono suishin keikaku)*, quickly became known as "the Blueprint." It hinted at the ability to predict earthquakes in ten years if its plans were fully funded. Strictly speaking, however, the Blueprint promised only that after ten years it would become possible to say whether specific earthquake warnings are a realistic goal. Moreover, "it will be at least ten years before the survey and observations under the present proposal really get under way," said the document. Fundamentally, the Blueprint was an appeal for the state to fund the collection of data: "If we aim at predicting earthquakes with magnitude greater than 6, it seems highly probable that we would be able to find some significant correlation between earthquake occurrence and observed phenomena merely by accumulating data for several years."[3] The idea that accumulating more data will surely reveal useful precursors or coseismic phenomena had been a theme in Japanese earthquake literature and science since the early nineteenth century. We have also seen it in the prewar research agenda of the Imperial Earthquake Investigation Committee and, after 1924, in the "catfish school" of seismology. The idea remains influential to this day. It is important to bear in mind that the Blueprint provided no path forward whereby accumulated observations might lead to successful prediction. The document proposes no theory of earthquake mechanics, and more important, it does not propose a testable hypothesis. Instead, it reflects faith that somehow, more data accumulation will lead to important insights.[4]

Given the relatively modest claims of the Blueprint, it might never have generated public funding. The earth intervened, however, in the form of the June 1964 Niigata earthquake (M7.5). Although this earthquake resulted in only twenty-six fatalities, it caused dramatic damage to facilities, and the new medium of television magnified its psychological impact. Scientists pushed hard to leverage this earthquake for funds and appealed to seven different government agencies. The result in 1965 was 170 million yen for earthquake prediction research and the establishment of the first of what would eventually become several government committees charged with earthquake prediction. The idea was to increase the capacity to observe and measure seismic activity and thereby detect any relevant earthquake precursors.

That same year in Nagano Prefecture, the Matsushiro swarm of earthquakes began, producing about 648,000 small earthquakes by the time it faded in 1970. At its peak, in the middle of April 1966, the swarm produced approximately six hundred earthquakes in a single day. The swarm remains a mystery, and it never produced a major earthquake. It was very effective, however, in keeping local residents on edge and focusing attention on earthquakes and earthquake prediction. A team of researchers from Tokyo University set up seismometers in four locations around the area and began monitoring seismic activity. In an interview, the mayor of Matsushiro famously appealed for more earthquake science. In 1967, the budget for earthquake prediction doubled.[5] One legacy of the Matsushiro swarm was scientific interest in the study of small earthquakes (much more numerous and easy to deal with) as a proxy for understanding large ones.[6] Writing critically of this trend, Shimamura Hideki has pointed out that the struggle for money tended to favor the businesslike, routine pursuit of data. The focus on garnering data from very small earthquakes, measuring changes in the earth's crust, and other routine observational work fit perfectly with this situation, but it did so at the expense of research on basic questions such as what happens at the hypocenter of an earthquake.[7]

The M7.9 Tokachi offshore earthquake of May 1968 originated to the northeast of Aomori and Iwate Prefectures. It killed fifty-two and was felt throughout most of the northeastern half of Honshū. One result of this event was the 1969 creation of the Coordinating Committee for Earthquake Prediction (CCEP, or Jishin yochi renraku kai, commonly known as Yochiren in Japan) within the Geospatial Information Authority (GSI, or Kokudo chiri in). Earthquake prediction appeared in the name of a government committee and became a topic of interest to the mass media, but genuine earthquake prediction remained completely outside the pale of scientific knowledge and know-how. Seismologists were reluctant to claim the power of prediction, but earthquake monitoring and data collection is expensive.

To appreciate some of the relevant expenses, consider that to establish an observation post, an agency must buy the land, build a structure to house the equipment, tunnel into rocks, and install an expensive device. The collected data must be transmitted to a central location via an expensive telemeter. Both the observation point and the central location must be staffed. Collecting earthquake data in the postwar era as called for in the Blueprint required a significant outlay of public funds, and to those building it, the observational network never seemed sufficient.[8] The lure of increased funding soon influenced claims about earthquake prediction.

FROM RESEARCH TO PREDICTION

The Tokachi offshore earthquake provided a context for the expansion of earthquake research in several respects. First was a change in nomenclature. The first government-funded plan for earthquake prediction, covering 1965–1968, was called "Plan for Earthquake Prediction Research" ("Jishin yochi kenkyū keikaku"). Most seismologists in 1969 sought to continue in the data collection mode, but public expectations in the wake of the Matsushiro earthquake swarm and the Tokachi offshore earthquake raced ahead of actual capabilities. According to Tsuneji Rikitake, in response to the Tokachi offshore earthquake, "The necessity of earthquake prediction was discussed at the cabinet level, and a drastic intensification of earthquake prediction was proposed. The public now required actual prediction rather than prediction research, wherever possible."[9] Although Rikitake most likely did not know this detail at the time he wrote, the key cabinet member was Nakasone Yasuhiro, then minister of transportation, later to become prime minister.

In a 1994 newspaper article, former director of Tokyo University's Earthquake Research Center Morimoto Ryōhei explained what occurred in 1969. At that time, the Japan Meteorological Agency was part of the Ministry of Transportation. Nakasone explained that the word "research" (*kenkyū*) was problematic. If the scientific community was willing to drop this word and propose an outright earthquake prediction plan, then its budget might increase ten times or more. Otherwise, it would stay approximately the same. In other words, the price for greatly increased funding was to imply that earthquake prediction is possible and that scientists would put it into effect. The committee members in charge of the plan agreed. Thus, Japan began to implement a program of earthquake prediction, even though scientifically, "We still do not have a clue about how to predict earthquakes, and barring some miracle, I do not think that we will," said Morimoto in 1994. In practice, the seismological community used the additional funds mainly to continue expanding their observational network.[10]

To guide this expansion, in 1969, the CCEP produced a map of Japan featuring nine areas selected for especially intense observation based on the occurrence of destructive earthquakes in the past, the location of known active faults, high rates of seismic activity, and sociopolitical significance. These initial nine areas did not include any of the Sanriku coast, but a revised version of the map in 1988 included the coastal areas of Fukushima and Miyagi Prefectures. Shimamura, a strong critic of official earthquake policy, says of the 1988 map that it better reflects political influence than academic knowledge.[11] He and others have leveled similar criticism at recent iterations of Japan's official earthquake hazard maps, as well as pointing out other problems with them.[12] There is considerable overlap between both the 1965 and 1988 maps and the areas of highest danger in recent government hazard maps.

Writing in 1992, when it had become apparent that the possibility of ever being able to predict earthquakes was remote, the first head of the CCEP kept the faith. He said, "Certainly we can expect that there are precursors of large earthquakes. After all, one hundred or two hundred kilometers of the earth's crust moves. It is hard to imagine that nothing happens before that."[13] This view encapsulates the basic logic of Japan's quest for earthquake prediction: if only we watch closely and carefully enough, surely we will find the precursors that we know must be there. The observation process has been under way since 1828.

During the 1960s and 1970s, many seismologists in different countries shared a similar view. Some in the United States, for example, supported an ambitious program of national support for earthquake research and hazard reduction, "promoted largely if not entirely on promises of earthquake prediction—promises that were, in retrospect, somewhere between optimistic and totally irresponsible," according to seismologist Susan Hough.[14] The same could be said about Japanese scientists' agreement to drop the word "research," thereby implying that they were capable of carrying out effective earthquake prediction.

WORLD TRENDS, 1970s AND BEYOND

Japanese optimism that greater data accumulation would lead to predictive capabilities was mirrored elsewhere in the world during the late 1960s and the decade of the 1970s. Particularly important were developments in the Soviet Union, China, and the United States. Here I briefly outline major developments.

The March 27, 1964, Good Friday earthquake in Alaska and the tsunami it generated received extensive television coverage, functioning much like the Niigata earthquake in Japan the same year. A panel of experts convened in the wake of the Alaska event and urged the government to adopt a ten-year, $137 million program for earthquake prediction and damage mitigation. No government funding was forthcoming, but the United States Geological Survey (USGS) successfully positioned itself as the leading agency in earthquake research, eclipsing the Coast and Geodetic Survey (CGS). The event that eventually dislodged money from Washington was the M6.6 Sylmar (San Fernando) earthquake of February 9, 1971. This event killed sixty-five in the northern San Fernando region, caused extensive property damage, produced a series of aftershocks, and generated numerous amateur predictions or prophesies of future earthquakes (none correct). This situation prompted Charles Richter to utter his famous words that those claiming to make a precise earthquake prediction are "charlatans, fakes, or liars." While no earth scientists came forward with specific predictions, in 1971 some implied publicly that earthquake prediction would soon become possible. Geologist Richard Berry, for example, said of earthquakes, "that within a decade we will have information that, within limits, will make it possible to predict what will happen."[15] Perhaps the most important words in this sentence are "within limits."

The Sylmar earthquake intersected with and reinforced Cold War concerns and rivalries. Most obviously, earthquake detection equipment was essential for monitoring underground nuclear weapons tests. More important for our purposes, by 1970, Soviet scientists claimed success in earthquake prediction using the Vp/Vs method, which measures changes in the ratio of the velocity of "p" (push-pull, pressure) waves and "s" (shear) waves. These claims came to the attention of seismologists around the world, including those in Japan and the United States. Initial visits to the Soviet Union by foreign scientists produced enthusiastic reports, and enthusiasm remained high in some circles as late as 1974. The Soviet results, however, proved impossible to replicate, and close examination of actual data revealed considerable room for interpretation in assigning velocity ratio anomalies.[16] Attempts to explain the Vp/Vs data led some American scientists to theorize a process of dilatancy.

In 1973 a team led by Christopher Scholz proposed that rocks dilate (expand in volume) when subject to stress. The basic idea was that stress shifts rock grains, generating new cracks, which can absorb groundwater. The result is an increase in rock volume. This dilatancy theory posited a physical explanation of what might occur prior to an earthquake and raised hopes that eventually the process leading up to an earthquake could be understood and possibly predicted. The dilatancy theory generated great enthusiasm in Japan, where it was known as the "Scholz theory." Indeed, the basic idea remains the foundation of official hopes for predicting a Tōkai earthquake. Soon after the Scholz theory began making waves in Japanese seismological circles, the earth produced another boon for prediction advocates: the M7.3 Haicheng earthquake in northeast China. The main shock occurred at 7:36 p.m. February 4, 1975, but a series of smaller preshocks had been occurring for several days.

The official story line at the time was that, mobilized by Chairman Mao to be on the lookout for earthquake signs, the people of the area noticed anomalies, most famously strange animal behavior. In consultation with specialists, local officials issued evacuation orders and warnings the morning of the earthquake, saving many lives. In short, local authorities, aided by masses of nonspecialist observers, had successfully predicted a major earthquake, according to government reports.[17]

The news spread in subsequent months, prompting foreign scientists to visit the region, often with difficulty. Debates raged in journals over whether and to what extent the party line was accurate in this case. New

Zealand seismologist Robin Adams was the first foreign scientist to visit the area. Although his hosts mentioned a number of questionable points, such as the issuing of warnings in prior years that were not followed by earthquakes, Adams concluded on an enthusiastic note:

> The achievements of the Chinese people relating to this earthquake are twofold. Technically, this is the first major earthquake anywhere in the world to have been adequately predicted by a systematic refining of the estimate of time, position, and magnitude. This achievement alone is outstanding whether or not there may have been an element of luck, but an even greater achievement, and one to which only a society such as that in China can currently aspire, is the education of the people to take part in prediction programmes, and to accept the disruption to their lives that must accompany any action taken following an earthquake prediction. In this aspect perhaps lies the greatest value of involving the people in mass prediction programmes.[18]

A delegation of scientists from the United States was similarly enthusiastic and concluded its report with five recommendations, including: "An earthquake volunteers program should be initiated through existing institutions and organizations."[19]

Haicheng was perhaps most influential in Japan, "renowned as the first successful example of earthquake prediction in a practical sense," wrote earthquake prediction advocate Kiyoo Mogi in 1987.[20] Writing much more recently, marine geologist Kimura Masaaki not only regards Haicheng as an unqualified success, but he even claims that the 1995 Kōbe earthquake closely resembled Haicheng and therefore could have been predicted.[21]

Haicheng also served as a general inspiration for mobilizing nonspecialist observers in Japan. Motoji Ikeya, for example, wrote approvingly of "the Chinese claim to have successfully predicted the 1976 [sic] Haicheng quake by analyzing laymen's observations of animal behavior," but he realized that in the twenty-first century, a program centered on schools would be more effective. His specific recommendation was to place catfish in aquariums in schools all over Japan for observation, with data sent via the Internet to Osaka University for analysis.[22] Prediction advocate Hagiwara Takahiro also regarded Haicheng as a great success, but he downplayed the role of well-water levels and animal behavior. For him, the observed preshocks were the decisive factor.[23]

It was uncommon in Japan to find criticism of the official narrative of the Haicheng earthquake. By contrast, some in the United States rejected Chinese claims on apparent ideological grounds, voicing skepticism about "the alleged accomplishments of Chinese Communist seismology under the guidance of Chairman Mao" or, more concisely, "Maoist seismology," in the words of one critic.[24] Assessment based on close study of relevant evidence, however, would have to wait decades until scholars had access to a wide range of documents. A detailed analysis by Kelin Wang and his colleagues in 2006 revealed a much less tidy picture of the event than the official narrative at the time asserted. Some localities did issue evacuation orders, but others did not. Basic terms are problematic in that the Chinese *yubao* covers both the English "prediction" and the less constrained "forecast," and certain key Chinese terms implied bureaucratic effectiveness, not scientific accuracy. The county-level official who ordered the evacuations apparently did so in part under the influence of folklore, which held that heavy autumn rains would cause an earthquake in the winter—a case of being "right for the wrong reasons." In any event, the most important warning was the series of foreshocks in the days before February 4. Moreover, the relatively low death toll is attributable not only to evacuations but also to the type of wood-frame houses common in that part of China.[25]

As Hough explains, "Haicheng leaves us with hints and perhaps promises, but in the end far more questions than answers."[26] We now know that parts of the official story line are inaccurate, but even if frogs and snakes emerged in the wintertime, pigs stopped eating, well-water levels fluctuated, and other alleged "precursors" actually happened, these things do not normally happen before large earthquakes. Precursors are useful only if they occur reliably before destructive earthquakes and occur only at those times. Significantly, while earthquake prediction advocates marveled at the Haicheng case, the July 28, 1976, M7.5 earthquake in the nearby Tangshan region came entirely without warning, killing at least 250,000 (according to official statistics) and probably more than twice that many. It was the most deadly earthquake of the twentieth century and possibly of all time. Moreover, there has been no successful prediction of a major earthquake since Haicheng. In retrospect, the brief time between the Haicheng and Tangshan earthquakes was the high-water mark of scientific interest in earthquake prediction.

One general pattern prevailing from the 1970s to the present is the announcement of some kind of new, promising method of earthquake prediction, always discovered retrospectively. Inevitably, on close inspection and in light of a wide range of data, these methods fail to predict earthquakes to a statistically significant degree compared with random chance. Each of these methods still has partisans, but the broader seismological community gradually lost interest in earthquake prediction as one method after another rose and fell and as the chaotic nature and complexities of earthquake geophysics became more apparent. If the 1970s are likened to a wild party, the 1980s was a decade in which the hangover set in, to use Hough's metaphor.[27]

Particularly dramatic was the prediction experiment at Parkfield, California. The USGS concluded that M6-class earthquakes occur on the San Andreas Fault near Parkfield on average every twenty-two years. It publicly predicted that the next earthquake would occur within four years of 1988, and scientists rushed to set up instrumentation, including even a computer-monitored box of cockroaches. The year 1992 came and went with no earthquake. Finally, on September 28, 2004, the earthquake occurred. Although Parkfield failed as a case of accurate earthquake prediction, a major purpose of the experiment was to ambush an earthquake with measuring devices. In this sense, Parkfield was a success.

Enough instrumentation remained in place in 2004 to conclude that this earthquake had no measurable precursors. There was no fault creep prior to the main shock, no warping of the crust, and no unusual magnetic signals, nor was there any major foreshock activity, in contrast to the 1934 and 1966 Parkfield earthquakes.[28] The 2004 Parkfield earthquake was another blow to advocates of prediction via precursors. As Hough points out, "The negative results from Parkfield do not prove that significant precursors don't precede some earthquakes, but they do prove that significant precursors don't precede all earthquakes."[29] To the list of recent large earthquakes that occurred without any significant precursors accepted by the scientific community we could add 1989 Loma Prieta (M6.9), 1993 Landers (M7.3)—both in California—1995 Kōbe, 2003 Tokachi offshore (M8.3), and 3/11.[30]

Just because seismologists were unable to detect any precursors with their instruments in these and other earthquakes does not mean that there were no claims of precursors. After every large earthquake, the popular press in Japan and elsewhere reports on strange phenomena, especially animal behavior, that some people claim in retrospect to have been seismic precursors. The range of these alleged precursors is overwhelmingly large. Claims include most of the classic precursors one might have found in writings from the 1820s onward as well as phenomena such as strange behavior of electronic gadgets. Tokyo University seismologist Robert Geller points out sarcastically that he has to read the popular press, including sensational tabloids, to keep up with the latest "advances" in earthquake prediction.[31] Shimamura points out that panels on earthquake prediction at meetings of the Seismological Society of Japan (SSJ) are almost entirely conducted and attended by amateurs. More to the point, despite the existence of more than one thousand monitoring stations throughout Japan, there has been no actual progress in the ability to predict earthquakes.[32] In short, the center of the discourse on earthquake prediction has shifted from the seismological community to the popular press. That said, however, some seismologists remain interested in and defenders of prediction research.

THE MAGIC MALLET

Many residents of Shikoku and coastal areas of Honshū from Osaka to the Izu Peninsula have been dreading a Tōkai earthquake since 1977. That year, seismologist Ishibashi Katsuhiko presented a report to the CCEP warning of an imminent Tōkai earthquake. Among the points he singled out as "especially important" was, "At the present stage, it would not be strange to think that precursory phenomena could begin at any moment. Because there is no guarantee that they would continue for a long period, we should immediately begin concentrated observation."[33] Word of Ishibashi's dire forecast spread fear, and the claim of the recent successful forecast of the Haicheng earthquake put pressure on Japanese seismologists similarly to protect the nation from the ravages of nature. The "Tōkai earthquake shift" had begun, and the mass media buzzed with talk of earthquake prediction. The governor of Shizuoka Prefecture pressed the national legislature for action, and it responded in what was record time by the standards of Japanese lawmaking.[34]

Before describing the passage of the Special Measures Law for Large-Scale Earthquakes, we should pause to consider the basic thinking behind the Tōkai earthquake theory. The Nankai Trough extends from Suruga Bay to offshore areas of Shikoku and Kyūshū and is the result of the

Philippine Sea Plate subducting under the Eurasian Plate. Seismologists have hypothesized three fault planes (from northeast to southwest), known as Tōkai, Tōnankai, and Nankai. Furthermore, they have divided the fault into four segments: A, B, C, and D, from southwest to northeast, respectively. Some accounts add a fifth segment, E. All four segments broke in 1707 to create the M8.6 Hōei earthquake and tsunami. Segments C and D broke to cause the M8.4 Ansei Tōkai earthquake in 1854, and less than two days later, segments A and B broke to cause the Ansei Nankai earthquake. In 1944, segment C broke, followed in 1946 by segments A and B. Segment D, the part that includes Suruga Bay, has not ruptured since 1854. In the typical (but possibly problematic) thinking of most seismologists and the public, Segment D is "overdue" for causing an earthquake. Moreover, if it ruptures, there is a chance that other segments or possibly the whole fault will rupture, increasing the likelihood of a catastrophic tsunami.[35]

As in the case of Parkfield, the earth often fails to cooperate with predictions and forecasts, and the earthquake that seemed imminent in 1977 has yet to occur as of this writing. At least one contrarian scientist claims that there is a good reason why this earthquake has not occurred.[36] For the most part, however, this thirty-five-year apparent delay has only added to fears that the earthquake may strike at any moment. Similarly, the large earthquakes that have shaken other parts of Japan since 1977 are reminders that the Tōkai earthquake is overdue, at least in the typical way we think about earthquakes. Moreover, prediction advocates can excuse the complete failure to predict any of Japan's other earthquakes owing to the relative lack of observational instruments in those areas because of the disproportionate focus on the region likely to be struck by a Tōkai earthquake.

Geller likens the constant threat of a Tōkai earthquake to the "magic mallet" (*uchide no kozuchi*) of Japanese folklore. When someone shakes the mallet, money flows from it. Geller's basic argument is that the continuous stoking of Tōkai earthquake fears preserves the budget and personnel needed for efforts to predict the event. Moreover, these efforts funnel considerable public money into the region likely to be shaken by such an earthquake, creating and perpetuating vested interests.[37] The other point of view, of course, is that the focus on a Tōkai earthquake is an appropriate channeling of resources. In any case, this focus is written into the law.

Similar to past examples, the earth itself served as a catalyst in producing the Special Measures Law. At a time of heightened anxiety about a Tōkai earthquake, the M7.0 Izu-Ōshima earthquake of January 14, 1978, occurred just outside the eastern edge of the Tōkai earthquake zone. Prime Minister Fukuda Takeo urged fast passage of the law, which sailed through the Diet in a mere two months, becoming law on June 7, 1978. The Special Measures Law is mainly concerned with the implementation of martial law, but it also states that the JMA will predict Tōkai earthquakes. Pursuant to the law, in 1979 the JMA created a committee whose sole purpose is to predict a Tōkai earthquake. It is commonly known as the Decision Committee (Hanteikai), an abbreviation of its long official name, the Jishin bōsai taisaku kansoku kyōka chiiki hantei kai. The Decision Committee evaluates volumetric strain gauge data with respect to four threat levels and the number of different locations of apparent crustal abnormalities.[38] Should it decide that a Tōkai earthquake will occur within three days, it can recommend that the JMA director ask the prime minister to invoke the emergency provisions in the Special Measures Law.[39]

These measures would apply to all of Shizuoka Prefecture and parts of Kanagawa, Yamanashi, Nagano, and Aichi Prefectures. The Tōkaidō Shinkansen trains would stop, the Tōmei Expressway would close, and the operation of buses and private automobile use in the zone would be prohibited. Banks, the post office, supermarkets, department stores, schools, offices—almost everything except hospitals—would close, and the self-defense forces would mobilize to evacuate the zone's residents. In short, the committee is expected to do something never done before, to predict a major earthquake, with no objective basis or formula to guide it. The economic consequences would be staggering in the event of a full invocation of the law, and if the earthquake did not occur on a particular day, lifting the emergency measures would be very difficult. Doing so would be an admission of error, and there would be the possibility of the predicted earthquake occurring soon after any all-clear declaration.[40] Given the dire consequences of a false alarm and the extreme difficulty of interpreting crustal movement data, it is hard to imagine that the law would ever be invoked.

If indeed a declaration of an imminent Tōkai earthquake is highly unlikely, is the Special Measures Law otherwise problematic? One adverse effect is that the law contributes to a distorted focus on the Tōkai region and on the pursuit of short-term earthquake prediction. Whether precise short-term prediction will ever be possible is arguable, but there is nearly unanimous agreement that it is currently impossible and will remain so in the foreseeable future.

The false premise of accurate short-term prediction built into the Special Measures Law imparts a schizophrenic quality to official statements. Consider the website of the JMA. The text under the subheading "Prediction of an Imminent Earthquake" reads:

> Prediction of an earthquake just before it occurs (at the longest, several days) is called imminent earthquake prediction (or short-term prediction).
>
> The present state of science should be regarded as still in the research stage of imminent earthquake prediction. One reason is that large earthquakes occur infrequently and the phenomena occurring prior to an earthquake at the focal area or nearby are not fully understood.
>
> Despite this situation, owing to reasons explained below, **a Tōkai earthquake is regarded as the only type of earthquake in present-day Japan for which there is a possibility of imminent prediction** (*however, even in the case of a Tōkai earthquake it is impossible to predict a specific day*).
>
> You might sometimes hear specific predictions like "A large earthquake will occur on X-month, X-day," but they either lack a scientific basis or they lack full scientific verification, so caution is necessary.[41]

The site goes on to explain the means by which it will predict the Tōkai earthquake (preslip), but the following subsection is entitled "Will we definitely succeed in predicting a Tōkai earthquake?" and the response begins, "Unfortunately, the answer is 'No.'"[42] So short-term earthquake prediction is impossible, except in the case of a Tōkai earthquake, but even then, it might not work.

Official pronouncements such as these are, on the one hand, typical examples of muddled bureaucratic language. On the other hand, the doublespeak required by the Special Measures Law creates confusion. Even in the second decade of the twenty-first century, many details of what occurs within the earth's crust prior to and during an earthquake remain unclear. To use a medical metaphor offered by Shimamura, today's seismology is like occasionally seeing symptoms without any idea of their causes. There are few examples of illness, each with apparently different symptoms. Establishing a perspective is difficult, and doing an autopsy is impossible.[43] Given the tendency of nonspecialists to overestimate the predictive abilities of seismology, it is desirable for government agencies and individual scientists unambiguously to stress that accurate short-term earthquake prediction is impossible for any earthquake anywhere. Owing to the law, however, researchers funded in full or in part by money designated for earthquake prediction must give lip service to the possibility of prediction, even if privately they acknowledge the futility of such a goal. In short, the Special Measures Law is a barrier to the dissemination of straightforward, accurate information on earthquakes.

The Special Measures Law also skews the distribution of resources, although the precise degree can be difficult to determine. At the time of the law's passage, earthquake prediction was consuming the majority of public funding for geophysics, and that entire budget was stagnating with respect to funding for outer space and nuclear energy projects. Maintaining and expanding the observational network was expensive, and the Special Measures Law, with its assumption of prediction and its mandate for close observation, was a boon to scientists and technicians working in this area. Thanks in large part to the law, therefore, the network in the Tōkai region has continued to expand. There has never been a serious debate about whether pouring funds into earthquake prediction is a wise allocation of resources. Moreover, the question of whether it is reasonable to concentrate equipment and facilities in one area of a country whose entire surface is subject to major earthquakes only rarely comes under consideration. After two hundred lives were lost in the 1993 Hokkaidō southwest offshore earthquake (M7.8), the press complained of deficiencies in the observation infrastructure. There was not even a single seismometer on the island of Okushiri, for example.[44]

There is at least one additional less obvious harm from the Special Measures Law. Shimamura points out that because funds spent on earthquake prediction almost all go toward expanding the observation network, earthquake prediction is not a field that attracts innovative young scientists. No Japanese universities offer courses on earthquake prediction, for example, and in 1999 when the journal *Nature* sponsored the debate forum "Is the Reliable Prediction of Individual Earthquakes a Realistic Scientific Goal?" no Japanese scientist participated despite that country spending more money on earthquake prediction than any other. As for the Tōkai area observational network, the dominant view is that it is not complete, and nobody has proposed any means of determining when it will be complete. The network consumes resources and grows with no end in sight.[45]

It might seem that the devastation of 3/11 would have raised such concerns, and to a small extent, it has. However, the dominant impact of 3/11 in this realm has been to raise Tōkai earthquake fears even higher. Not only is the Tōkai event "overdue" in terms of time, but it also seems next in line in terms of geography. Moreover, the widespread underestimation of the magnitude of 3/11 has prompted an upward estimate of tsunami wave size and likely damage estimates of a Tōkai earthquake. Consider, for example, the following lead paragraph from a *Daily Yomiuri* article reporting on recent expert forecasts:

> A tsunami of ten meters or higher could strike eleven prefectures, including Tokyo, and an earthquake with an intensity of 7—the highest level on the Japanese seismic scale—could devastate an area twenty times larger than previously predicted if the Nankai Trough triggers a triple quake simultaneously, according to a revised forecast by the Cabinet Office.[46]

In other words, 3/11 has intensified Tōkai earthquake fears.

Tectonic plates keep moving, and a megathrust earthquake originating somewhere along the Pacific Coast between Suruga Bay and approximately offshore from northern Kyūshū is inevitable. Such an earthquake is likely to be severe and to generate destructive tsunami waves. However, experts cannot say when it will occur. Preparing for this event is prudent, but the obsession with it since 1977 has produced serious opportunity costs that have largely evaded public discussion. Funding constantly to expand the observation network might have been better spent on basic research, emergency response infrastructure, antiseismic engineering, or perhaps an observational network more evenly distributed across the country. In the United States, the bureaucratic focus on the New Madrid seismic zone centered in southeastern Missouri bears some resemblance to the Tōkai earthquake situation in Japan, except that a future repeat of the 1811 and 1812 main shocks in that region is much less certain.[47]

THE IZU-ŌSHIMA (IZU PENINSULA) EARTHQUAKE AND PROBLEMS WITH PRECURSORS

The Earthquake Prediction Research Consultation Committee (Jishin yochi kenkyū kyōgi kai, now the Jishin, kazan funka yochi kenkyū kyōgi kai) of Tokyo University is a major beneficiary of earthquake prediction funding. In 1991, it issued a booklet with the misleading title *Earthquake Prediction Is Now (Jishin yochi wa ima)*. The booklet touts the familiar line of thinking that apprehending precursors is the key to short-term prediction, and it claimed 790 instances of precursors in Japan. Of these, 40 percent were small and medium earthquakes that in retrospect were regarded as foreshocks, 27 percent were other kinds of changes in earthquake activity, 14 percent were abnormal changes in the earth's crust, 8 percent were electromagnetic anomalies, 6 percent were about radon gas, temperature, and other changes in groundwater, and 5 percent were uplift or subsidence of the earth's crust. In other words, 67 percent of the cases were abnormal seismic activity. The remaining 33 percent were phenomena that typically exhibit natural variability.[48]

The prime piece of evidence discussed in the booklet was abnormal levels of radon gas in wells prior to the 1978 Izu-Ōshima earthquake. Not only did this earthquake serve as a catalyst for passage of the Special Measures Law, it also produced a large number of alleged precursors. Radon gas levels generated the most interest. When the International Union of Geodesy and Geophysics (IUGG) sponsored a contest in 1991 in which scientists from around the world presented cases of earthquake precursors evaluated by a panel of referees, twenty-eight of the thirty-one entries failed outright and three tentatively passed, based solely on the data submitted. Two were from Haicheng, and the other was the radon gas anomalies from Izu-Ōshima.[49] It turns out that the key to getting past the panel of referees and becoming the prime exhibit in the booklet was submitting a suitably narrow segment of data.

Looking at a graph of changes in radon levels over a half-year period, there is indeed an abnormality just before the 1978 earthquake. If we look at the data for measurements over the subsequent eight years, however, there are similar irregularities here and there, entirely independent of seismic activity. Moreover, when the 1980 Izu Peninsula Tōhō Offshore earthquake struck, no radon irregularities were detected. In other words, the alleged 1978 precursor was a random occurrence. Despite the presence of thirteen years of radon data, *Earthquake Prediction Is Now* selected only the six-month period that suited its claims.[50]

This situation points to several problems connected with retrospective reporting of precursors. So many phenomena vary randomly that it is quite possible to find something increasing, decreasing, or otherwise changing prior to an earthquake. This coincidence seems significant only because the earthquake occurred. It is largely for this reason that earthquake prediction advocates list a bewilderingly large and diverse array of supposed precursors. Moreover, when a particular item such as radon gas becomes well known, it attracts closer scientific scrutiny. This increased attention typically reveals the item unreliable as a precursor. Although it is possible that genuine precursors preceded some earthquakes, nobody has yet discovered a precursor or set of precursors that can reliably predict a destructive earthquake.

As proof that surely precursors must be real and at least some of them must be known, some might point to the extensive journalistic and popular writings (and even some scientific writings) that advance one or another item among literally thousands as a possible precursor. The ultimate test, however, is the use of a specific item repeatedly to predict serious earthquakes accurately with respect to the time, location, and strength of the event. Despite all the reported precursors out there, our ability to predict earthquakes today is only slightly better than that of the 1830 authors of *Thoughts on Earthquakes*.

POST KŌBE PIVOT

The January 17, 1995, M7.3 Kōbe earthquake is officially known in Japan as the Hyōgo-ken Nanbu earthquake and more commonly known there as the Hanshin-Awaji earthquake. This intraplate earthquake struck without warning, originating at a previously unknown fault system now known as the Rokkō-Awaji fault system. It caused 6,434 deaths and 43,792 injuries, and its economic cost amounted to over 10 percent of the national budget.[51] It was the first seismic event since the 1948 Fukui earthquake that caused fatalities in the thousands and the deadliest earthquake since 1923.[52] For the first time ever, people all over Japan watched the aftermath of a major deadly earthquake in their country on television.

One consequence of this earthquake was a revision of the JMA seismic intensity scale, resulting in the current scale of seven levels, with levels 5 and 6 subdivided into "strong" and "weak."[53] More significantly, it prompted a reorganization of the multiagency earthquake bureaucracy and the establishment of what was supposed to be a new, overall earthquake coordinating entity, the Headquarters for Earthquake Research Promotion (Jishin chōsa kenkyū suishin honbu). However, the Decision Committee (Hanteikai, 1979) of the JMA and the CCEP (Yochiren, 1969) continued to perform their previous functions. Now there are three major earthquake-related organizations within the government. Others deal with volcanoes or with disasters in general, especially the Central Council for Disaster Prevention (Chūō bōsai kaigi, 1959). Very few Japanese know the differences between these entities. Moreover, multiple agencies sometimes issue separate, divergent comments on events, as was the case with the Miyakejima eruption of 2000.[54]

Damage to structures was dramatic in the Kōbe earthquake, approximately thirteen times worse than in the 1948 Fukui earthquake. Following freeway collapses during the 1989 Loma Prieta and 1994 Northridge (Los Angeles) earthquakes, experts in Japan testified that no such collapse would occur there. Sure enough, the main freeway running through Kōbe collapsed.[55] During Japan's long period of relative postwar seismic calm, complacency had become a problem. Tsuneo Katayama, president of the National Research Institute for Earth Science and Disaster Prevention, commented on this phenomenon:

> For almost fifty years a seismically quiescent period had continued in Japan's urbanized areas, and this period was a golden time for the advancement in earthquake engineering research and technology in Japan. These two independent facts were misused to establish the safety myth, a myth that the time had come when Japanese structures would not collapse even [when] subjected to strong earthquakes.[56]

Repeatedly in Japan's past, periods of relative seismic calm have led to overconfidence that science and technology had managed to gain control of, or at least contain, the power of an unruly earth. Repeatedly, the earth has shattered such illusions.

Failures, however, do not tell the full story of the Kōbe earthquake. Seismic provisions in building codes underwent major revisions in 1971 and 1981, and damage patterns followed these changes precisely. Referring to Kōbe, journalist David McNeill points out, "I volunteered to help deliver water after that quake and walked around the city, noting how the shaking had left the newer, middle-class suburban housing projects almost untouched but had decimated older, poorer neighborhoods with their wooden frames and heavy tiled roofs."[57] In the central part of Kōbe, over 55 percent of structures built before 1970 collapsed or suffered irreparable damage. This figure drops to 30 percent for those built between 1971 and 1975, 10 percent for those built between 1976 and 1980, and none for those built after 1980.[58] A report issued by Risk Management Solutions points out: "Code changes in the early 1980s prohibited the use of non-ductile reinforced concrete structures in favor of ductile reinforced concrete structures. These newer structures provided greater flexibility, allowing structures to withstand the strong ground shaking levels experienced in Kobe."[59] In short, the Kōbe earthquake provided both positive and negative examples of the importance of antiseismic engineering using ductile (flexible) materials. The dramatic and effective swaying of tall buildings in Tokyo and elsewhere during 3/11 was in part a result of lessons learned or confirmed in 1995.

Optimism about earthquake prediction suffered a severe blow in 1995. Many of the government agencies dealing with earthquakes had "prediction" in their names. Although there was some actual reorganization of agencies in the wake of the Kōbe earthquake, the major change was in nomenclature. During the Tokugawa era, major earthquakes sometimes prompted a change of era names. In 1995, agencies scrambled to remove words like "prediction" and "precursor" from their names, replacing them with terms such as "investigation" (*chōsa*) or "research." Prediction became so unfashionable that it dropped out of some agencies charged with monitoring volcanic eruptions, even though prediction in this realm is possible under some circumstances.[60] Perhaps it was only coincidental, but in 1995 in the United States, the National Earthquake Prediction Council "quietly disappeared," although the USGS revived it ten years later.[61]

Incidentally, a similar rechristening and reshuffling process took place in the nuclear regulatory bureaucracy after 3/11:

> In September 2012, Japan's two discredited nuclear regulatory institutions, the Nuclear and Industrial Safety Agency (NISA) and the Nuclear Safety Commission (NSC) were disbanded and replaced by the Nuclear Regulatory Authority (NRA) with a staff of 480. But the NRA is

more a reorganization than a significant reform as 460 of its staff were transferred from NISA and the NSC.[62]

When things go wrong, reshuffling the same basic deck of cards seems to be a common approach to "reform," not only in Japan, of course, but also in other bureaucratic environments.

Vested interests in Japan's earthquake bureaucracy sought an alternative to "prediction" that would facilitate continuation of the project of expanding the observational network concentrated in the anticipated Tōkai earthquake zone. Rhetorically, the solution was to abandon "prediction" (*yochi*) and pursue "forecasting" (*yosoku*) instead. Forecasting manifests itself in the issuing of probabilistic seismic hazard maps, and we have seen that the details of these maps depend on the assumptions of the mapmakers. Moreover, Geller and others have pointed out that when recent deadly earthquakes, including 3/11, are placed on the government's 2010 map, they all occurred in seemingly safe areas. Similarly, Shimamura sees little practical difference between prediction and forecasting. For example, a common estimate such as a 0.9 percent to 9 percent chance of a fault's rupture in thirty years is of little or no practical value, even if accurate. In any case, the public budget for earthquake research more than doubled in 1995. Although it dropped in 1996, it remained higher than pre-1995 levels thereafter.[63]

The failure to predict the Kōbe earthquake also contributed to a partial revision of the Special Measures Law in 2003 and a pragmatic realization that a Tōkai earthquake might well occur without warning.[64] At the time of 3/11, all of Japan was covered by GPS observation devices. Although the northeast coast was not as closely monitored as the projected Tōkai earthquake region, it was nevertheless well covered by a network of instruments. Although 3/11 was a subduction zone earthquake like the anticipated Tōkai earthquake, data from just before the main shock reveal no precursors with respect to crustal movement or anything else.[65] Like Kōbe in 1995 and all other recent destructive earthquakes, 3/11 was an example of Hough's conclusion, "We cannot say it will always be the case, but given the state of earthquake science at the present time, earthquakes are unpredictable."[66] An equally if not more important lesson from Kōbe and 3/11 is that antiseismic engineering can be an effective way of preserving life and property. In the next chapter, I pull together the major points from our study of earthquakes in Japan, offer some concluding remarks, and look to the future.

NOTES

1. Musha Kinkichi, *Jishin namazu* (1957; Meiseki shoten, 1995), 150.

2. "Daikibo jishin taisaku tokubetsu sochi hō," accessed September 24, 2012, http://law.e-gov.go.jp/htmldata/S53/S53HO073.html.

3. Quoted in Tsuneji Rikitake, *Earthquake Prediction* (New York: Elsevier Scientific, 1976). See also Robert Geller (Robaato Geraa), *Nihonjin wa shiranai "Jishin yochi" no shōtai* (Futabasha, 2011), 87; and Hagiwara Takahiro, *Jishingaku hyakunen* (Tōkyō daigaku shuppankai, 1982), 177–79. According to Hagiwara, the blueprint also influenced seismological research in China and the United States.

4. Geller, *Jishin yochi*, 85–86.

5. Shimamura Hideki, *Nihonjin ga shiritai jishin no gimon rokujūroku: Jishin ga ōi Nihon dakara koso chishiki no sonae mo wasurezu ni* (Soft Bank Creative, 2008), 70; Shimamura Hideki, *"Jishin yochi" wa uso darake* (Kōdansha, 2008), 97–98; Rikitake, *Earthquake Prediction*, 35; and Hagiwara, *Jishingaku hyakunen*, 179–85.

6. Hagiwara, *Jishingaku hyakunen*, 184–93.

7. Shimamura, *Jishin yochi*, 122.

8. Shimamura, *Jishin yochi*, 113.

9. Rikitake, *Earthquake Prediction*, 36.

10. The article appeared in the August 31, 1994, evening edition of the *Sankei shinbun*. It is quoted in Geller, *Jishin yochi*, 90–91. See also Shimamura, *Jishin yochi*, 103–6, for a detailed discussion of this matter.

11. See Rikitake, *Earthquake Prediction*, 36–37, for the original map and an explanation of it. For the 1988 map and explanation, see Shimamura Hideki, "Jishin yochi no kanōsei, genjitsusei," in *Jishin yochi to shakai*, ed. Kaminuma Katsutada and Hirata Kōji (Kokon shoin, 2003), 68–69.

12. In Japanese, these maps are known as "probabilistic earthquake motion calculation maps" (*kakuritsuronteki jishindō yosoku chizu*). For a critique of these maps, see Geller, *Jishin yochi*, 159–64; and Shimamura, *Jishin yochi*, 314–16. Stein, Geller, and Liu argue that these maps are often inaccurate in that they underpredict or overpredict actual seismic hazards. In many cases, the maps are products of overly simplified or inaccurate models of earthquake occurrence and a dearth of accurate historical data. One problematic assumption brought into sharp relief by 3/11 was the idea that M9-class earthquakes could occur only where young lithosphere was rapidly subducting. Moreover, only since about 1950 have the instruments existed to record M9-class earthquakes. These problems result in poorly constrained parameters. The product is hazard maps that reflect the preconceptions of the mapmakers. See Seth Stein, Robert J. Geller, and Mian Liu, "Why Earthquake Hazard Maps Often Fail and What to Do about It," *Tectonophysics* 562–63 (2012): 1–25.

13. Asada Toshi in *Nyūton*, September 9, 1992, quoted in Geller, *Jishin yochi*, 99.

14. Susan Hough, *Predicting the Unpredictable: The Tumultuous Science of Earthquake Prediction* (Princeton, NJ: Princeton University Press, 2011), 69.

15. Hough, *Predicting the Unpredictable*, 62–65.

16. Hough, *Predicting the Unpredictable*, 65–68. Rikitake, writing closer in time to these events and generally more sanguine about earthquake prediction, says, "There was little doubt about the importance of the Soviet finding to earthquake prediction," and provides details of numerous instances in which decreases in Vp/Vs ratios alleg-

edly preceded earthquakes, typically hundreds or even thousands of days in advance. See Rikitake, *Earthquake Prediction*, 189–96.

17. For a study of citizen earthquake observers in several countries of the Western world, see Deborah R. Coen, *The Earthquake Observers: Disaster Science from Lisbon to Richter* (Chicago: University of Chicago Press), 2013.

18. R. D. Adams, "The Haicheng, China, Earthquake of 4 February 1975: The First Successfully Predicted Major Earthquake," *Earthquake Engineering and Structural Dynamics* 4 (1976): 437. See also Hough, *Predicting the Unpredictable*, 69–85 (70–71 re Adams).

19. Haicheng Earthquake Study Delegation, "Prediction of the Haicheng Earthquake," *Eos* 58 (1977): 269.

20. Kiyoo Mogi, "Comparison of Precursory Phenomena before the 1975 Haicheng (China) Earthquake and the 1978 Izu-Oshima-kinkai (Japan) Earthquake: The Possible Effect of Stress History on Precursory Phenomena," *Tectonophysics* 138 (1987): 33.

21. Kimura Masaaki, *Daijishin no zenchō o toreata! Keikai subeki chiiki wa dokoka* (Daisan bunmeisha, 2008), 223–29.

22. Motoji Ikeya, *Earthquakes and Animals: From Folk Legends to Science* (River Edge, NJ: World Scientific, 2004), 229, 231.

23. Hagiwara, *Jishingaku hyakunen*, 208.

24. Ian O. Huebsch, "Comment," *Eos* 59 (1978): 2.

25. Kelin Wang et al., "Predicting the 1975 Haicheng Earthquake," *Bulletin of the Seismological Society of America* 96, no. 3 (June 2006): 757–95; and Hough, *Predicting the Unpredictable*, 69–85.

26. Hough, *Predicting the Unpredictable*, 82.

27. Hough, *Predicting the Unpredictable*. See chapter 9, "Hangover," 108–24. Similarly, Shimamura describes the 1970s (and, to some extent, the 1980s) in Japan as a "rose-colored" era that faded. See, for example, *Jishin yochi*, 65. Geller likens the situation in Japan during the 1970s to a narcotics (*mayaku*) addict increasing the dose. See *Jishin yochi*, 92.

28. Hough, *Predicting the Unpredictable*, 50–54. Regarding the cockroaches, see Ikeya, *Earthquakes and Animals*, 230. Seth Stein points out that the twenty million dollar cost of the experiment caused some to call it "Porkfield." Moreover, when the USGS formally abandoned prediction efforts, "Some joked that the USGS motto 'science for a changing world' was now 'science for a change.'" See Seth Stein, *Disaster Deferred: How Science Is Changing Our View of Earthquake Hazards in the Midwest* (New York: Columbia University Press, 2010), 37–38.

29. Hough, *Predicting the Unpredictable*, 54.

30. Geller, *Jishin yochi*, 100–101, 123–32, 169.

31. Geller, *Jishin yochi*, 123.

32. Shimamura, *Jishin yochi*, 123–24.

33. Ishibashi Katsuhiko, "Tōkai chihō no yosōsareru daishinsai no saikentō: Suruga-wan jishin no kanōsei" ("Re-Examination of a Great Earthquake Expected in the Tokai District, Central Japan—Possibility of the 'Suruga Bay Earthquake'"), Jishin yochi renraku kai report 17 (1977), 127–28, http://cais.gsi.go.jp/YOCHIREN/report/kaihou17/04_13.pdf.

34. For discussion of these events, see Geller, *Jishin yochi*, 92–98; and Shimamura, *Jishin yochi*, 107–12.

35. For the geophysical details, see Stein, Geller, and Liu, "Hazard Maps," esp. figure 1 (p. 3) and figure 3(e) (p. 5).

36. Kimura Masaaki claims to have developed an effective prediction method based largely on the clustering of preshocks into a discernible "seismic eye," located within a telltale doughnutlike pattern. He claims that a Tōkai earthquake in the near future is unlikely because there is no discernible seismic eye in any of the hypothesized fault planes. See *Dijishin no zenchō*, esp. the chapter "Tōkai jishin wa naze konai" ("Why Hasn't the Tōkai Earthquake Occurred?"), 162–92.

37. Geller, *Jishin yochi*, 98.

38. See Mizoue Megumi, "Jishin yochi to shakai," in *Jishin yochi to shakai*, ed. Kaminuma Katsutada and Hirata Kōji (Kokon shoin, 2003), 38–40, for a detailed description of the levels and the number of different locations. Despite the appearance of quantification, these levels do not provide precise numerical guidelines, nor is it always easy to determine how many different locations are in an anomalous state. It ultimately comes down to interpretation by the members of the committee—their "gut feeling" (*kan*), according to Shimamura (*Jishin yochi*, 194–95).

39. Geller, *Jishin yochi*, 105–6, 150–51.

40. For a thorough discussion of these matters, including estimates of the economic cost and problems with volumetric strain gauges, see Shimamura, *Jishin yochi*, 87, 194–212.

41. Japan Meteorological Agency (JMA) website, page "Jishin yochi ni tsuite," heading "Jishin yochi to wa," subheading "Jishin no chokuzen yochi nit suite," accessed October 5, 2012, http://www.seisvol.kishou.go.jp/eq/tokai/tokai_eq4.html. Emphasis here follows the original, with the italicized text appearing as bold red type on the website.

42. Japan Meteorological Agency (JMA) website, page "Jishin yochi ni tsuite," heading "Jishin yochi to wa," subheadings "Zenchō-suberi (puresurippu) to wa" and "Tōkai jishin wa kanarazu yochi dekiru no ka?" accessed October 5, 2012, http://www.seisvol.kishou.go.jp/eq/tokai/tokai_eq4.html.

43. Shimamura, *Jishin yochi*, 119–20. See also Geller, *Jishin yochi*, 151–53, for a critique of the overly simplistic medical metaphor advanced by some prediction advocates.

44. Geller, *Jishin yochi*, 76–77. For a broader analysis of these issues, see Shimamura, *Jishin yochi*, 110–15.

45. Shimamura, *Jishin yochi*, 79–84, 116–18, 121–24, 129–30. For the 1999 *Nature* forum, "Is the Reliable Prediction of Individual Earthquakes a Realistic Scientific Goal?" see *Nature Debates*, http://www.nature.com/nature/debates/earthquake/equake_frameset.html. Staunch critic of earthquake prediction Robert Geller was the sole participant based in Japan.

46. "Massive Tsunami Projected/Panel Forecasts Nankai Trough Quakes Could Affect 11 Prefectures," *Daily Yomiuri Online*, April 2, 2012.

47. In *Disaster Deferred*, Stein argues that GPS data indicate that the faults in the New Madrid fault zone appear to be shutting down and that there is no imminent threat of an earthquake. The USGS, on the other hand, maintains that GPS data might not be indicative of what is occurring at focal depth. This same point is a reason for doubting the effectiveness of measuring preslip in the Japanese context, although geology of the two zones is quite different. For the USGS statement on New Madrid, see "Earthquake Hazard in the New Madrid Seismic Zone Remains a Concern," USGS Fact Sheet 2009-3071, http://pubs.usgs.gov/fs/2009/3071/.

48. Shimamura, *Jishin yochi*, 45–51.

49. Shimamura, *Jishin yochi*, 46–47, 77–79.

50. Geller, *Jishin yochi*, 100.

51. Shutō Nobuo and Koshimura Shun'ichi, "Meiji Sanriku jishin tsunami ni yoru higai," in *1896 Meiji Sanriku jishin tsunami hōkokusho*, ed. Chūō bōsai kaigi (2005), 44–45.

52. The 1944 Tōnankai earthquake caused 1,223 deaths, the 1945 Mikawa earthquake killed 2,306, the 1946 Nankaidō earthquake killed 1,362, and fatalities resulting from the 1948 Fukui earthquake were 3,769. Earthquakes near Hokkaidō killed 202 in 1993 and 437 in 1994.

53. For details of this revision and for past iterations of the scale, see Shimamura, *Jishin no gimon*, 56–58. The scale changed in 1898 owing to the Nōbi and Meiji Sanriku earthquakes, in 1936 owing to the Shōwa Sanriku earthquake, and in 1949 owing to the Fukui earthquake.

54. Shimamura, *Jishin yochi*, 98–101.

55. Shimamura, *Jishin yochi*, 134–36.

56. Quoted in Amos Nur with Dawn Burgess, *Apocalypse: Earthquakes, Archaeology, and the Wrath of God* (Princeton, NJ: Princeton University Press, 2008), 271.

57. Lucy Birmingham and David McNeill, *Strong in the Rain: Surviving Japan's Earthquake, Tsunami, and Fukushima Nuclear Disaster* (New York: Palgrave Macmillan, 2012), xiv.

58. Riley M. Chung. *The January 17, 1995, Hyogoken Nanbu (Kobe) Earthquake: Performance of Structures, Lifelines, and Fire Protection Systems*, NIST Special Report 901 (Gaithersburg, MD, 1996), 87, accessed October 6, 2012, http://www.fire.nist.gov/bfrlpubs/build96/PDF/b96002.pdf.

59. "1995 Kobe Earthquake 10-Year Retrospective" (Risk Assessment Models paper, Risk Management Solutions, January 2005), 11, accessed October 6, 2012, http://www.rms.com/publications/KobeRetro.pdf.

60. Shimamura, *Jishin yochi*, 141–46; and Geller, *Jishin yochi*, 156–59.

61. Hough, *Predicting the Unpredictable*, 124.

62. Jeff Kingston, "Power Politics: Japan's Resilient Nuclear Village," *Asia-Pacific Journal* 10, issue 43, no. 1 (October 29, 2012), accessed October 30, 2012. http://japanfocus.org/-Jeff-Kingston/3847.

63. Stein, Geller, and Liu, "Hazard Maps"; Shimamura, *Jishin yochi*, 144–46, 159–69; and Geller, *Jishin yochi*, 156–72.

64. For details, see Shimamura, *Jishin yochi*, 175–222.

65. Geller, *Jishin yochi*, 169.

66. Hough, *Predicting the Unpredictable*, 222.

SIX

Conclusions

Much like generals fighting the previous war, societies tend to prepare for the previous natural disaster. For example, 3/11 has already influenced perceptions of the future Tōkai earthquake, the one originally scheduled to arrive at any moment in the late 1970s. In the preceding chapters, we have encountered a variety of earthquake disasters, each with unique histories. Here I revisit the arguments that I stated in skeletal form in the introduction, fleshing them out with specific cases. I then conclude by examining several problems, successes, and possible future changes suggested by this study. Although focused on Japan, many of these issues are applicable to other societies.

NATURE OF EARTHQUAKES AS NATURAL DISASTERS

We have seen repeated attempts to, in essence, regularize earthquakes by creating organizational frameworks into which people think they fit (or wish they would). The behavior of the earth, however, frequently makes a mockery of these frameworks, sometimes with tragic results. Whether at the level of folk wisdom or scientific knowledge, we assign recurrence intervals and other temporal characteristics to earthquakes. The feared Tōkai earthquake is far overdue, both in the scientific and popular minds. It could happen tomorrow—or not for decades. The earth moves on its own schedule. Notice that not a single earthquake we have examined, even Haicheng in China, was successfully predicted. Geological time and

159

human time do not match up well, and there seems little point in trying to assign temporal characteristics to major earthquakes.

If I were to "predict" that within fifty years, Japan would suffer a serious earthquake, I would probably be right. Such a prediction, however, would be meaningless in practical terms. Imamura Akitsune claimed credit for, and often is credited with, "prediction" of the Great Kantō Earthquake, but it hardly matters that the event fell within the broad period Imamura specified. The important aspect of Imamura's disaster prediction was his fearless message that Tokyo was unprepared to deal with an earthquake. The condition of the city (crowded, narrow roads, lack of water mains, abundant flammable materials, etc.) made it ripe for a catastrophe when, inevitably, a major earthquake would occur. Such an argument was not earthquake prediction in the sense that most people use the term but a sensible assessment of risk. Imamura was willing to face inconvenient facts and sought to stir up healthy concern. Ōmori, by contrast, seems to have dreaded social alarm more than seismic risk. The events of 1923 worked to shine a heroic spotlight on Imamura, but the matter is not simple. Consider more recent cases.

Ishibashi Katsuhiko sounded the alarm regarding a Tōkai earthquake in the 1970s. To be fair, the press and politicians amplified Ishibashi and participated in a sense of panic—precisely the sort of situation Ōmori earlier sought to avoid. Moreover, this process led to what is arguably a problematic law and skewed resource allocation. That the earthquake did not happen (though it surely will) is simply an indication that we do not possess the means to ascertain the earth's timetable. In connection with his concern about a Tōkai earthquake, Ishibashi also warned of the dangers of seismicity and nuclear power. On that point, even his critics applaud his foresight.[1] Consider, too, the willful and repeated ignoring of warnings by TEPCO officials regarding the possibility of an M9-class earthquake and tsunami. Notice again the important distinction that I pointed out first with respect to Imamura. Ishibashi's warning of the Tōkai earthquake was problematic because he, in essence, tried to predict its timing. His warning about nuclear power plants was like Imamura's warning about narrow streets and gas lanterns in Tokyo, a sensible assessment of seismic risks—warnings few heeded until it was too late. From these points, we can see that there is little or no benefit in trying to time earthquakes. Predicating how earthquake disasters will play out in society is possible, but only to a limited extent. The key to beneficial social prediction seems to be identifying major vulnerabilities. It is in this realm that past earthquakes can be especially valuable: as examples of disastrous vulnerabilities, both structural and behavioral.

The various earthquakes we examined caused a range of social effects. Looting and profiteering, for example, was a problem in some places in 1896 and, to a smaller degree, in 1933. Social behavior was generally exemplary in the hardest hit areas of Edo in 1855 and the Tōhoku region after 3/11. However, it was murderous in 1923 Tokyo. The food shortages (and hoarding) in places like Tokyo after 3/11 and the general sense of panic regarding nuclear contamination suggest a variety of possible and potentially severe vulnerabilities should an event with destructiveness similar to 3/11 strike a densely populated area. In 1855, the relevant agencies of the *bakufu*, acting as a de facto local government, responded very effectively in providing relief. In 1891, the central government moved quickly to initiate and fund the relief and recovery project. The central government was much less helpful in 1896, and in 1995 (Kōbe) it was especially inept.[2]

Although earthquakes are unpredictable, unique phenomena whose timing and social trajectory is unknowable, the record of past earthquakes provides a valuable guide to the range of potential natural hazards and at least some possibilities about how those hazards might interact with society. M9 subduction zone earthquakes are possible, tsunami wave heights of about thirty-eight meters in some areas are possible, M7-class or stronger earthquakes can shake Tokyo or almost any city in Japan, and no part of Japan is seismically safe. This seismic danger has been an impetus for improvement in both building design and other potential vulnerabilities. Indeed, many of the obvious infrastructure vulnerabilities evident in past disasters have been remedied to various degrees. The successes of 3/11, discussed below, provide several good examples.

Some generalizations are applicable regarding the potential for natural disasters to produce fundamental social or political change. J. Charles Schencking points out that in the opinions of some, "disasters possess the potential to change everything." Moreover, with respect to 3/11 and the view that it would transform Japan:

> Some argued that rising to the challenge of recovery would instill citizens with a newfound confidence and make people once again proud to be Japanese. Many predicted that reconstruction spending would

> provide the economic stimulus necessary to end two lost decades of
> deflation. Still others posited notions that the Japanese people might
> lose their faith in science and demand a reorientation of the nation's
> economy, or that humanitarian aid from China might help resolve
> long-standing disputes between both countries. Will these transforma-
> tions ever materialize or will contestation and resistance limit policy
> outcomes? History suggests the latter.[3]

This study strongly affirms Schencking's conclusion.

Natural disasters in general and earthquakes in particular lack the power to change society in any fundamental way. Although the economic damage can appear tremendous at the time, in the large picture, major disasters often have approximately the same economic impact as business cycle recessions—significant but not a stimulus for major change. Susan Elizabeth Hough and Roger G. Bilham have analyzed GNP data for Japan between 1880 and 1964. Both the Great Kantō Earthquake and the Great Depression "caused short-lived dips in the GNP figures, yet both dips were indeed only blips: no bigger than the usual sorts of fluctuations seen in the curve." By contrast, the Pacific War caused a much sharper and more pronounced decline in Japan's GNP.[4] War may have the power to change a society fundamentally, but modern earthquakes apparently do not. None of the major modern earthquakes that we have examined resulted in fundamental change, despite optimistic rhetoric to the contrary. As for early modern earthquakes, Ansei Edo was somewhat unusual in that the common people of Edo tended to interpret it as an instance of "world renewal" (*yonaoshi*). What they usually meant by this term, however, was a brief period of windfall profits for laborers. As a rule, early modern earthquakes produced rhetoric of reassurance but not rhetoric or expectation of change.

Given the nature of earthquake disasters, how should we prepare for them? We should assume that major earthquakes will happen but that their occurrence cannot be timed. Judicious use of the historical record for guidance in a realistic assessment of major risk factors and contingency plans that are viable and permit a flexible response seems the prudent course for ensuring that the term "*sōteigai*" (unimaginable) will not figure prominently in future disasters. This study also affirms the conclusions of Richard J. Samuels in his analysis of 3/11 that the key to effective disaster response lies in effective local governments in cooperation with one another, nongovernmental organizations (NGOs), and the central government.[5] Local governments were always on the front lines of disaster relief in the early modern era, and they often performed very well. In the major modern earthquakes we have examined, local governments provided relief and leadership, and local newspapers played key roles in communications and mobilizing citizens for voluntary contributions. In the digital age, of course, other forms of communication are likely to play roles analogous to that of the newspapers of former times. The most important central government entity was the military, which was in a position to move large quantities of material aid quickly and in 1923 was also instrumental in restoring social order. The military also played a key role in the aftermath of 3/11 and will surely be an essential component of recovery from future disasters.

SCIENCE AND TECHNOLOGY

The history of earthquakes is inextricably connected with the history of attempts to understand and explain these events. In medieval times around the world, such attempts were mainly in the realm of religion. Beginning in the early modern era, nonreligious theories of earthquake mechanics began to develop. At what point academic knowledge about earthquakes can be called "seismology" is debatable and not particularly important for our purposes. The formal origins of seismology in Japan go back to the early Meiji period, but academic and popular literature on earthquakes extends back much further. Although not uniquely a Japanese phenomenon, seismology in that country was inevitably grounded in older ideas.

Much of the early modern lore about earthquakes, and especially about earthquake precursors, made sense in the intellectual context of its day. There was a strong consensus in the early modern era that earthquakes were explosive phenomena caused by the accumulation of yang energy, mainly from wind and the rays of the sun, within the earth. We have seen that by the end of the early modern era, observers of earthquakes routinely reported almost exactly the same precursory phenomena, as if they were reading from a common script. Throughout the Meiji period, the fundamental framework for understanding earthquakes gradually changed, but much early modern lore carried over into the modern era, in part because the actual mechanisms of earthquakes were so poorly understood.

All of the major modern earthquakes in Japan helped advance science and technology to varying degrees. The Nōbi earthquake highlighted the prominence of faults, although it would take seven more decades before it became clear that faulting causes earthquakes, not vice versa. The peculiar 1896 Meiji Sanriku earthquake and tsunami prompted a sustained scientific debate about the causes of tsunamis, including five different theories (electricity, wind/atmospheric conditions, undersea volcano, seafloor uplift, and liquid pendulum). Imamura even proposed the idea of slow earthquakes, which Hiroo Kanamori further developed in the 1970s. In this realm as well, verification occurred several decades later. Antiseismic engineering was part of the original Anglo-Japanese seismology project in the early Meiji period. The Great Kantō Earthquake helped advance antiseismic engineering, especially the use of ferroconcrete. The use of ductile materials in buildings in the 1980s was a major advance in this realm, and the Kōbe earthquake dramatically highlighted the potential effectiveness of antiseismic construction. Some sixteen years later, 3/11 dramatically demonstrated the effectiveness of seismic isolation (or base isolation) in buildings as well as safety features such as automatic shutoff systems in trains. In postwar Japan, a peculiar combination of seismicity, politics, hubris, and unrealistic public expectations resulted in Japan leading the world in funding for earthquake prediction research, a program that has not demonstrated useful results whether in the guise of short-term prediction or longer-term forecasting.

APPROACHES TO SEISMIC HAZARDS

One psychological barrier to dealing effectively with seismic hazards is the tendency to seek order, regularity, or recurring characteristics in seismic events. Owing to the relative rarity of major earthquakes in a local area, the most recent past major earthquake often serves as a de facto model of earthquake characteristics. Another potential barrier is the flow of money. Postwar Japan's earthquake research, with its focus on data collection in the hope of finding a useful precursor, creates vested interests that resist change. These interests adroitly jumped from the "prediction" to the "forecasting" bandwagon after 1995 but carried on largely as they had before. After 3/11, we have seen Japan's so-called nuclear village attempt a similar feat. Approaching the matter historically, the project of earthquake prediction or forecasting seems unlikely to yield useful results. The search for a reliable precursor has been going on since 1828 or earlier, thus far without practical success.

In the remainder of this chapter, I expand on some of the insights that a history of earthquakes provides with respect to approaches to seismic hazards and resource allocation. My approach is to bring together material already discussed and add relevant new material to shed light on a series of problems and successes. Finally, I look to the future, both in Japan and in North America, which faces a seismic hazard similar to that of 3/11.

MISTAKEN CORRELATIONS

The trial of the Italian scientists mentioned in the introduction ended in a guilty verdict. The press in Japan and elsewhere characterized the offense as failure in earthquake prediction (*jishin yochi shippai*). In a newspaper interview, Abe Katsuyuki, chair of the Decision Committee, which is charged with predicting a Tōkai earthquake, expressed shock at the verdict. He pointed out that although predicting a Tōkai earthquake is possible, doing so for any other earthquake is "difficult" (*muzukashii*), which in Japanese essentially means impossible. However, "in principle it is not the case that earthquake prediction is proven to be impossible," he pointed out, adding, "I think it is a worthy challenge for research."[6] Abe's statements echo the bizarre government line that all earthquakes are impossible to predict at present except Tōkai earthquakes. What the article never mentions is that the reason for this peculiar position is the Special Measures Law.

As we have seen, earthquake prediction in Japan has always been based on the search for a reliable precursor. Let us return to the "catfish school," briefly discussed in chapter 3, to highlight the most common problems with this approach. Musha Kinkichi and others claim that prior to the 1856, 1896, and 1933 earthquakes and tsunamis, fishermen along the Sanriku coast pulled in vast quantities of sardines just before the earthquakes struck. Moreover, in the aftermath of the tsunamis, they caught unusually large quantities of squid. Conversely, in 1896 prior to the tsunami, fishermen could catch no cod or sharks, and in 1933, sea cucumbers became almost impossible to find just before the earthquake and tsunami. Musha regarded these reported observations as likely earthquake precursors, and the possibility of large squid catches as a precursor appeared in the mass media in the wake of 3/11.[7] Suppose that these reported excesses or dearth of sea life were real, as opposed to people thinking they saw what they expected to see. If sardines, for example, really increased in the days, weeks, or months before the tsunami, surely the sardines must have been reacting to something? Perhaps, but they were not necessarily reacting to something seismic. Do large sardine catches only precede earthquakes and never occur in years with no earthquakes?

Fluctuations in fish populations in Japan's northern waters occur naturally because of shifts in water temperature. These temperature shifts are the result of currents and other conditions.[8] Herein lies the basic problem with so many apparent earthquake precursors. They vary randomly or in relation to factors other than seismicity. The fact of the earthquake's occurrence makes an observed increase, decrease, or other change seem significant in hindsight. Such associations are the root of superstitious beliefs, and it seems that the human mind has evolved to overassociate in this way.

Shimamura Hideki, drawing on the work of psychologist Kikuchi Satoru, highlights the problem of "mistaken correlation" (*sakugo sōkan*). For many with preconceived notions about the nature of certain events, the occurrence of that event suddenly makes ordinary, mundane phenomena seem significant in hindsight. In extreme cases, people can manufacture earthquake "precursors" in the wake of confusing events vaguely remembered.[9] More broadly, according to psychologist Thomas Gilovich:

> We humans seem to be extremely good at generating ideas, theories, and explanations that have the ring of plausibility. We may be relatively deficient, however, in evaluating and testing our ideas once they are formed. One of our biggest impediments to doing so is in our failure to realize that when we do not precisely specify the kind of evidence that will count in support for our position, we can end up "detecting" too much evidence for our preconceptions.[10]

The history of the quest for earthquake precursors abounds with this kind of excess evidence.

One need only page through the books on earthquake precursors produced over the years to be overwhelmed by the quantity of supposed evidence. According to Motoji Ikeya, for example, before the Kōbe earthquake, dogs, cats, sea lions, hippopotami, squirrels, rats, hamsters, rabbits, crows, cocks, eggs (double yolks), seagulls, sparrows, pigeons, parrots, pheasants, peacocks, parakeets, four kinds of reptiles, and over six varieties of marine life were reported (source unspecified) to have behaved strangely. The pre-earthquake vibes, ambiances, ether—or whatever—allegedly even rubbed off on humans. For example, "a local professor noted in his diary a day before the quake that he felt uncommonly irritable that day."[11] The list of anecdotal precursor candidates goes on for dozens of pages. Just as Gilovich explains, such lists of precursor candidates are useless owing to the open-ended nature of the "investigation" and the bewildering array of unconstrained "evidence."

In summarizing the scientific data on catfish, Rikitake Tsuneji wrote circa 1995 that the idea of fish as earthquake predictors is "not absurd" and should be considered in future research on earthquake prediction.[12] At the time that taxpayer-funded catfish research was shut down in 1993, Rikitake said, "In ancient times and the present, east and west, people have reported such things as dogs barking before earthquakes. Even if only one in a hundred such reports are accurate, we should pursue them."[13] Should this pursuit go on indefinitely? "Earthquake prediction is a seductive mirage—forever beckoning but always out of reach," says Andrew Robinson.[14] After nearly two centuries of failure, perhaps it is time for the scientific community and government agencies to say loudly, clearly, and frequently to the public that major earthquakes can occur anywhere in the Japanese islands and nobody can predict any of them.

CHARACTERISTIC PARADIGMS

Dynamic systems are all around us. Examples include bathtubs, a swinging clock pendulum, a pot of boiling water, or outbreaks of epidemic disease. Mathematical rules can precisely describe the flow and possible accumulation of water into a bathtub via the faucet and drain. Pendulum motion varies predictably as a function of time and space. Heat applied to a pot of water will produce steam in a well-defined process according to the flow of energy as the water absorbs it. Even the changes within many biological systems, such as the spread of epidemic diseases, can be described according to fixed rules.

Earthquakes are different. Although in an obvious sense they are dynamic systems through which energy flows, they are also chaotic. Chaotic systems "can exhibit elaborately complex, indeed unpredictable, behavior" even if governed by mathematically simple equations.[15] Chaotic behavior is the main reason that neither the onset of an earthquake nor the effects of its release of energy can be known in advance. As Ian Main pointed out in introducing the 1999 *Nature* debate on earthquake prediction, "Even simple nonlinear systems can exhibit 'chaotic' behavior, whereas more 'complex' nonlinear systems, with lots of interacting elements, can produce remarkable statistical stability while retaining an inherently random (if not completely chaotic) component."[16] Weather is a classic example of a chaotic system, but compared with meteorologists, seismologists know much less about the interacting variables associated with earthquakes. Moreover, most atmospheric phenomena occur more frequently than large earthquakes, and it is often possible to measure them directly. It is mainly for these reasons that specific short-term earthquake prediction is impossible and even long-term forecasting has proved to be problematic.

People tend to dislike chaos, and this aversion has helped produce a vast, useful body of scientific knowledge, among other things. Antipathy to chaos, however, can be problematic. The assumption that earthquakes—not necessarily all earthquakes, but certain subsets of them—exhibit characteristic behavior has been deeply ingrained in seismology since its inception in approximately the eighteenth century. Conceptions of characteristic earthquakes dominate scientific circles today, typically in notions of seismic cycles or seismic gaps. Pioneering seismologists such as John Milne assumed that there must be regular laws or patterns to which earthquakes conform. He and his Japanese associates put great emphasis on compiling catalogues of past earthquakes as raw data and subjecting those data to statistical analysis to try to find correlations. In a chapter entitled "Seismic Frequency and Periodicity," Milne examined possibilities of earthquakes correlating with tides, phases of the moon, seasons, barometric pressure gradients, and other measurable phenomena.[17] He was, in effect, on a fishing expedition, looking for the orderliness he knew must be there.

Another manifestation of this basic idea was a tendency to imagine that earthquakes operate according to anniversaries or human time cycles. Consider, for example, an article that appeared in the daily newspaper *Yomiuri shinbun* in 1915. The first part dismisses the idea of earthquake weather as "mere superstition." Next, citing a recent presentation by Imamura Akitsune, the article mentions the popular notion that earthquakes occur in sixty-year cycles, based on the old zodiac cycle. The topic was timely because 1915 was the sixty-year anniversary of the Ansei Edo earthquake. The article reports that Imamura confirmed that there was some basis to this idea, but he did so by means of a statistical analysis of past data. Moreover, volcanic eruptions also tend to follow a sixty-year cycle. Reminiscent of the old idea of trapped yang energy beneath the earth, the article explains that major volcanic activity keeps earthquakes mild and vice versa. Because the relative prominence of each type of geological activity alternates, producing something more like a 120-year cycle, any earthquakes occurring around 1915 should be mild, the piece concluded.[18] Knowing Imamura's views, it seems odd that he would forecast mild seismicity for Tokyo, but the key point here is the appeal of the belief that earthquakes occur with statistical regularity. Imamura often endorsed this idea, while his rival Ōmori was more likely to express skepticism.

The imposition of order on chaotic events by assuming characteristic patterns that may not exist takes other forms. Chaotic systems are unstable and aperiodic. Human history is a superb example, as Stephen H. Kellert points out in his classic study of chaos theory:

> Although broad patterns in the rise and fall of civilizations may be sketched, events never repeat exactly—history is aperiodic. And history books teem with examples of small events that led to momentous and long-lasting changes in the course of human affairs. The standard examples of unstable aperiodic behavior have always involved huge conglomerations of interacting units.[19]

Human history in general and the history of earthquakes in particular provide examples of what is possible and, under limited circumstances, what is probable, but they cannot foretell the future. The variables are too many and the possible interactions too complex. As geophysicist Amos Nur puts the matter concisely, "Most people have difficulty accepting" that "the earth beneath our feet . . . moves irregularly and unpredictably."[20]

Not only do some scientists tend to find characteristic patterns where none may exist, but so, too, does everyone else. The living memory of the 1856 tsunami, for example, was not helpful in 1896. The lack of urgency for long-term change after 1896 was in part because of a belief that the characteristic pattern in the area was that massive tsunamis struck only every few centuries. After all, the previous one was in 1611. People extrapolated this tiny sample size of two into a characteristic pattern. The tsunami of 1933 demolished that idea, but it did not prepare the region for an event like 3/11. Indeed, the 1960 Chile tsunami helped reinforce the idea that seawalls could now fend off an angry ocean.

Such simplistic extrapolations have been common throughout the world. For example, when two modest earthquakes shook London precisely four weeks apart in 1750, rumors spread that a third earthquake would destroy the city four weeks after the second event. The population panicked, and as many as one-third of the city's residents evacuated.[21] Lest we be tempted to relegate unfounded earthquake panic to the distant past, it is worth pausing to recall a more recent case. By December 3, 1990, the small town of New Madrid, Missouri, had filled with television trucks from the news networks, covering a predicted earthquake that never occurred. On the strength of a dubious claim by business consultant and amateur climatologist Iben Browning that he had predicted the 1989 Loma Prieta earthquake, major news outlets gave his December 3 prediction of a big earthquake at New Madrid serious attention.[22] As a result:

> By late November, much of the new Madrid area was preparing for a large earthquake. Many schools held earthquake drills, and authorities made preparations like parking fire trucks outside. Businesses closed or took special precautions. . . . In Missouri alone, homeowners spent $22 million on earthquake insurance.[23]

On the big day, many schools closed, local officials established an emergency center, and the governor paid a visit. However, the only casualty was a family who decided to spend the night of December 2 sleeping in a camper instead of their home. A gust of wind rolled the camper over, sending three of the family to the hospital with injuries.[24] Perhaps it is because earthquakes, even imaginary ones, conjure up strong inchoate fears that people have long sought to make them conform to some kind of orderly scheme.

Despite the christening of 3/11 as a "thousand-year earthquake," we do not know when the next large earthquake and tsunami will strike the area or what its characteristics will be. We can say with certainty that potentially destructive tsunamis will strike the area relatively often and that there is a possibility that weak ground motion in an earthquake could nevertheless produce a powerful tsunami. Moreover, we know that M9-class earthquakes are possible. Other than these broad parameters, however, predicting the seismic future in a precise way is speculative at best. A rebuilding plan that takes this chaotic, unpredictable aspect of the seismic environment seriously will require unconventional thinking.

In a different but related realm of characteristic paradigms, 3/11 prompted extensive commentary about national character. One typical headline read, "Japanese Culture Prevents Looting, Price-Gouging after Disaster." The article relied on a retired professor, Thomas Lifson, who trotted out the usual stock of stereotypes, some dating back to the 1940s. For example, "He described the main difference between American culture and Japanese culture as 'guilt' versus 'shame.'" Moreover, "Lifson said that Japanese culture abhors theft, has a deep respect for private property and admires stoicism."[25] This reliance on cultural stereotypes and its implication of a characteristic response to disasters by "the Japanese" is problematic. We would be better off focusing on material circumstances of the environment.

Price gouging and looting, for example, were problems in 1896, and price gouging took place the wake of the 1855 Ansei Edo earthquake, although the main "victims" of it seem to have been wealthy merchants, local lords (*daimyō*), and government officials. Neither of these events featured deadly violence, however, unlike the Great Kantō Earthquake. A tendency to value social order, hardly unique to Japan, probably did influence behavior after 3/11. Cultural values do vary in emphasis from one society to another, and they do influence behavior in times of stress. In life-and-death situations, however, material circumstances usually trump cultural values. If there had been mass starvation in the wake of 3/11, orderly behavior might not have prevailed. Hoarding of goods and shortages of necessities were a distinct problem in Tokyo, although it never reached the point of desperation. A major earthquake striking Tokyo or Osaka might engender very different kinds of behavior than we saw in the Tōhoku region after 3/11. The behavior of crowds, especially under duress, is also an example of a chaotic system, whose outcomes are unpredictable. We should not assume that 3/11 is socially characteristic of Japanese earthquake disasters.

CYCLES OF COMPLACENCY

Although problematic when used to find characteristic patterns or make predictions, historical data often reveal aspects of human psychology at work behind the scenes. One especially important force is complacency.

We have seen repeatedly that the psychological shock of even the most deadly seismic event soon fades, and there is a tendency for people to resume risky behavior, such as dwelling in lowland areas previously devastated by tsunami waves. Let us take a closer look at the Sanriku coast during the postwar years as an additional example.

The increasingly common use of automobiles in the 1960s freed fishing families from the requirement of living near the coast. On the other hand, postwar prosperity brought with it a desire to increase living space and an increase in nuclear families, which functioned to spread out the population. Houses located in upland areas were difficult to expand, and overbuilt upland areas were subject to landslides owing to heavy rain or earthquakes. The overall tendency, therefore, was for people to find or build larger houses in low-lying areas. The population of the Sanriku coast living in vulnerable areas increased during the decades of postwar prosperity. Construction of seawalls, such as the Great Wall of Tarō, increased along with the population, although not in perfect synchronization.[26]

By the time of 3/11, the former town of Tarō had become a part of Miyako City. After the 1933 tsunami, a report issued by an investigative committee under the Ministry of Education stated, "It is impossible to confront a tsunami directly. The only option is to flee to high ground." The same report singled out Tarō and recommended that the village relocate to higher ground in the north that is at least twelve meters high.[27] As we have seen, however, Tarō chose to confront tsunamis directly and began seawall construction. After the 1960 Chile tsunami, this approach seemed viable, and Tarō became a model of success. The town grew, and people began building on the ocean side of the first wall, most of which was set back from the water's edge. Matsumoto Yūki, manager of the Tarō Tourist Hotel, was typical of the expanding population. After 1933, his family relocated to high ground. In 1972, they moved back to the town. His hotel, built in 1986, was near the ocean, but Matsumoto felt safe because it was behind a newly constructed part of the seawall.[28]

New construction spilled over into areas outside the seawall. When former mayor Nonaka Ryōichi was asked after 3/11 why the town did not move to prohibit such construction, he said that the increase in nuclear families was such that no more land remained behind the wall, so the town remained silent on the matter. Moreover, some of the roughly two hundred residents who died in 3/11 were not late in fleeing. Instead, they did not flee at all. The network of walls, which the tsunami waves over-topped, provided a false sense of security. Safe high ground was accessible by foot less than ten minutes from anywhere in Tarō. Had everyone moved to such locations after the initial shaking, nearly all of the two hundred would have survived.[29] The 1960 Chile tsunami was a unique event, not necessarily characteristic of other tsunamis. That the wall worked then was no guarantee it would be sufficient to protect against future events, but people tend toward complacency when danger does not seem near.

The nuclear component might well push the 3/11 disaster toward the forefront of social awareness longer than had it been only an earthquake and deadly tsunami. Nevertheless, even 3/11 is bound to recede in urgency. A new cycle of overconfidence or complacency will almost certainly develop as attention to risk fades over time.

UNREALISTIC ATTITUDES TOWARD SCIENCE

In 1913, today's Japan Meteorological Agency was the Central Meteorological Observatory (Chūō kishōdai). From June 1913, residents near Sakurajima, an active volcano in Kagoshima Bay in southern Kyūshū, began to feel mild earthquakes and notice emissions of steam from coastal areas. By early January 1914, residents feared an eruption was imminent. Local officials made inquiries to the local weather bureau office, and the bureau maintained that there would be no eruption. The mayor of Sakurajima Village therefore assured residents that there was no need for evacuation. The explosive eruption on January 12 trapped people between the lava flows and the sea. It wiped out villages and killed or injured hundreds.

A monument to the disaster located at Sakurajima elementary school is commonly called the "distrust science monument" (*kagaku fushin no hi*). As a warning to future generations, it reads in part, "It is essential that residents put no trust in theory, but make preparations to evacuate immediately after detecting abnormalities."[30] When a scientific bureaucracy confidently provides tragically incorrect information, it is only reasonable to expect an angry reaction from the victims. In the case of Sakurajima, the weather bureau overestimated its capabilities, and local residents vowed to trust their intuitions, not science. Closer to the present, one resident of L'Aquila, Italy, bitterly blamed the loss of his wife on "using the Internet, television, science" and thus remaining indoors because of official assurances.[31] Moreover, "Some blamed 3.11 on science—particularly Western Science—that smugly assumed human beings could control nature."[32] When science fails to live up to expectations, people feel betrayed. Rejecting science, however, is not an effective strategy for dealing with its limitations or for dealing with natural hazards.

When in 2011 city officials in Susaki decided to monitor animal behavior and well-water levels as a method of earthquake prediction, they, too, rejected science. Although they are surely justified in their skepticism of the JMA's claim that it can predict a Tōkai earthquake, relying on folklore is hardly a viable alternative. Indeed, the example of Susaki should serve to highlight a serious problem with the unrealistic assumptions of the Special Measures Law. That some patients stricken with incurable diseases seek "alternative" therapies is a manifestation of the urge to retain some sense of control. Nevertheless, in almost every such case, the disease runs its course.

In the case of earthquakes and many other kinds of natural hazards, it is possible to retain a genuine, albeit limited, degree of control by directing all available social resources into sensible disaster mitigation and emergency response projects. Depending on the location, these measures might include zoning, upgraded building codes, building and highway reinforcement, antilandslide netting, the creation of safe evacuation areas, better firefighting equipment and infrastructure, disaster response drills, and stores of emergency food, water, and shelter that can be readily transported to disaster zones. Realistic understanding of what is possible and what is not, honest risk assessment, and establishing sensible priorities for allocating resources is the best approach to reducing vulnerabilities and thus maintaining some control over the course of future disasters. While it is valuable to retain a healthy skepticism of entrenched bureaucracies, scientific or otherwise, there is no benefit in rejecting science in favor of folklore or superstition.

Closely related to unrealistic expectations of science are unrealistic expectations of the state. My intention in making these points is not to excuse the shortcomings of the scientific community or the state, two entities that are closely connected in Japan and many other countries. It is simply to point out another manifestation of the tendency toward complacency. Although relatively few, those in Tarō who chose not to flee surely placed too much confidence in the wall that engineering technology and state funding helped create. Similarly, the long history of Japan's citizens believing state assurances about the safety of nuclear power came to an abrupt end in 3/11. A related aspect of unrealistic expectations of the state is the notion that legislation or other government action can ensure complete safety from natural hazards.

The Nōbi and Meiji Sanriku earthquakes stimulated a demand for the scientific study of earthquakes, and these events indeed served as catalysts for advancements in seismology. Moving into the twentieth century, confidence in the expertise of earthquake scientists grew, and Japanese seismologists themselves exhibited confidence that they had cracked the code of what was occurring inside the earth. A newspaper article in 1917 explaining a presentation by Ōmori conveyed reassurance to Tokyo's residents. Entitled "Tokyo and Earthquakes—No Need to Worry" ("Tōkyō to jishin: Shinpai no oyobazu"), it sought to calm jittery nerves caused by many recent small earthquakes felt in the capital. Ōmori explained that the origins of these small earthquakes were in the Tsukuba Mountains to the northeast of Tokyo. Moreover, he explained that such earthquakes were entirely different from the 1855 Ansei Edo earthquake, which occurred directly under the city. Therefore, Tokyo's residents need not fear a major earthquake.[33] Ōmori continued to make such reassuring claims right up to the occurrence of the Great Kantō Earthquake. We have seen that one result was to discredit "Ōmori seismology." If the disasters of the 1890s produced a call for science, 1923 produced a call for better science. The long period of relative quiescence between 1948 and 1995 also nurtured overconfidence, often abetted by a scientific community eager to receive largesse from the state.

SUCCESSES

In a history of earthquakes, it is perhaps inevitable to focus on problems. The nuclear disaster component of 3/11 especially shone a spotlight on problems and shortcomings. However, it is equally important to take note of successes. Considerations of success and failure in the wake of seismic events are not always simple. Tarō's Great Wall, for example, became a model of success after its performance in 1960, and Hamaguchi's original seawall protecting Hiro has performed well so far. Seawalls might make sense in some circumstances, but 3/11 has dramatically revealed their shortcomings. Moreover, seawall construction has not been simply a matter of disinterested risk-benefit analyses. Close ties between the construction industry and government have influenced the process and continue to do so.

Local communities with strong memories of the past often did well in 3/11. Recall that most residents of Murohama avoided being caught between two tsunami waves in 2011 based on local lore, possibly dating from 869. The small hamlet in Aneyoshi in Miyako City that heeded the warnings on stone monuments erected in 1933 is another example of the importance of maintaining a constant awareness of what is possible in the future based on what has happened in the past. As one reporter noted, "Thanks to an old stone tablet on a nearby hillside, erected as a warning after a deadly 1896 [*sic*] tsunami, no Aneyoshi residents erected houses close to the water, and none perished there March 11. But many other communities failed to heed the lessons of history, and lived on the seafront behind man-made barricades."[34] Just below the homes in the Aneyoshi neighborhood, a 132.5-foot wave crashed ashore.

Given the extensive photographic and video record of the 3/11 destruction, it would not take much imagination to conceive of ways to incorporate this material into local monuments for future generations. Indeed, such monuments could be combined with networks of signs pointing out the swiftest route to safety. In most cases, the relatively simple act of fleeing to high ground after an earthquake would be more consistently effective in saving lives than other approaches to tsunami defense, as the Shōwa Sanriku tsunami demonstrated particularly well. There is probably considerable room for innovation in ways to keep this message in the public eye.

Another realm of success that 3/11 highlighted was advances in antiseismic engineering. As we have seen, the Kōbe earthquake demonstrated that even modest attention to antiseismic building techniques dramatically lowers destruction rates. There are other cases of engineering success, such as the Trans-Alaska Pipeline:

> When the designers of the Trans-Alaska Pipeline realized that their pipe had to cross the Denali Fault, they engineered an ingenious solution that allowed sections of the pipe to move on skids. The investment paid off when a magnitude 7.9 quake struck on the Denali Fault on November 3, 2002. The pipeline sustained some damage but did not rupture, averting what would have otherwise been a massive economic and environmental disaster. It was and is nothing short of a poster

child for the cause of earthquake risk mitigation, the up-front cost that pays for itself many times over.[35]

Built in the 1970s, the pipeline employed relatively simple, albeit expensive, technology. Advances in antiseismic building design, in Japan especially, have been dramatic over the past fifteen years or so.

When 3/11 struck, skyscrapers in Tokyo swayed but did not break, owing to seismic isolation (or base isolation). There are now more than five thousand structures in Japan that employ this technology. Moreover, an entire community near Tokyo consists of twenty-one residential buildings atop a base-isolated artificial foundation. The use of massive rubber bearings, lead-rubber bearings, ball bearings (typically in the case of single-family homes), viscous dampers, and oil dampers enables base isolation of individual buildings or portions of buildings such as a single story that houses especially sensitive equipment. It is possible to retrofit crucial infrastructure, including power plants, using this technology. Even some cultural heritage sites such as the Daigokuden in Nara are being retrofitted to provide base isolation.[36] Here is an example of advanced technologies that, while still very expensive, are already paying safety dividends. Many other less expensive mitigation projects, such as the construction of safe evacuation areas or the erection of netting to prevent rockslides, are also potentially effective uses of resources.

Finally, the JMA early earthquake warning system worked reasonably well in 3/11, its first major test. Depending on their location, many Tōhoku residents had between ten and twenty seconds of warning time before strong shaking began. Anecdotal evidence suggests that these seconds often made a difference and probably reduced deaths and injuries from the shaking. The system also shut down bullet trains and elevators. Its main flaw was that it underestimated the magnitude because its algorithms assume an earthquake originating at a single point, not a vast slip along a long plate boundary.[37] Another problem was that because the earthquake shaking disabled electric power in many areas, residents who depended on conventional devices such as television and radio would not have been able to receive earthquake updates or the tsunami warning.[38]

LOOKING AHEAD: JAPAN

In an island country located at a complex junction of several plate boundaries, it is impossible to say what the next earthquake will be like geographically, geologically, or socially. The realistic approach is to assume a major earthquake can strike anywhere and to devise flexible responses. I am not suggesting that there be no planning for specific scenarios, only that we cannot actually know how specific future events will play out. It is therefore necessary to have the capacity to adapt.

The official earthquake bureaucracy is redundant and confusing. Adding agencies that deal with volcanoes and general disasters to the mix makes the situation all the more byzantine. The public has little idea what each entity does, and different entities issue separate reports on the same events and maintain their own networks of equipment. Some degree of redundancy, of course, can be desirable. Nevertheless, Japan would surely benefit from streamlining its convoluted earthquake bureaucracy and from functioning with greater transparency. Doing so would disrupt vested interests, so capable political and administrative leadership would be a requirement for progress in this area.

Similarly, some laws and regulations governing earthquakes and nuclear power are in need of overhaul or repeal. The basic regulations governing the nuclear power industry are products of a time when M9-class earthquakes were largely unknown and other seismic hazards poorly understood compared with today. The Special Measures Law was the result of panic and was created at a time when there was unwarranted zeal for earthquake prediction. Ideally, legislation and regulation that depends on science and technology would undergo periodic review and revision to ensure that it better reflects prevailing knowledge. To a small extent, such revision does occur now and then on an ad hoc basis, but ideally, it would be regularized. Regular review and possible revision is likely to be imperfect, of course, but it is probably a step in the right direction.

In the wake of the 1896 tsunami, we have seen that some communities relocated, but many rebuilt in the same low-lying areas as before, in part thinking that no serious tsunami would come along until centuries in the future. The 1933 tsunami shattered that illusion but replaced it with the illusion that barriers could protect the region from a wrathful sea. After the Great Kantō Earthquake, there was considerable difference of opinion about the details, but nearly everyone agreed that Tokyo could and should be rebuilt. 3/11 is different in several ways. First, it happened at a time when Japan was no longer enjoying rapid economic growth. Second, it severely curtailed Japan's energy options owing to the public reaction against nuclear power. This energy crunch then exacerbated the relatively slow economic growth. For these and other reasons, 3/11 is a vexing challenge that may not be as easily overcome as past disasters.

There is no obvious course of action for rebuilding the devastated areas. Should the costly seawalls be rebuilt or rebuilt higher? Should tsunami-devastated areas remain unoccupied? If so, what happens to the land, and who pays for which costs? Apparently, in at least some cases, plans to reconstruct failed seawalls have become part of the approach to economic revitalization of the region. For example, in the case of the seawall at Kamaishi, now in ruins:

> Its performance that day, coupled with its past failure to spur the growth of new businesses, suggested that the breakwater would be written off as yet another of the white elephant construction projects littering rural Japan. But Tokyo quickly and quietly decided to rebuild it as part of the reconstruction of the tsunami-ravaged zone, at a cost of at least $650 million. . . .
>
> As details of the government's reconstruction spending emerge, signs are growing that Japan has yet to move beyond a postwar model that enriched the country but ultimately left it stagnant for the past two decades. As the story of Kamaishi's breakwater suggests, the kind of cozy ties between government and industry that contributed to the Fukushima nuclear disaster are driving much of the reconstruction and the fight for a share of the $120 billion budget expected to be approved in a few weeks.[39]

These and many other questions confront the region in the years ahead, at a time when China is pressing Japan hard as an economic and potentially military competitor. The challenges of 3/11 will almost certainly be greater than any previous seismic disaster, but thus far, the disaster does not seem to have stimulated innovative approaches to Japan's problems or any fundamental change.

LOOKING AHEAD: NORTH AMERICA

Many of the points in this study of the history of earthquakes in Japan are applicable to other places. It is my hope that readers will find the information and arguments here thought provoking in comparative studies involving other parts of the world. I conclude with a note of caution about the Pacific coast of North America.

3/11 is directly relevant to the Pacific Northwest coast of the United States and southern Canada, an area known as Cascadia.[40] In this region, M9-class megathrust earthquakes and large tsunamis have occurred in a subduction zone near the eastern end of the Pacific Plate. In Cascadia, the small Juan de Fuca Plate pushing underneath the North American Plate creates the problematic subduction zone. The most recent major earthquake in the Cascadia subduction zone took place on January 26, 1700. Estimates of the earthquake's magnitude range from 8.7 to 9.2. Extensive Japanese records of an "orphan tsunami" led investigators to discover that an earthquake and tsunami had devastated coastal areas of the Pacific Northwest, even submerging entire forests.[41] Tsunami evacuation signs are now common in coastal areas of Oregon and Washington State, and researchers have discovered extensive evidence in the myths and legends of native peoples of massive earthquakes and tsunamis in the past.[42]

As one of the researchers who helped uncover the 1700 event pointed out:

> Once we admit this earthquake happened in the past . . . we also have to accept that the same earthquake will happen in the future. Because earthquakes in subduction zones—we know that they repeat. So the most significant thing—the most important thing that comes out of this research—is that now we know that this earthquake can happen in the future.[43]

Of course, the next earthquake and tsunami might not be identical to that of 1700, but there will be a next one, and any subduction zone earthquake is likely to be large and destructive. To make a point, one expert referred to the deadly 2004 Sumatra earthquake and tsunami and declared, "*Sumatra is Cascadia.*"[44] Outside of Native American lore, however, today's Pacific Northwest possesses no collective memory of disastrous seismic events and is in many other ways less prepared for the possibility of a disaster than its cross-Pacific neighbors in the Tōhoku region of Japan.

NOTES

1. Robert Geller (Rōbaato Geraa), *Nihonjin wa shiranai "jishin yochi" no shōtai* (Futabasha, 2011), 56.

2. For a fine analysis of the problematic government response to Kōbe, see Richard J. Samuels, *3.11: Disaster and Change in Japan* (Ithaca, NY: Cornell University Press, 2013), 57–63.

3. J. Charles Schencking, *The Great Kantō Earthquake and the Chimera of National Reconstruction in Japan* (New York: Columbia University Press, 2013), xv–xvi.

4. Susan Elizabeth Hough and Roger G. Bilham, *After the Earth Quakes: Elastic Rebound on an Urban Planet* (New York: Oxford University Press, 2006), 181–82.

5. Samuels, *3.11*, esp. 151–79.

6. "Jishin yochi shippai de jikkei, Tōkai jishin 'Hanteikaichō' odoroki," *Yomiuri shinbun*, October 24, 2012.

7. Musha Kinkichi, *Jishin namazu* (1957; Meiseki shoten, 1995), 31–35; Yoshimura Akira, *Sanriku kaigan ōtsunami* (Bungei shunjū, 2004), 16–20, 81–82; and "Ika no toresugi wa daijishin no zenchō? Tokushima de 4-bai mo," *Yomiuri Online*, May 1, 2011.

8. "Saba hōryo Hokkaidō ihen," *Yomiuri shinbun*, October 11, 2012, evening edition.

9. Thomas Gilovich, *How We Know What Isn't So: The Fallibility of Human Reason in Everyday Life* (New York: Free Press, 1993), 72; and Shimamura Hideki, *Nihonjin ga shiritai jishin no gimon rokujūroku: Jishin ga ōi Nihon dakara koso chishiki no sonae mo wasurezu ni* (Soft Bank Creative, 2008), 102–3. For a detailed analysis of this and related psychological phenomena, in addition to Gilovich, see Kikuchi Satoru, *Chōetsu genshō o naze shinjiru no ka: Omoikomi o umu "taiken" no ayausa* (Kōdansha, 1998).

10. Gilovich, *How We Know What Isn't So*, 58.

11. Motoji Ikeya, *Earthquakes and Animals: From Folk Legends to Science* (River Edge, NJ: World Scientific, 2004), 23–26.

12. For full details on this research, see Rikitake Tsuneji, "Deeta ni miru namazu to jishin," in *Namazue: Shinsai to Nihon bunka*, ed. Miyata Noboru and Takada Mamoru (Ribun shuppan, 1995), 148–56. For details on research in the 1920s, see Musha, *Jishin namazu*, 16–22. Regarding animals other than fish, see 23–51.

13. Quoted in Geller, *Jishin yochi*, 134–35. Geller points out critically that if one in a hundred is a suitable yardstick, then every superstition or fantasy ever connected with earthquakes deserves public funding.

14. Andrew Robinson, *Earthquake: Nature and Culture* (London: Reaktion, 2012), 152.

15. Stephen H. Kellert, *In the Wake of Chaos: Unpredictable Order in Dynamic Systems* (Chicago: University of Chicago Press, 1993), ix.

16. Ian Main, "Is the Reliable Prediction of Individual Earthquakes a Realistic Scientific Goal?" Introduction to a *Nature* debate, February 25, 1999, accessed October 31, 2012, http://www.nature.com/nature/debates/earthquake/equake_frameset.html.

17. John Milne, *Seismology* (London: Kegan Paul, Trench, Trübner and Co., 1898), 203–18.

18. "Tsūzoku jishin monogatari (*jō*)," *Yomiuri shinbun*, November 19, 1915, morning edition, 5.

19. Kellert, *In the Wake of Chaos*, 4–5.

20. Amos Nur with Dawn Burgess, *Apocalypse: Earthquakes, Archaeology, and the Wrath of God* (Princeton, NJ: Princeton University Press, 2008), 16.

21. Nur, *Apocalypse*, 247.

22. Robinson, *Earthquake*, 166–67.

23. Seth Stein, *Disaster Deferred: How Science Is Changing Our View of Earthquake Hazards in the Midwest* (New York: Columbia University Press, 2010), 13.

24. Susan Hough, *Predicting the Unpredictable: The Tumultuous Science of Earthquake Prediction* (Princeton, NJ: Princeton University Press, 2010), 190.

25. "Japanese Culture Prevents Looting, Price-Gouging after Disaster," *Hawaii News Now*, March 16, 2011 (updated May 15, 2011; accessed October 31, 2012), http://www.hawaiinewsnow.com/Global/story.asp?S=14266637.

26. Yamashita Funio, *Tsunami no kyōfu: Sanriku tsunami denshōroku* (*The Horrors of Tsunami—The Documents and Histories of Sanriku-Tsunami of the Tohoku Area*) (Sendai, Japan: Tōhoku daigaku shuppankai, 2005), 158–67.

27. Mainichi shinbun "shinsai kenshō" shuzai han, eds., *Kenshō "daishinsai:" Tsutaenakereba naranai koto* (Mainichi shinbunsha, 2012), 96.

28. Mainichi shinbun "shinsai kenshō" shuzai han, *Kenshō "daishinsai,"* 96–97.

29. Mainichi shinbun "shinsai kenshō" shuzai han, *Kenshō "daishinsai,"* 97–100.

30. Yanagawa Yoshirō, *Sakurajima funkaki: Jūmin wa riron ni shinraisezu* (Nihon hōsō shuppankai, 1984), 9–10 for the text of the monument. See also Shimamura Hideki, *"Jishin yochi" wa usodarake* (Kōdansha, 2008), 219–21.

31. Robinson, *Earthquake*, 153.

32. Samuels, *3.11*, 188.

33. "Tōkyō to jishin: Shinpai no oyobazu," *Yomiuri shinbun*, October 18, 1917, morning edition, 5.

34. Calum Macleod, "Japanese Towns Reconsider Sea Walls after Deadly Tsunami," *USA Today*, August 11, 2011 (Chie Matsumoto contributing).

35. Hough, *Predicting the Unpredictable*, 212.

36. Takayoshi Kamada and Takafumi Fujita, "State of the Art of Development and Application of Antiseismic Systems in Japan," *American Institute of Physics Conference Proceedings* 1020 (2008): 1255–71, accessed October 29, 2012, http://link.aip.org/link/doi/10.1063/1.2963748. See also Japan Society of Seismic Isolation, ed., *How to Plan and Implement Seismic Isolation for Buildings* (Ohmsha, 2013).

37. Erika Yamasaki, "What We Can Learn from Japan's Early Earthquake Warning System," *Momentum* 1, no. 1 (April 18, 2012): 11–12, accessed November 2, 2012, http://repository.upenn.edu/cgi/viewcontent.cgi?article=1022&context=momentum.

38. Satake Kenji, "Kyodai tsunami no mekanizumu," in *Kyodai jishin, kyodai tsunami: Higashi Nihon daishinsai no kenshō*, ed. Hirata Naoshi, Satake Kenji, Meguro Kimirō, and Hatakemura Yōtarō (Asakura shoten, 2011), 82.

39. Norimitsu Onishi, "Japan Revives a Sea Barrier That Failed to Hold," *New York Times*, November 2, 2011.

40. For a comprehensive account of the discovery of this seismic hazard, see Jerry Thompson, *Cascadia's Fault: The Coming Earthquake and Tsunami That Could Devastate North America* (Berkeley, CA: Counterpoint, 2011).

41. For a detailed analysis of the orphan tsunami, see Brian F. Atwater et al., *The Orphan Tsunami of 1700: Japanese Clues to a Parent Earthquake in North America* (*Minashigo Genroku tsunami: Oya-jishin wa Hokubei seikaigan ni ita*) (Reston, VA: United States Geological Survey/University of Washington Press, 2005).

42. R. S. Ludwin and G. J. Smits, "Folklore and Earthquakes: Native American Oral Traditions from Cascadia Compared with Written Traditions from Japan," in *Myth and Geology*, ed. L. Piccardi and W. B. Masse (London: Geological Society, 2007), 67–78,

86–91; and Ruth S. Ludwin et al., "Dating the 1700 Cascadia Earthquake: Great Coastal Earthquakes in Native Stories," *Seismological Research Letters* 76, no. 2 (March 2005): 140–48. See also Satake, "Kyodai tsunami," 87–89.

43. Kenji Satake quoted in Thompson, *Cascadia's Fault*, 211.

44. Garry Rogers quoted in Thompson, *Cascadia's Fault*, 277.

Glossary of Terms and Entities

aftershock. A smaller earthquake following a larger one on or near the fault plane that slipped during the main shock.

Blueprint, The. *See Prediction of Earthquakes: Progress to Date and Plans for Further Development*.

Central Council for Disaster Prevention (Chūō bōsai kaigi). A government entity established in 1959 that assists the cabinet in formulating natural disaster policy. It deals with earthquakes and other natural disasters.

characteristic earthquake theory (*koyū jishin setsu*). The controversial proposal that large earthquakes with similar geological attributes occur periodically along certain faults, based on historical and/or paleoseismological observations.

chaotic process. A dynamic system highly sensitive to initial conditions and/or affected by a range of unconstrained or poorly constrained variables such that prediction, especially long-term prediction, becomes impossible. Weather is widely regarded as a chaotic process, and many specialists regard earthquakes and human history as chaotic processes.

Coordinating Committee for Earthquake Prediction (CCEP) (Jishin yochi renraku kai). A committee created in 1969 in the wake of the Tokachi offshore earthquake. It is commonly known as "Yochiren," and its charge is to pursue earthquake prediction.

crust. The outermost layer of the earth's upper shell of solid rock.

Daishinhō. *See* Special Measures Law for Large-Scale Earthquakes.

Decision Committee (Jishin bōsai taisaku kansoku kyōka chiiki hantei kai). A committee created within the JMA in 1979 whose job is to predict a Tōkai earthquake. In Japanese, it is commonly known as the Hanteikai.

dilatancy. Volume increase of rocks when subject to stress, caused by changes in crack and pore distribution.

displacement. Shifting of ground surface during an earthquake.

earthquake. A sudden release of accumulated stress along a fault that produces seismic waves.

earthquake disaster. A natural disaster caused by seismic hazards interacting destructively with human society.

Earthquake Prediction Research Consultation Committee (Jishin yochi kenkyū kyōgi kai, now the Jishin, kazan funka yochi kenkyū kyōgi kai). An academic committee at Tokyo University that pursues earthquake prediction research and that issued the controversial booklet *Earthquake Prediction Is Now* in 1991.

epicenter. The location on the surface directly above the hypocenter of an earthquake.

fault. A plane of weakness in the earth's crust that manifests itself as a discontinuity across which there has been shear displacement. Energy stored in the rocks around a fault causes earthquakes when one side of the fault overcomes friction and slips past the other side in a vertical or horizontal direction.

fault scarp. A linear ridge of uplifted crust caused by vertical displacement.

focus. *See* hypocenter.

foreshock. A small earthquake that sometimes occurs as precursor to larger shocks, usually recognized in retrospect.

Fukushima Daiichi Nuclear Power Plant. A light-water reactor built in 1971 and shut down by the end of April 2011. The 3/11 tsunami disabled the reactor cooling systems, leading to nuclear radiation leaks and a thirty-kilometer evacuation zone surrounding the plant and giving rise to popular opposition to nuclear power.

galileo (Gal). A unit of acceleration defined as one centimeter per second squared.

Headquarters for Earthquake Research Promotion (Jishin chōsa kenkyū suishin honbu). An entity established in 1995 to serve as a master coordinating agency within the government bureaucracy. In practice, it did not displace the Decision Committee or the CCEP, resulting in three major entities within the government that deal specifically with earthquakes.

hypocenter. The point within the earth on a fault where rocks begin to slip past one another in an earthquake.

Imperial Earthquake Investigation Committee (IEIC) (Shinsai yobō chōsakai). An organization of scientists and engineers within the

Ministry of Education created in 1892 to pursue goals such as earthquake prediction and earthquake hazard mitigation. It dissolved in 1924.

intensity (*shindo*). The effect of earthquakes on humans and human structures.

intraplate earthquake (*chokkagata jishin*). An earthquake that occurs at a point removed from plate boundaries, in the interior of a plate.

Japan Meteorological Agency (JMA) (Kishōchō). The lead agency in monitoring seismic activity, charged with the task of predicting a Tōkai earthquake.

JMA. *See* Japan Meteorological Agency.

JMA seismic intensity scale. A scale for measuring seismic intensity used in Japan. It has been modified following past major earthquakes, and the current scale dates from 1995. The scale consists of whole numbers 1–7, with 5 and 6 subdivided into "weak" and "strong."

local magnitude. *See* magnitude.

magnitude (Mw or M). A measure of the quantity of energy an earthquake releases based on seismic moment. Magnitude is expressed using a logarithmic scale.

megathrust earthquake. Earthquakes at subduction zones caused by slipping of the locked plate boundary. This seismic activity produces the world's largest earthquakes.

moment magnitude. *See* magnitude.

Nankai earthquake. A megathrust earthquake originating in the Nankai Trough in which segments A and B of the fault boundary break.

natural disaster. The destructive intersection of natural hazards and human society.

natural hazard. A potentially destructive force in nature.

near-field earthquake. *See* intraplate earthquake.

NRA. *See* Nuclear Regulatory Authority.

Nuclear Regulatory Authority (NRA). Japan's nuclear regulatory agency, created in September 2012 from two discredited agencies in the wake of 3/11.

-oki. A suffix in many Japanese earthquake names translated in this book and elsewhere as "offshore."

Parkfield experiment. An attempt to predict an earthquake and "ambush" it by placing equipment in the vicinity. According to USGS prediction, an M6-class earthquake would occur in Parkfield, California, by 1992. Instead, it occurred in 2004. Most of the measuring equipment was in place at that time, and it revealed no precursors.

Plan for Earthquake Prediction Research (Jishin yochi kenkyū keikaku). The first funding by the state to promote earthquake prediction, 1965–1968. In subsequent iterations, the word "research" disappeared, thus implying that earthquake prediction was a practical possibility.

plate tectonics. The theory that the solid earth's surface consists of a small number of large plates (as well as some smaller ones) that are in relative motion. Movement of plates causes most of the earth's seismic activity.

precursor (precursory phenomenon) (*zenchō*). Any of a wide range of phenomena occurring prior to an earthquake that at least some people regard as connected with the earthquake. Precursors are usually recognized in retrospect, after an earthquake has occurred. While genuine coseismic precursors may exist, no reliable precursor (one that occurs consistently in close temporal proximity to major earthquakes and only prior to earthquakes) has been discovered.

Prediction of Earthquakes: Progress to Date and Plans for Further Development (Jishin yochi, genjō to sono suishin keikaku). A 1965 document outlining a preliminary program of inquiry into earthquake prediction. It is commonly called "the Blueprint."

preslip (*purii surippu* or *zenchō-suberi*). The idea that prior to a megathrust earthquake in the Nankai Trough, the fault will slip slightly, and this slippage will deform the crust enough to register in JMA strain gauges. Preslip is the official basis for predicting a Nankai Trough earthquake, although some seismologists have expressed doubt about whether preslip actually exists.

recurrence interval. The average time between major earthquakes on a fault.

Richter scale. A logarithmic magnitude scale developed in 1935 to measure earthquakes in California and gradually discontinued in the late 1970s, replaced by moment magnitude.

Scholz theory. A dilatancy theory proposed by Christopher Scholz that became especially influential in Japan.

seiche. Standing wave in a lake or partially enclosed body of water.

seismic gap hyphothesis. The proposition that over long periods of time, the displacement on any segment of a fault must be equal to that experienced by all the other parts of the fault.

seismic moment. A measurement of earthquake strength that reflects the size of the fault rupture, the strength of the rocks, and the amount of displacement across the fault. It is converted into magnitude using a formula.

seismic sea wave. *See* tsunami.

seismic wave. An elastic wave traveling within the earth, propagating outward from a slipping fault plane. The fastest seismic waves are P waves (push-pull waves), which are sound waves traveling through the earth. S waves (shear waves) are slower and more destructive, shaking the earth perpendicular to their direction of travel (i.e., sideways). S waves cannot travel through liquids. Other types of seismic waves include Love waves (lateral waves) and Rayleigh waves (which cause ground roll).

seismicity. Earthquake activity.

seismograph. An instrument that records the shaking that occurs in an earthquake.

seismometer. *See* seismograph.

slip. The motion when two sides of a fault move past each other.

slow earthquake. *See* tsunami earthquake.

Special Measures Law for Large-Scale Earthquakes (Daikibo jishin taisaku tokubetsu sochi hō). A 1978 law granting vast powers to the state to implement emergency measures in areas subject to damage from a Nankai Trough megathrust earthquake. The law explicitly requires a committee of scientists in the JMA to predict such an earthquake. Also known as the Special Measures Act for Large-Scale Earthquakes.

strain gauge (volumetric strain gauge). An oil-filled cylinder used by the JMA to detect crustal deformation and thereby predict a megathrust earthquake originating in the Nankai Trough.

stress. Force per unit area acting on the surface of a solid and the equal and opposite reaction of the material.

subduction zone. A convergent tectonic plate boundary in which the denser plate thrusts under the lighter plate. Subduction zones are the sites of most of the world's seismic activity and of megathrust earthquakes.

tectonic plate. *See* plate tectonics.

TEPCO. *See* Tokyo Electric Power Company.

tidal wave. An inaccurate alternative name for a tsunami.

Tōkai earthquake. A megathrust earthquake originating in the Nankai Trough in which segments C and D of the fault boundary break. More casually, this term can serve as a generic name for any megathrust earthquake originating in the Nankai Trough.

Tokyo Electric Power Company (TEPCO or Tepco). A power company that operates several nuclear power plants, including the Fukushima Daiichi plant that failed as a result of 3/11.

Tōnankai earthquake. A megathrust earthquake originating in the Nankai Trough in which segments B and C of the fault boundary break.

trench (ocean trench, deep sea trench). Long but narrow topographic depressions of the seafloor caused by convergent plate boundaries at which the less dense of two tectonic plates pushes (subducts) beneath the denser plate.

trough (ocean trough). A less steep and less deep version of a trench.

tsunami (seismic sea wave). A long-wavelength water wave usually caused by vertical movement of the ocean floor from an earthquake. Literally, "harbor wave."

tsunami earthquake (*tsunami jishin*). Also known as slow earthquakes, sliding earthquakes, and other terms. It is sometimes used simply to mean a tsunamigenic earthquake but as a technical term indicates an earthquake that causes mild shaking but generates a large tsunami.

tsunami magnitude (Mt or Mt0). A logarithmic measure of the size of a tsunami as a function of crest-to-trough wave amplitude (height) and distance from the epicenter. Tsunami magnitude formulas are specific to oceans and regions. They usually correspond to earthquake magnitudes except in the case of tsunami earthquakes.

tsunamigenic earthquake. An earthquake that generates a tsunami.

Vp/Vs method. An approach developed in the Soviet Union during the 1970s that measures changes in the ratio of the velocity of P (push-pull, pressure) waves and S (shear) waves as a way of predicting earthquakes. This method has led to theories of dilatancy.

yochi. Japanese term for short-term prediction.

yosoku. Japanese term for long-term prediction; forecasting.

Bibliography

Note: The place of publication for Japanese books is Tokyo unless otherwise specified.

Abe, Katsuyuki. "Estimate of Tsunami Run-Up Heights from Earthquake Magnitudes." In *Tsunami: Progress in Prediction, Disaster Prevention, and Warning,* edited by Yoshihito Tsuchiya, 21–35. Leiden: Kluwer Academic, 1995.

Adams, R. D. "The Haicheng, China, Earthquake of 4 February 1975: The First Successfully Predicted Major Earthquake." *Earthquake Engineering and Structural Dynamics* 4 (1976): 423–37.

Akabane Sadayuki and Inoue Kimio. "Saigai no jōkyō." In *1847 Zenkōji jishin hōkokusho,* edited by Chūō bōsai kaigi (Nihon shisutemu kaihatsu kenkyūsho, 2007), 22–42, 222.

Ansei kenmonshi. 3 vols. Illustrations by Utagawa Kuniyoshi et al. Author(s) and publisher unknown, 1856.

Arakawa Hidetoshi, ed. *Jitsuroku, Ō-Edo kaimetsu no hi: Ansei kenmonroku, Ansei kenmonshi, Ansei fūbunshū.* Kyōikusha, 1982.

Atwater, Brian F., Musumi-Rokkaku Satoko, Satake Kenji, Tsuji Yoshinobu, Ueda Kazue, and David K. Yamaguchi. *The Orphan Tsunami of 1700: Japanese Clues to a Parent Earthquake in North America (Minashigo Genroku tsunami: Oya-jishin wa Hokubei seikaigan ni ita).* Reston, VA: United States Geological Survey/University of Washington Press, 2005. Also available in digital form at http://pubs.usgs.gov/pp/pp1707.

Birmingham, Lucy, and David McNeill. *Strong in the Rain: Surviving Japan's Earthquake, Tsunami, and Fukushima Nuclear Disaster.* New York: Palgrave Macmillan, 2012.

Bolitho, Harold. "The Tempō Crisis." In *The Cambridge History of Japan: Volume 5, The Nineteenth Century,* edited by Marius B. Jansen, 116–167. New York: Cambridge University Press, 1989.

Borland, Janet. "Capitalising on Catastrophe: Reinvigorating the Japanese State with Moral Values through Education following the 1923 Great Kantô Earthquake." *Modern Asian Studies* 40, no. 4 (October 2006): 875–907.

————. "Stories of Ideal Japanese Subjects from the Great Kanto Earthquake of 1923." *Japanese Studies* 25, no. 1 (May 2005): 21–34.

Busch, Noel Fairchild. *Two Minutes to Noon: The Story of the Great Tokyo Earthquake and Fire.* New York: Simon and Schuster, 1962.

"Chōsakai no kyūsai hōhō." *Ōu nichinichi shinbun,* July 28, 1896. Accessed May 9, 2013. http://tsunami-dl.jp/newspaper/OouNichinichiM29/OouNichinichiM29_July28_02.

Chung, Riley M. *The January 17, 1995, Hyogoken Nanbu (Kobe) Earthquake: Performance of Structures, Lifelines, and Fire Protection Systems* (NIST Special Report 91). Gaithersburg, MD, 1996. Accessed October 6, 2012. http://www.fire.nist.gov/bfrlpubs/build96/PDF/b96002.pdf.

Chūō bōsai kaigi, ed. *1854 Ansei tōkai jishin, Ansei nankai jishin.* 2005.

————. *1891 Nōbi jishin hōkokusho*. Nihon shisutemu kaihatsu kenkyūsho, 2008.

————. *1896 Meiji Sanriku jishin tsunami hōkokusho*. 2005.

————. *1923 Kantō daishinsai hōkokusho, dai ippen*. Nihon shisutemu kaihatsu kenkyūsho, 2006.

"City Looks to Base Tsunami Warnings on Animal Behavior." *Japan Times*, June 3, 2012.

Clancey, Gregory. *Earthquake Nation: The Cultural Politics of Japanese Seismicity, 1868–1930*. Berkeley: University of California Press, 2006.

Coen, Deborah R. *The Earthquake Observers: Disaster Science from Lisbon to Richter*. Chicago: University of Chicago Press, 2013.

"Daikibo jishin taisaku tokubetsu sochi hō." Accessed September 24, 2012. http://law. e-gov.go.jp/htmldata/S53/S53HO073.html.

Dai-Nippon yūbenkai Kōdansha, comps. *Taishō daishinsai, daikasai*. Dai-Nippon yūbenkai Kōdansha, 1923.

"Echigo jishin kudoki" (blog). Accessed October 28, 2010. http://blogs.yahoo.co.jp/ gojukara11/2937035.html.

Enomoto Yūji. "Kotō ronbun no Nōbi jishin Neodani dansō shashin ni tsuite." *Rekishi jishin* 21 (2006): 219–22.

"Fujisawa gichō no kaishō higaichi saisatsudan (shōzen)." *Ōu nichinichi shinbun*, July 28–29, 1896. Accessed May 13, 2013. http://tsunami-dl.jp/newspaper/ OouNichinichiM29/OouNichinichiM29_July28_02 (July 28); and http://tsunami-dl. jp/newspaper/OouNichinichiM29/OouNichinichiM29_July29_02 (July 29).

Fujita Hiroshige. "Kenkai giin kokuyūrin nai ni wa kanjin no yōzai ga kiwamete kinshō." *Kahoku shinpō*, March 20, 1933. Accessed May 14, 2013. http://tsunami-dl. jp/newspaper/KahokuShinpouS8/KahokuShinpouS8_March20_08.

————. "Kenkai giin ōjishin attara tsunami shūrai o kakugo." *Kahoku shinpō*, March 14, 1933. Accessed May 14, 2013. http://tsunami-dl.jp/newspaper/KahokuShinpouS8/ KahokuShinpouS8_March14_08.

"Fukkō wa kaki no yōshoku kara tanekaki haikyū no tairyō mōshikomi ni me o mawasu Watanoha shuishi." *Kahoku shinpō*, April 15, 1933. Accessed May 14, 2013. http:// tsunami-dl.jp/newspaper/KahokuShinpouS8/KahokuShinpouS8_April15_08.

"Fuku-tabemono oyobi jiyōhin no ketsubō." *Ōu nichinichi shinbun*, June 27, 1896. Accessed May 8, 2013. http://tsunami-dl.jp/newspaper/OouNichinichiM29/ OouNichinichiM29_June27_02.

"Futatabi, kainai no jinjin ni uttau." *Ōu nichinichi shinbun*, July 15, 1896. Accessed May 9, 2013. http://tsunami-dl.jp/newspaper/OouNichinichiM29/OouNichinichiM29_ July15_02.

Geller, Robert (Rōbaato Geraa). *Nihonjin wa shiranai "jishin yochi" no shōtai*. Futabasha, 2011.

Geller, Robert J., David D. Jackson, Yan Y. Kagan, and Francesco Mulargia. Response to "Cannot Earthquakes Be Predicted?" *Science* 278 (October 17, 1997): 488–90.

Gilovich, Thomas. *How We Know What Isn't So: The Fallibility of Human Reason in Everyday Life*. New York: Free Press, 1993.

"Gisonkin boshū enki kōkoku." *Ōu nichinichi shinbun*, July 28, 1896. Accessed May 7, 2013. http://tsunami-dl.jp/newspaper/OouNichinichiM29/OouNichinichiM29_ July28_03.

"Gisonsha rikuzoku tari." *Ōu nichinichi shinbun*, June 23, 1896.

Guidoboni, Emanuela, and John E. Ebel. *Earthquakes and Tsunamis in the Past: A Guide to Techniques in Historical Seismology*. New York: Cambridge University Press, 2009.

Hagiwara Takahiro. *Jishingaku hyakunen*. Tōkyō daigaku shuppankai, 1982.

Haicheng Earthquake Study Delegation. "Prediction of the Haicheng Earthquake." *Eos* 58 (1977): 236–72.

"Hakodate yori beikoku o yunyū su." *Iwate kōhō*, June 21, 1896. Accessed May 8, 2013. http://tsunami-dl.jp/newspaper/IwateKouhouM29/IwatekouhouM29_June21_02.

Hall, Stephen S. "Scientists on Trial: At Fault?" *Nature* 477 (2011): 264–69. Accessed October 10, 2012. http://www.nature.com/news/2011/110914/full/477264a.html.

Hammer, Joshua. *Yokohama Burning: The Deadly 1923 Earthquake and Fire That Helped Forge the Path to World War II*. New York: Free Press, 2006.

Harada Kazuhiko. "Matsushiro-han de sakusei sareta jishinzuerui ni tsuite." In *1847 Zenkōji jishin hōkokusho*, edited by Chūō bōsai kaigi, 134–49. Nihon shisutemu kaihatsu kenkyūsho, 2007.

Haruo Matuo [Matsuo]. "Estimation of Energy of Tsunami and Protection of Coasts." *Jishin kenkyūjo ihō bessatsu*, no. 1 (March 3, 1934), 55–64.

Hashimoto Manpei. *Jishingaku no kotohajime: Kaituakusha Sekiya Seikei no shōgai*. Asahi shinbunsha, 1983.

Hashimoto Mitsuo, ed. *Geology of Japan*. Tokyo: Terra Scientific, 1991.

Hatamura Yōtarō. "Higashi Nihon daishinsai ni omō." In *Kyodai jishin, kyodai tsunami: Higashi Nihon daishinsai no kenshō*, edited by Hirata Naoshi, Satake Kenji, Meguro Kimirō, and Hatamura Yōtarō, 151–55 (Asakura shoten, 2011).

Hatano, Jun. "Edo's Water Supply." In *Edo and Paris: Urban Life and the State in the Early Modern Era*, edited by James L. McClain, John W. Merriman, and Ugawa Kaoru, 234–50. Ithaca, NY: Cornell University Press, 1994.

Hermanns, William. *Einstein and the Poet: In Search of the Cosmic Man*. Wellesley, MA: Branden Books, 1983.

"Higaichi to eisei." *Iwate kōhō*, June 19, 1896. Accessed May 7, 2013. http://tsunami-dl.jp/newspaper/IwateKouhouM29/IwatekouhouM29_June19_04.

"Higaisha kyūjo no ippō." *Ōu nichinichi shinbun*, June 24, 1896. Accessed May 9, 2013. http://tsunami-dl.jp/newspaper/OouNichinichiM29/OouNichinichiM29_June24_02.

"Higashi Nihon daishinsai: Senjin wa shitteita 'rekishi gaidō' shinsui sezu." *Mainichi shinbun*, April 19, 2011.

Hirakawa Sukehiro. *Koizumi Yakumo: Seiyō dasshutsu no yume*. Shinchōsha, 1981.

Hirata Naoshi, Satake Kenji, Meguro Kimirō, and Hatakemura Yōtarō. *Kyodai jishin, kyodai tsunami: Higashi Nihon daishinsai no kenshō*. Asakura shoten, 2011.

"Hi to mizu no naka kara umareta kokusai bidan Sanriku shinsai aiwa no hitotsu." *Mainichi shinbun*, March 8, 1933.

Holguín-Veras, José. "Japan's 1,000-Year-Old-Warning." *Los Angeles Times*, March 11, 2012.

"Honnendo shitsugyō kyūsai shikō hōshin kettei." *Mainichi shinbun*, April 2, 1933. Accessed May 14, 2013. http://tsunami-dl.jp/newspaper/S8Mainichi/MainichiS8_April02_02.

"Honsha imon dai-ni han, Sanriku higaichi no mukau torakku no Hitsujuhin o mansai shite hikitsuzuki dai-san han o soshiki." *Kahō shinpō*, March 6, 1933. Accessed May 14, 2013. http://tsunami-dl.jp/newspaper/KahokuShinpouS8/KahokuShinpouS8_March06_07.

Hough, Susan Elizabeth, and Roger G. Bilham. *After the Earth Quakes: Elastic Rebound in an Urban Planet*. New York: Oxford University Press, 2006.

Hough, Susan. *Predicting the Unpredictable: The Tumultuous Science of Earthquake Prediction*. Princeton, NJ: Princeton University Press, 2010.

Hough, Susan Elizabeth. *Earthshaking Science: What We Know (and Don't Know) about Earthquakes*. Princeton, NJ: Princeton University Press, 2002.

Huebsch, Ian O. "Comment." *Eos* 59 (1978): 2.

"Ika no toresugi wa daijishin no zenchō? Tokushima de 4-bai mo." *Yomiuri Online*, May 1, 2011. http://www.yomiuri.co.jp/national/news/20110501-OYT1T00194.htm

Ikeya, Motoji. *Earthquakes and Animals: From Folk Legends to Science*. River Edge, NJ: World Scientific, 2004.

Iki Tsunenaka. "Sanriku chihō tsunami jistujō torishirabe hōkoku." In *Shinsai yobō chōsakai hōkoku, dai 7 gō* (Shinsai yobō chōsakai, 1896), 4–34.

Imamura Akitsune. "Futatabi tsunami no gen'in ni tsuki." *Chishitsugaku zasshi* 4 (1897): 116–19.

———. "Jishin tsunami no gen'in ni tsuite." *Chigaku zasshi* 17 (1905): 792–801.

———. "Jisuberi ni tsuite ronji jinari oyobi tsunami no gen'in ni oyobu." *Chishitsugaku zasshi* 4 (1897): 65–69.

———. "Jo." In *Taishō daishinsai, daikasai,* unpaginated front matter. Dai-Nippon yūbenkai Kōdansha, 1923.

———. "Sanriku tsunami ni tsuite." *Chigaku zasshi* 11 (1899): 801–10.

———. "Sanriku tsunami ni tsuite." *Chigaku zasshi* 12 (1900): 142–58.

"Imonhin bunpai gunkan *Itsukushima* no tsundekita Yokosuka chinfu kizōhin." *Kahō shinpō*, March 7, 1933. Accessed May 14, 2013. http://tsunami-dl.jp/newspaper/KahokuShinpouS8/KahokuShinpouS8_March07_02.

Inamura no hi website. Accessed October 17, 2012. http://www.inamuranohi.jp.

"Ishi mōsei wo unagasu." *Iwate kōhō*, June 24, 1896. Accessed May 8, 2013. http://tsunami-dl.jp/newspaper/IwateKouhouM29/IwatekouhouM29_June24_02.

Ishibashi Katsuhiko. *Daijishinran no jidai*. Iwanami shoten, 1994.

———. "Tōkai chihō no yosōsareru daishinsai no saikentō: Suruga-wan jishin no kanōsei" ("Re-Examination of a Great Earthquake Expected in the Tokai District, Central Japan—Possibility of the 'Suruga Bay Earthquake'"). Jishin yochi renraku kai report 17 (1977), 127–128. Accessed October 10, 2012. http://cais.gsi.go.jp/YOCHIREN/report/kaihou17/04_13.pdf.

Itō Kazuaki. *Jishin to funka no Nihonshi*. Iwanami shoten, 2002.

Ito, Takashi. "Were There Precursors of March 11 Quake?" *Daily Yomiuri Online*, July 25, 2011.

Japan Meteorological Agency (JMA) website. Page "Jishin yochi ni tsuite," heading "Jishin yochi to wa," subheading, "Jishin no chokuzen yochi ni tsuite." Accessed October 5, 2012. http://www.seisvol.kishou.go.jp/eq/tokai/tokai_eq4.html.

———. Page "Jishin yochi ni tsuite," heading "Jishin yochi to wa," subheadings "Zenchō-suberi (puresurippu) to wa" and "Tōkai jishin wa kanarazu yochi dekiru no ka?" Accessed October 5, 2012. http://www.seisvol.kishou.go.jp/eq/tokai/tokai_eq4.html.

Japan Society of Seismic Isolation, ed. *How to Plan and Implement Seismic Isolation for Buildings*. Ohmsha, 2013.

"Japanese City to Watch Animal Behaviour for Disaster Signs." *Tokyo Times*, 2012.

"Japanese Culture Prevents Looting, Price-Gouging after Disaster." *Hawaii News Now*, March 16, 2011 (updated May 15, 2011). Accessed October 31, 2012. http://www.hawaiinewsnow.com/Global/story.asp?S=14266637.

Jishin chōsa kenkyū suishin honbu. "Budget Related to Earthquake Research for FY 2012." Accessed October 5, 2013. http://www.jishin.go.jp/main/yosan-e/yosan2012b.pdf.

———. "Budget Request Related to Earthquake Research for FY 2013." Accessed October 5, 2013. http://www.jishin.go.jp/main/yosan-e/yosan2013a.pdf.

———. "Rokkō-Awajishima dansō-tai." Accessed October 8, 2012. http://www.jishin.go.jp/main/yosokuchizu/katsudanso/f079_rokko_awaji.htm.

"Jishin yochi shippai de 4 nen kyūkei, Itaria kensatsu, gakushara 7 nin ni 'iinkai no handan ga hitobito no shi ni musubitsuita." *MSN-Sankei nyūsu*, September 26, 2012.

"Jishin yochi shippai de jikkei, Tōkai jishin 'Hanteikaichō' odoroki." *Yomiuri shinbun*, October 24, 2012.

"Jiyūtō no tame ni tsurushi, Shinpotō no tame ni keisu." In *Ōu nichinichi shinbun*, July 18–19, 1896. Accessed May 9, 2013. http://tsunami-dl.jp/newspaper/OouNichinichiM29/OouNichinichiM29_July18_02 (July 18); and http://tsunami-dl.jp/newspaper/OouNichinichiM29/OouNichinichiM29_July19_02 (July 19).

Kagan, Yan Y., and David D. Jackson. "Seismic Gap Hypothesis: Ten Years After." *Journal of Geophysical Research* 96, no. 13 (December 10, 1991): 21, 419–21, 431.

Kagan, Yan Y., David D. Jackson, and Robert J. Geller. "Characteristic Earthquake Model, 1884–2011, R.I.P." *Seismological Research Letters* 83 (November–December 2012): 951–53.

"Kaigun kyūjutsuhin *Yakaze* yori juryō tadachini risai mura e." *Kahō shinpō*, March 8, 1933. Accessed May 14, 2013. http://tsunami-dl.jp/newspaper/KahokuShinpouS8/KahokuShinpouS8_March08_07.

"Kaishō jisshiroku ni Shizugawa-chō, honsha tokuha'in Imazumi Torajirō." *Ōu nichinichi shinbun*, June 15, 1896.

"Kaishō no sangai gikin no boshū." *Ōu nichinichi shinbun*, June 17, 1896. Accessed May 7, 2013. http://tsunami-dl.jp/newspaper/OouNichinichiM29/OouNichinichiM29_June17_02.

"Kaishō no zengosaku to jiyūtō no kakaku reigan kyoshi." *Ōu nichinichi shinbun*, July 2, 1896. Accessed May 9, 2013. http://tsunami-dl.jp/newspaper/OouNichinichiM29/OouNichinichiM29_July04_02.

Kamada, Takayoshi, and Takafumi Fujita. "State of the Art of Development and Application of Antiseismic Systems in Japan." *American Institute of Physics Conference Proceedings* 1020 (2008): 1255–71. Accessed October 29, 2012. http://link.aip.org/link/doi/10.1063/1.2963748.

Kaminuma Katsutada. "Jishin yochi to kazan funka yochi no kenkyūsha no yakuwari." In *Jishin yochi to shakai*, edited by Kaminuma Katsutada and Hirata Kōji, 1–18. Kokon shoin, 2003.

Kaminuma Katsutada and Hirata Kōji, eds. *Jishin yochi to shakai*. Kokon shoin, 2003.

Kellert, Stephen H. *In the Wake of Chaos: Unpredictable Order in Dynamic Systems*. Chicago: University of Chicago Press, 1993.

Kikuchi Satoru. *Chōjō genshō o naze shinjiru no ka: Omoikomi o umu "taiken" no ayausa*. Kōdansha, 1998.

Kimura Masaaki. *Daijishin no zenchō o toraeta! Keikaisubeki chiiki wa dokoka?* Daisan bunmeisha, 2008.

Kingston, Jeff. "Power Politics: Japan's Resilient Nuclear Village." *Asia-Pacific Journal* 10, issue 43, no. 1 (October 29, 2012). Accessed October 30, 2012. http://japanfocus.org/-Jeff-Kingston/3847.

Kitahara Itoko. *Saigai jaanarizumu, mukashi hen*. Sakura, Japan: Rekishi minzoku hakubutsukan shinkōkai, 2001.

Kitō Yasuyuki and Nagase Satoshi. "Saigai to kyūsai: Machi to mura." In *Zenkōji jishin ni manabu*, edited by Akahane Sadayuki and Kitahara Itoko, 75–94. Nagano-shi, Japan: Shinano mainichi shinbunsha, 2003.

"Kōen Sanriku kashō no ippashi o kataru ato roku no nigo Sendai kara." *Kahoku shinpō*, March 26, 1933. Accessed May 14, 2013. http://tsunami-dl.jp/newspaper/ KahokuShinpouS8/KahokuShinpouS8_March26_05.

Koizumi Kinmei. "Chōshin hiroku." In *"ihon no rekishi jishin shiryo" shuī, Saiko 2-nen yori Shōwa 21-nen ni itaru*, vol. 3, edited by Usami Tatsuo, 210–41. Watanabe tansa gijutsu kenkyūjo, 2005.

Kojima Tōzan and Tōrōan-shujin. *Jishinkō*. Kyoto: Saiseikan, 1830.

"Kokka shōbi no kyūmu." *Iwate kōhō*, June 18, 1896. Accessed May 9, 2013. http:// tsunami-dl.jp/newspaper/IwateKouhouM29/IwatekouhouM29_June18_02.

"Kōkoku." *Ōu nichinichi shinbun*, July 3, 1896. Accessed May 7, 2013. http://tsunami-dl. jp/newspaper/OouNichinichiM29/OouNichinichiM29_July03_04.

Kondō Hiroyuki, ed. *Meiji, Shōwa, Heisei, kyodai tsunami no kiroku*. Mainichi shinbunsha, 2011.

Koshimura Shun'ichi. "Sanriku chihō no tsunami saigai gaiyō." In *1896 Meiji Sanriku jishin tsunami hōkokusho*, 3–6. Chūō bōsai kaigi, 2005.

Kotô, Bundjiro [Kotō Bunjirō]. "On the Cause of the Great Earthquake in Central Japan, 1891." *Tōkyō teikoku daigaku kiyō, rika* 5, no. 10 (1893): 295–353.

Kotō Bunjirō. "Takanami no yūin." *Tōyō gakugei zasshi* 13 (1896): 441–44.

Kusakabe Shirōta. *Shinkō butsuri angya*. Dai-Nippon yūbenkai, Kōdansha, 1924.

"Kyūjohi no kafu." *Ōu nichinichi shinbun*, July 14, 1896. Accessed May 9, 2013. http:// tsunami-dl.jp/newspaper/OouNichinichiM29/OouNichinichiM29_July14_02.

Ludwin, Ruth S., Robert Dennis, Deborah Carver, Alan D. McMillan, Robert Losey, John Clague, Chris Jonientz-Trisler, J. Bowechop, J. Wray, and K. James. "Dating the 1700 Cascadia Earthquake: Great Coastal Earthquakes in Native Stories." *Seismological Research Letters* 76, no. 2 (March, 2005): 140–48.

Ludwin, R. S., and G. J. Smits. "Folklore and Earthquakes: Native American Oral Traditions from Cascadia Compared with Written Traditions from Japan." In *Myth and Geology*, edited by L. Piccardi and W. B. Masse, 67–94. London: Geological Society, 2007.

Macleod, Calum. "Japanese Towns Reconsider Sea Walls after Deadly Tsunami." *USA Today*, August 11, 2011 (Chie Matsumoto contributing).

Main, Ian. "Is the Reliable Prediction of Individual Earthquakes a Realistic Scientific Goal?" Introduction to a *Nature* debate, February 25, 1999. Accessed October 31, 2012. http://www.nature.com/nature/debates/earthquake/equake_frameset.html.

Mainichi shinbun "shinsai kenshō" shuzai han, eds. *Kenshō "daishinsai:" Tsutaenakereba naranai koto*. Mainichi shinbunsha, 2012.

"Massive Tsunami Projected/Panel Forecasts Nankai Trough Quakes Could Affect 11 Prefectures." *Daily Yomiuri Online*, April 2, 1012.

Matsutani, Minoru. "Nuclear Crisis Man-Made, Not 'an Act of God': Experts, Government, Tepco Blamed for Failure to Prepare for Tsunami." *Japan Times*, April 6, 2011.

Matuo [Matsuo], Haruo. "Estimation of Energy of Tsunami and Protection of Coasts." In *Jishin kenkyūjo ihō bessatsu*, no. 1 (March 3, 1934): 55–64. Accessed October 15, 2012. http://hdl.handle.net/2261/13772.

McClain, James L., John W. Merriman, and Ugawa Kaoru, eds. *Edo and Paris: Urban Life and the State in the Early Modern Era*. Ithaca, NY: Cornell University Press, 1994.

Meguro Kimirō. "Higashi Nihon daishinsai no jinteki higai no tokuchō to tsunami ni yoru giseisha no tsuite." In *Kyodai jishin, kyodai tsunami: Higashi Nihon daishinsai no kenshō*, by Hirata Naoshi, Satake Kenji, Meguro Kimirō, and Hatakemura Yōtarō, 93–145. Asakura shoten, 2011.

Mikami Sanjin. "Jo." In *Taishō daishinsai, daikasai*, unpaginated front matter. Dai-Nippon yūbenkai Kōdansha, 1923.

Miki Haruo. *Kyōto daijishin*. Shibunkaku shuppan, 1979.

Milne, John. *Seismology*. London: Kegan Paul, Trench, Trübner and Co., 1898.

"Miyagi kenpō kokuji dai hachijūroku gō." *Ōu nichinichi shinbun*, July 9, 1896. Accessed May 9, 2013. http://tsunami-dl.jp/newspaper/OouNichinichiM29/OouNichinichiM29_July09_01.

Miyake Yūjirō [Setsurei]. "Jo." In *Taishō daishinsai, daikasai*, unpaginated front matter. Dai-Nippon yūbenkai Kōdansha, 1923.

Miyata Noboru and Takada Mamoru, eds. *Namazue: Shinsai to Nihon bunka*. Ribun shuppan, 1995.

Mizoue Megumi. "Jishin yochi to shakai." In *Jishin yochi to shakai*, edited by Kaminuma Katsutada and Hirata Kōji, 19–46. Kokon shoin, 2003.

Mogi, Kiyoo. "Comparison of Precursory Phenomena before the 1975 Haicheng (China) Earthquake and the 1978 Izu-Oshima-kinkai (Japan) Earthquake: The Possible Effect of Stress History on Precursory Phenomena." *Tectonophysics* 138 (1987): 33–43.

Mukherjee, Saumitra, ed. *Earthquake Prediction*. Leiden: Brill, 2006.

Murayama Masataka. *Shinden kōsetsu* [1856]. Edo josei bunko, vol. 49. Ōzorasha, 1994 (no pagination).

Musha Kinkichi. *Jishin namazu*. Meiseki shoten, 1995. First published 1957.

"Nabe, tetsubin, kondensu miruku, kanzume rui." *Ōu nichinichi shinbun*, July 2, 1896. Accessed May 8, 2013. http://tsunami-dl.jp/newspaper/OouNichinichiM29/OouNichinichiM29_July02_02.

"Nagaretekita iwashi kasu o shūtoku kansōsasete baikyakusu." *Kahō shinpō*, April 26, 1933.

Nakamura, David, and Chico Harlan. "Japanese Nuclear Plant's Safety Analysts Brushed off Risk of Tsunami." *Washington Post*, March 23, 2011.

Namegaya Yūichi, Tsuji Yoshinobu, and Ueda Kazue. "Kansei go-nen (1793) Miyagi-ken-oki ni hasseishita jishin no shōsai shindo bunpu to tsunami no jōkyō" ("Detailed Distributions of Seismic Intensity and Tsunami Heights of the Kansei off Miyagi Prefecture Earthquake of February 17, 1793"). *Rekishi jishin*, no. 11 (2003): 75–106.

"Nigeashiosoi rōjin, kodomoni gisei ga ōi." *Kahoku shinpō*, March 7, 1933. Accessed May 7, 2013. http://tsunami-dl.jp/newspaper/KahokuShinpouS8/KahokuShinpouS8_March07_07.

Nihon gakushiin, eds. *Meiji-zen Nihon butsuri kagakushi*. Nihon gajutsu shinkōkai, 1964.

Nosengo, Nicola. "Prosecution Asks for Four-Year Sentence in Italian Seismology Trial." *Nature Newsblog*. Accessed October 10, 2012. http://blogs.nature.com/news/2012/09/porsecution-asks-for-four-year-sentence-in-italian-seismology-trial.html.

Nur, Amos, with Dawn Burgess. *Apocalypse: Earthquakes, Archaeology, and the Wrath of God*. Princeton, NJ: Princeton University Press, 2008.

Obara, Kuzushige, Hitoshi Hirose, Fumio Yamamizu, and Keiji Kasahara. "Episodic Slow Slip Events Accompanied by Non-volcanic Tremors in Southwest Japan Subduction Zone." *Geophysical Research Letters*, vol. 31, L23602. doi:10.1029/2004GL020848 (2004). 4 pages.

Ochibe Chūshō. "Sanriku chihō tsunami ni tsuki chishitsugakujō no kōsetsu." In "furoku" (supplement), *Chigaku zasshi* 8 (1896): 1–17.

Ōishi Hisakazu. *Kokudo to Nihonjin: saigai taikoku no ikikata. Chūō kōron shinsha,* 2012. ISBN978-4-12-102151-9.

Okada Yoshimitsu. *Saishin Nihon no jishin chizu.* Tōkyō shoseki, 2006.

Ōmori Fusakichi. "Nihon ni okeru tsunami ni tsuite." *Shinsai ybō chōsakai hōkoku, dai 34 gō* (January 1901), 5–81.

———. "Tsunami ni tsuite." *Tōyō gakugei zasshi* 18 (1901): 13–25.

O'Neill, Brendan. "A Disaster That Science Brought upon Itself." *Spiked,* November 6, 2012. Accessed November 6, 2012. http://www.spiked-online.com/site/printable/ 13016.

Onishi, Norimitsu. "Japan Revives a Sea Barrier That Failed to Hold." *New York Times,* November 2, 2011.

Rikitake Tsuneji. "Deeta ni miru namazu to jishin." In *Namazue: Shinsai to Nihon bunka,* edited by Miyata Noboru and Takada Mamoru, 148–56. Ribun shuppan, 1995.

———. *Earthquake Prediction.* New York: Elsevier Scientific, 1976.

Risk Management Solutions. "1995 Kobe Earthquake 10-Year Retrospective." Risk Assessment Models paper, January 2005. Accessed October 6, 2012. http://www.rms. com/publications/KobeRetro.pdf.

Robinson, Andrew. *Earthquake: Nature and Culture.* London: Reaktion, 2012.

Rogaski, Ruth. *Hygienic Modernity: Meanings of Health and Disease in Treaty-Port China.* Berkeley: University of California Press, 2004.

Rowan, Chris. "Earthquake 'Precursors' and the Curse of the False Positive." *Highly Allochthonous: News & Commentary from the World of Geology and Earth Science* (blog). Accessed October 15, 2012. http://all-geo.org/highlyallochthonous/2011/05/ earthquake-precursors-and-the-curse-of-the-false-positive.

"Saba hōryo Hokkaidō ihen." *Yomiuri shinbun,* October 11, 2012, evening edition.

Samuels, Richard J. *3.11: Disaster and Change in Japan.* Ithaca, NY: Cornell University Press, 2013.

Sangawa Akira. *Jishin no Nihonshi: Daichi wa nani wo kataru no ka?* Chūōkōron shinsha, 2007.

———. *Nihonjin wa donna daijishin o keikenshitekita no ka: Jishin kōkogaku nyūmon.* Heibonsha, 2011.

"Sanshin hitotaba." *Iwate kōhō,* June 25, 1896. Accessed May 9, 2013. http://tsunami-dl. jp/newspaper/IwateKouhouM29/IwatekouhouM29_June25_02.

Satake Kenji. "Kyodai tsunami no mekanizumu." In *Kyodai jishin, kyodai tsunami: Higashi Nihon daishinsai no kenshō,* edited by Hirata Naoshi, Satake Kenji, Meguro Kimirō, and Hatakemura Yōtarō, 55–91. Asakura shoten, 2011.

Schencking, J. Charles. *The Great Kantō Earthquake and the Chimera of National Reconstruction in Japan.* New York: Columbia University Press, 2013.

Scidmore, Eliza Ruhamah. "The Recent Earthquake Wave on the Coast of Japan." *National Geographic* 8, no. 9 (September 1896), 285–89.

"Seishi o hōtai shite okashikin o yūkō ni saigai fukkō ni tsutomu beshi shingaichi jūshichi chōsonchō ni kokuyu o hassu." *Kahoku shinpō,* March 21, 1933. Accessed May 14, 2013. http://tsunami-dl.jp/newspaper/KahokuShinpouS8/ KahokuShinpouS8_March21_07.

Shimamura, Hideki. "Jishin yochi no kanō sei, genjitsusei." In *Jishin yochi to shakai,* edited by Kaminuma Katsutada and Hirata Kōji, 47–74. Kokon shoin, 2003.

———. *"Jishin yochi" wa usodarake.* Kōdansha, 2008.

————. *Nihonjin ga shiritai jishin no gimon rokujūroku: Jishin ga ōi Nihon dakara koso chishiki no sonae mo wasurezu ni.* SoftBank Creative, 2008.

Shinano mainichi shinbunsha kaihatsukyoku shuppanbu, ed. *Kōka yonen Zenkōji daijishin.* Nagano-shi: Shinano mainichi shinbunsha, 1977.

Shinsai yobō chōsakai, eds. *Dai-Nihon jishin shiryō.* 2 vols. Shibunkaku, 1973.

————. "Sanriku chihō tsunami ihō (sanshō dai-yon)." *Shinsai yobō chōsakai hōkoku,* no. 11 (1896): 41–49. Accessed October 19, 2012. http://hdl.handle.net/2261/16746.

Shou, Zhongshao. "Earthquake Vapor, a Reliable Precursor." In *Earthquake Prediction,* edited by Saumitra Mukherjee, 21–51. Leiden: Brill, 2006.

Shutō Nobuo and Koshimura Shun'ichi. "Gyōsei no ōkyū taiō." In *1896 Meiji Sanriku jishin tsunami hōkokusho,* edited by Chūō bōsai kaigi, 47–68, 2005.

————. "Meiji Sanriku jishin tsunami saigai kara no fukkō." In *1896 Meiji Sanriku jishin tsunami hōkokusho,* edited by Chūō bōsai kaigi, 91–92, 2005.

————. "Meiji Sanriku jishin tsunami ni yoru higai." In *1896 Meiji Sanriku jishin tsunami hōkokusho,* edited by Chūō bōsai kaigi, 33–46, 2005.

Smits, Gregory. "Conduits of Power: What the Origins of Japan's Earthquake Catfish Reveal about Religious Geography." *Japan Review* 24 (2012): 41–65. http://shinku.nichibun.ac.jp/jpub/pdf/jr/JN2402.pdf.

————. "Earthquakes as Social Drama in the Tokugawa Period." In *Environment and Society in the Japanese Islands,* edited by Philip Brown and Bruce Batten. Eugene: University of Oregon Press, forthcoming.

————. *Seismic Japan: The Long History and Continuing Legacy of the Ansei Edo Earthquake.* Honolulu: University of Hawaii Press, 2013.

Stein, Seth. *Disaster Deferred: How Science Is Changing Our View of Earthquake Hazards in the Midwest.* New York: Columbia University Press, 2010.

————. "Seismic Gaps and Grizzly Bears." *Nature* 356 (April 2, 1992): 387–88.

Stein, Seth, Robert J. Geller, and Mian Liu. "Why Earthquake Hazard Maps Often Fail and What to Do about It." *Tectonophysics* 562–63 (2012): 1–25.

"Suisaigo eiseijō no chūi." *Iwate kōhō,* June 20, 1896. Accessed May 7, 2013. http://tsunami-dl.jp/newspaper/IwateKouhouM29/IwatekouhouM29_June20_01.

Sutton, Gerard K., and Joseph A Cassalli, eds. *Catastrophe in Japan: The Earthquake and Tsunami of 2011.* New York: Nova Science, 2011.

Suzuki Tōzō and Koike Shōtarō, eds. *Fujiokaya nikki.* Kinsei shomin seikatsu shiryō, vol. 15. San'ichi shobō, 1995.

"Taiwan ijū o shōrei seyo." *Ōu nichinichi shinbun,* June 28, 1896. Accessed May 13, 2013. http://tsunami-dl.jp/newspaper/OouNichinichiM29/OouNichinichiM29_June28_02.

Takahashi Katsumine. "Bun'en: Daikaishō kiji (Sensha kadai)." *Ōu nichinichi shinbun,* July 22, 1896. Accessed May 7, 2013. http://tsunami-dl.jp/newspaper/OouNichinichiM29/OouNichinichiM29_July22_01.

Tanakadate Hidezō. "Sankakuten 'tsunami hinan dōro.'" *Mainichi shinbun,* March 25, 1933. Accessed May 13, 2013. http://tsunami-dl.jp/newspaper/S8Mainichi/MainichiS8_March25_03.

"Tatsuta-kan no kaken." *Iwate kōhō,* June 21, 1896. Accessed May 7, 2013. http://tsunami-dl.jp/newspaper/IwateKouhouM29/IwatekouhouM29_June21_02.

Tennant, H. *The Great Earthquake in Japan, October 28, 1891: Being a Full Description of the Disasters Resulting from the Recent Terrible Catastrophe.* Kessinger, 2007. First published 1892.

Thompson, Jerry. *Cascadia's Fault: The Coming Earthquake and Tsunami That Could Devastate North America*. Berkeley, CA: Counterpoint, 2011.

Toishi Shirō. *Tsunami o tatakatta hito: Hamamura Goryō den*. Shin-Nihon shuppansha, 2005.

Tōkyō daigaku jishin kenkyūjo, eds. *Shinshū Nihon jishin shiryō*, vol. 2. Nihon denki kyōkai, 1982.

Tōkyō kagaku hakubutsukan, ed. *Edo jidai no kagaku*. Meicho kankōkai, 1980. First published 1934.

"Tōkyō to jishin: Shinpai no oyobazu." *Yomiuri shinbun*, October 18, 1917, morning edition, 5.

"Toreru sakana no henka ga arō jishin to Sendai akana ichiba, ichi, ni ryōshi no hanashi." *Kahoku shinpō*, March 4, 1933. Accessed May 14, 2013. http://tsunami-dl.jp/newspaper/KahokuShinpouS8/KahokuShinpouS8_March04_06.

Tsu, Timothy Yun Hui. "Making Virtues of Disaster: 'Beautiful Tales' from the Kobe Flood of 1938." *Asian Studies Review* 32, no. 3 (June 2008): 197–214.

Tsuchiya, Yoshihito, ed. *Tsunami: Progress in Prediction, Disaster Prevention, and Warning*. Leiden: Kluwer Academic, 1995.

Tsuji Yoshinobu. *Sennen shinsai: Kurikaesu jishin to tsunami no rekishi ni manabu*. Daiyamondo sha, 2011.

———. *Zukai, naze okoru? Itsu okoru? Jishin no mekanizumu*. Nagaoka shoten, 2010.

Tsukuda Tameshige. *Jishin yochi no saishin kagaku: Hassei no mekanizumu to yochi kenkyū no saizensen*. SoftBank Creative, 2007.

"Tsunami Alert Softened Days before 3/11." *Japan Times Online*, February 27, 2012.

Tsunami Education Booklet "Inamura no Hi" web page (part of the Asian Disaster Reduction Center web site). Accessed January 17, 2012. http://www.adrc.asia/publications/inamura/list.html.

"Tsunami o fusegu yūkina mōza hoanrin no hitsuyō o toku Akabayashi Sendai eirinshō-chō." *Kahoku shinpō*, March 11, 1933. Accessed May 13, 2013. http://tsunami-dl.jp/newspaper/KahokuShinpouS8/KahokuShinpouS8_March11_06.

"Tsunami sanjuppun mae ni SOS tsūshin Onagawa Enoshima-kan no muden sōchi iyoiyo kōshōsaru." *Kahoku shinpō*, March 11, 1933. Accessed May 13, 2013. http://tsunami-dl.jp/newspaper/KahokuShinpouS8/KahokuShinpouS8_March11_06.

"Tsūzoku jishin monogatari (jō)." *Yomiuri shinbun*, November 19, 1915, morning edition, 5.

Udagawa Kōsai. *Jishin yobōsetsu*. Edo: Suhara Yaihachi, 1856.

Ulusoy, Ülkü, and Himansu Kumar Kundu, eds. *Future Systems for Earthquake Early Warning*. New York: Nova Science, 2008.

United States Geological Survey (USGS). "Earthquake Hazard in the New Madrid Seismic Zone Remains a Concern" (fact sheet 2009–3071). Accessed October 6, 2012. http://pubs.usgs.gov/fs/2009/3071.

Usami Tatsuo. *Nihon higai jishin sōran [416]–2001, Saishinpan (Materials for a Comprehensive List of Destructive Earthquakes in Japan, [416]–2001 [Latest Edition])*. Tōkyō daigaku shuppankai, 2003.

———, ed. *"Nihon no rekishi jishin shiryō" shūi*. Nihon denki kyōkai, 1998.

Wang, Kelin, Qi-Fu Chen, Shihong Sun, and Andong Wang. "Predicting the 1975 Haicheng Earthquake." *Bulletin of the Seismological Society of America* 96, no. 3 (June 2006): 757–95.

Watanabe Hideo. *Nihon higai tsunami sōran, dai-2 han (Comprehensive List of Tsunamis to Hit the Japanese Islands)*. Tōkyō daigaku shuppankai, 1998.

Weiner, Michael A. *The Origins of the Korean Community in Japan, 1910–1923*. Manchester, UK: Manchester University Press, 1989.

Weisenfeld, Gennifer. *Imaging Disaster: Tokyo and the Visual Culture of Japan's Great Earthquake of 1923*. Berkeley: University of California Press, 2012.

World Nuclear Association. "Earthquakes and Seismic Protection for Japanese NPPs." Accessed October 11, 2012. http://www.world-nuclear.org/fukushima/earthquakes_seismic_protection_japan.html.

———. "Fukushima Accident." Accessed October 11, 2012. http://www.world-nuclear.org/info/Safety-and-Security/Safety-of-Plants/Fukushima-Accident/.

Yamanaka, Chihiro, Hiroshi Asahara, Yutaka Emoto, and Yuko Esaki. "Earthquake Precursors—From Legends to Science and a Possible Early Warning System." In *Future Systems for Earthquake Early Warning*, edited by Ülkü Ulusoy and Himansu Kumar Kundu, 201–8. New York: Nova Science, 2008.

Yamasaki, Erika. "What We Can Learn from Japan's Early Earthquake Warning System." *Momentum* 1, no. 1 (April 18, 2012): 1–26. Accessed November 2, 2012. http://repository.upenn.edu/cgi/viewcontent.cgi?article=1022&context=momentum.

Yamashita Fumio. *Tsunami no kyōfu: Sanriku tsunami denshōroku* (*The Horrors of Tsunami—The Documents and Histories of Sanriku-Tsunami of the Tohoku Area*). Sendai, Japan: Tōhoku daigaku shuppankai, 2005.

———. *Tsunami tendenko: Kindai Nihon no tsunamishi*. Shin Nihon shuppansha, 2008.

Yanagawa Yoshirō. *Sakurajima funkaki: Jūmin wa riron ni shinraisezu*. Nihon hōsō shuppankai, 1984.

"Yobu karasu, sunahama ni kujira . . . shinsai mae ni dōbutsu ihen." *Yomiuri shinbun* (Yomiuri Online), July 2, 2011, 2:41 p.m. http://www.yomiuri.co.jp/science/news/20110702-OYT1T00504.htm

Yoshimura Akira. *Sanriku kaigan ōtsunami*. Bungei shunjū, 2004.

Index

About the Author

A specialist in Japan and East Asia, **Gregory Smits** received his PhD in history from the University of Southern California in 1992. His early research focus was intellectual history of the Ryukyu Kingdom (present day Okinawa Prefecture, Japan). More recently he has been researching the history of earthquakes in Japan, both with respect to the impact of earthquakes on history and from the standpoint of the history of science. Dr. Smits is the author of *Visions of Ryukyu: Identity and Ideology in Early-Modern Thought and Politics* (1999) and *Seismic Japan: The Long History and Continuing Legacy of the Ansei Edo Earthquake* (2013). He is coeditor with Bettina Gramlich-Oka of *Economic Thought in Early-Modern Japan* (2010) and the author of numerous articles on the history and culture of earthquakes. He is currently associate professor of history and Asian studies at Pennsylvania State University.